To Peter,
Best Wishes
GJMills
Geoffrey Stevens.
7th October, 1996.

A·J·S

of WOLVERHAMPTON

S.J. Mills

Published by the Author, 1994.

ISBN 0–9523338–0–5.

Copies may be obtained from:

S.J. Mills.
'Robinia House',
2, St. Andrews Road,
Sutton Coldfield,
West Midlands.
B75 6UG.

Copyright © S.J. Mills, 1994.

All rights reserved. No part of this publication may be reproduced, stored in a retrieval system, or transmitted in any form or by any means, electronic, mechanical, photocopying, recording or otherwise without the prior written permission of the copyright holder.

Designed by John Llewelyn Graphics.
21, Hagley Hall Mews.
Stourbridge,
West Midlands.
DY9 9LQ

Printed by Elton & Brown Ltd.
Unit 17, Thornleigh Trading Estate,
Dudley,
West Midlands.
DY2 8UB.

Bound by J.W. Braithwaite & Son Ltd.
Pountney Street,
Wolverhampton.
West Midlands.
WV2 4HY.

Contents

Foreword — 5
Preface — 7
Introduction — 9
Acknowledgements — 10

Part I

Chapter 1	*The Early Years*	13
Chapter 2	*1914… A Turning Point*	30
Chapter 3	*1915–1919 Ideas on Hold*	46
Chapter 4	*1920–1925 The Golden Years*	55
Chapter 5	*1926–1930 Times of Change*	77
Chapter 6	*1931*	99

Part II

Chapter 7	*Sidecars*	109
Chapter 8	*Big Port*	122
Chapter 9	*Wireless*	135
Chapter 10	*Overhead Camshaft*	146
Chapter 11	*Commercial Vehicles*	159
Chapter 12	*A.J.S. Light Car*	172
Chapter 13	*Stevens*	181

Appendices

A.J.S. Transfer Details — 193
Patents held by A.J.S. & Stevens Bros. (Wolverhampton) Ltd. — 194
A.J.S. Commercial Vehicles Chassis lists — 195
A.J.S. Motorcycle, Wireless, Commercial Vehicle & Car Specifications — 201
Map of Factory Locations — 212
Club Information — 214

Index — 215

FOREWORD

My generation of the Stevens family, have long felt the need for a comprehensive book about the A.J.S., particularly as many articles written about my father and uncles perpetuate certain errors. Most stories so far printed are about A.J.S. motor bikes; some include the cars, but very little has been published about the radios, or the commercial vehicles and certainly no existing publication covers the whole story.

My brother and I have tried to produce a history of the A.J.S. to remedy this, but we lack the necessary skill, so we regretfully gave up on the idea and resigned ourselves to accept that nobody would get the story right.

Then I met Steve Mills. The manner of our meeting was interesting. Steve's two main hobbies are photography and vintage motorcycles; he has been an enthusiastic motorcyclist all his life and has more recently turned his hand to restoring a 1928 Austin Seven 'Chummy', a 1920 Triumph motorcycle and, to my joy, a 1928 V-twin A.J.S. All are now in immaculate original condition and are entered successfully in rallies, with Steve in the saddle or driver's seat.

Being an expert photographer, Steve has produced an audio-visual show of his vintage vehicles, which he exhibits for various charities. It was in order to discuss the commentary on this, that I was invited to his home, I took along my collection of books and photographs to help him with his presentation. This widened Steve's interest from just A.J.S. motorcycles, to the other products of the Stevens brothers, bringing to light their tremendous drive, inventive ability and their great zest for life.

At this point, Steve decided the story should be told and that he would like to produce a book, giving the history of the brothers, from their early experiments at the end of the nineteenth century, to the manufacture of the last Stevens van and motorcycle of the 1930's. In order to obtain the greatest possible accuracy and a great variety of insights, I have had the pleasure of accompanying Steve on many visits to A.J.S. enthusiasts, for bikes, cars, coaches, and radio all over the country. In this way we have obtained details and photographs of all these varied products. We have also interviewed ex-employees or their descendants, riders and family connections, also vintage enthusiasts, to research, check and counter check the accuracy of the stories which have now been included in this book. Steve has delved into the archives of libraries and museums to research the many activities of the brothers, so that the book can pass on to the reader, as it has done for me, a feeling for the lives of the Wolverhampton engineers in the years when the motor industry was founded.

This is not only a reference book of facts and figures about the various factories and different models, often with engine and chassis numbers, production quantities etc., but it also contains many interesting stories about the Stevens brothers and their associates.

The research after so many years has not been easy, but I and the rest of my family are most grateful to Steve Mills for his efforts and his total commitment to detail. This book would have delighted my father, uncles and grandfather. I believe it has unfolded the complete story, and I commend it to the reader.

Geoff Stevens astride 1924 2¾ h.p. model 'B3' A.J.S. Photo: Author.

Geoffrey Stevens

PREFACE

The year is 1957, it is autumn. Everyone was still worried about the Suez crisis. I was twelve years old and my world in Handsworth, Birmingham was a long way from Egypt and Mr.Nasser.

My journeys to and from school took me past the local veterinary clinic. For the past two years, not a school day had gone by when I hadn't peeked over the wall into the vet's yard, where the object of my attention, a pair of deflated tyres, were peeping beneath a khaki tarpaulin. Being somewhat obsessed about motorcycles I had often fantasized about what lay beneath the sheets. I resolved to knock on the door and ask.

I had plucked up the courage to knock on the clinic door during the lunch-break. The vet's wife answered the door. I had only intended to ask if I could look beneath the sheets, but somehow the words came out as, "Can I have the old motorbike please?" With what seemed like an eternity - but must have been immediate, she responded. "You can take it out of my way, I would be glad to see the back of it." I didn't know what to say. "Call back after school and see my husband," she added. I nodded, speechless, and went back to school. Whatever the teachers had in mind for me that afternoon must have fallen on stoney ground: a matter which was brought to my attention when attempting that evening's homework.

Later as I approached the clinic, I noticed the machine had been moved. The vet saw me and directed me into the yard by the back gate. There in the corner was the shrouded machine. In the manner of a great unveiling the sheet was whisked off. "It's an A.J.S.," I heard myself say. "It's yours," said the kindly vet, "it hasn't run for some years, but I've pumped up the tyres and they seem to be holding." He gave me a warning about riding on the road and various other interdictions, but my confused twelve year old mind was not listening. The prize was all mine, I owned a motorbike.

Having got the machine, there remained one obstacle. My parents, or rather my mother. Dad would have no objection, but mum and motorcycles just didn't get on. It was dusk when I got home. I crept down the garden path and hid my latest acquisition in the Anderson shelter. It was my intention to explain the whole episode, but like many a good intention, the opportunity did not arise that evening. I never did get a definite 'yes' from mum when I eventually asked if I could keep it, but as time passed I grew more confident that this would be the case.

At last the weekend arrived and the 'Ajay' was brought out into the open. It still had petrol in the tank, which was just as well, as it was rationed at the time. Most of the morning was spent wiping away the grease and grime before polishing the black paintwork. Around lunchtime our neighbour popped his head over the fence and volunteered to start the engine. With hindsight I am glad I let him carry on. Dressed in smart grey flannels and a new sweater he was hardly suited for the occasion. After becoming quite breathless working the kickstart, he muttered something about the petrol not getting through. Off came the filler cap and all at once he began to blow for all his worth into the tank. The carburettor was tickled and petrol began to drip. He was beginning to enjoy himself. With a dirty black ring around his mouth he sat astride the 'Ajay' and resumed kicking with all his might. Without warning the engine backfired, the saddle was rapidly vacated, its former occupant did a lot of hopping and one twelve year old learnt a number of new words that day. In the fullness of time, the air cleared and the cripple, not to be outdone, decided to give it another go - 'if at first you don't succeed, try, try, again'... With a loud bang followed by a cloud of smoke and dust, the old 'Ajay' coughed into life. Before I could utter a word he was away, up the garden path and onto the road. I sat on the kerb to await his return, the sound of the exhaust rattling away in the distance. When at last he put in an appearance, he was all smiles, well as best as you can smile with a black ring around your mouth. There was a price to pay for his outing however, as his left hand trouser bottom had been reduced to an oily shred, the material having become enmeshed in the primary chain. He decided to call it a day and no doubt put it down to experience. For my part I was grateful, he had at least got it going.

Over the next few years, I rode that old 'Ajay' around a nearby farm, until she would go no more. I left her for scrap. Since then it has been my pleasure to own over sixty machines - but I shall always remember the kindly vet, the crippled neighbour and mainly that lovely old 'Ajay'.

INTRODUCTION

This book serves to illustrate an important, although often overlooked chapter of industrial history set in the Black Country town of Wolverhampton. It follows a truly remarkable story of achievement and success, brought about by the extraordinary talents and skills of the Stevens brothers born to a blacksmith's family.

The beginning, set during the Victorian unfolding of the industrial revolution, deals with the early years leading up to the birth of A.J.S. There follows the Company's incredible rise to world-wide fame through its unique record in motorcycle trials and road racing during the early 1920's.

As well as dealing with that most famous of A.J.S. products, motorcycles, important chapters are included which explore in depth the Company's diversification, producing wireless, sidecars, commercial vehicles, cars and a chronicle of the Stevens family history.

The shock voluntary liquidation of A.J.S. in 1931 and the subsequent sale of its motorcycle business to Matchless Motorcycles (Colliers) Ltd of Plumstead, South East London, came as a bitter blow to many at the time. The Company had become recognized as one of Wolverhampton's largest and most respected employers.

Although the famous initials would continue to grace the petrol tanks of machines produced at Plumstead, the Stevens brothers were not part of it. They chose to form a new business in 1932 and produce a three wheel van and an impressive range of motorcycles under the 'Stevens' name until 1938; when, due to the pressures of work leading up to the war effort, production ceased.

Sadly the last remaining Stevens link with engineering in Wolverhampton was finally broken, when the Stevens Screw Company Ltd. founded in 1906, by Joe Stevens Senior, finally closed its doors in December 1992.

In researching and writing this story, I have had the help of many people, not least of whom is Geoff Stevens. These good folk are mentioned in the acknowledgements. I hope there are no errors, but should any be found, I would be pleased to know so that they can be corrected.

Over the past few years, the story has taken up a great part of my life, it has been enjoyable and frustrating, but always rewarding. I shall be happy to return to normal family life. My wife Irene and daughter Cara have had to contend with papers and books around the house, long 'phone calls and messages and many interruptions to the family routine. Their encouragement stimulated the work and kept me going. I hope the book will give the reader and researcher of years to come, as much pleasure as it has given me to write.

Stephen J. Mills
Sutton Coldfield.

October 1994

ACKNOWLEDGEMENTS

The author gratefully acknowledges the following people and organisations for their valuable assistance in supplying information, articles and photographs without which it would have been impossible to write this book.

John Allen
Titch Allen
Peter Allman
Jack Baines
Geoff Baker
Mark Baker
Patrick Braithwaite
Harry Buisst
Dr. Joseph Bayley
Jim Boulton
Eric Bradley
Tony Bullock
Ron Bubb
Ray Carter
Ralph Cartwright
Noel Clark
Robert Cordon Champ
Pat Craddock
Leo Davenport
Jim Davies
Lilian Deadman
Larry Devlin
David Delapp
David Evans
Chris Eyres
Terry Eden
Martin Flower
Stan Greenway
Arthur Griffiths
Ken Hallworth
Robert Hawes
David Hawtin
Phil Heath

Les Henshaw
Jonathan Hill
Alec Holder
Doug Hough
Rick Howard
Peter Hubbard
Ron Hughes
Wesley Hunt
David L. G. Hunter
Robin James
Ray Jones
Paul Lefevre
John Llewelyn
Bruce Main-Smith
Clive Mason
George Mildenhall
John Moore
John Mudge
David Nunns
Gordon Parish
Danae Parker
Barry Pook
Elizabeth Reece
Tom Ridgewell
Ian Robinson
Mary Robinson
Angela Rogers
Beverley Shingler-Day
Desmond Southgate
Geoffrey St. John
Alec Stevens
Eric Stevens
Jim Stevens

Joan Stevens
Geoff Stevens
Peter Stevens
Chris Taylor
Susan Taylor
Phillip Tooth
Peter Waine
Charles Weight
Gerald Wells
Reg Westworth
Peng Wilkinson
Charles Williams
Jimmy Wingfield
Peter Watson
Eric Wooley

A.J.S. and Matchless Owners Club
Birmingham Museum of Science and Industry
Birmingham Post and Mail
Black Country Bugle
British Vintage Wireless Society
Classic Bike Magazine
The Classic Motor Cycle Magazine
Ever Ready Limited
Express and Star
Historic Commercial Vehicle Society
S.R. Keig Ltd.
The National Motor Cycle Museum
The National Motor Museum
Old Bike Magazine
Radio West Midlands
The PSV Circle
The Vintage Motor Cycle Club Ltd.
The Vintage Wireless Museum
Wolverhampton Reference Library

Special thanks are recorded to:
John Allen, Jim Boulton, Ray Carter, Les Henshaw, Ray Jones, Paul Lefevre, Clive Mason and the Stevens family for their tremendous assistance and encouragement during the production of this book.

Photographs
Where possible, the photographs shown in this book are both contemporary, unpublished and are individually acknowledged.

A.J.S. *of* WOLVERHAMPTON

Part I

Chapter 1
The Early Years

The origins of A.J.S. really go back to 1856, when Joseph Stevens was born in Wednesfield, although it would be fifty-three years before the famous initials were used. Wednesfield was a small industrial town situated outside Wolverhampton, in the 'Black Country'.

In 1874 he became self-employed as an engineering blacksmith with premises in Cross Street under the title of J.Stevens & Co. 'Joe' had begun his trade amidst times of great change when Britain was clearly recognized as the 'Workshop of the World'. The railway age had arrived and with it new businesses and factories were opening, in all directions. Most manufacturing trades found themselves working flat out in order to cope with the vast volume of external trade reaching our shores. Against this background, Joe established an enviable reputation as a highly skilled craftsman, who would undertake to repair or make all manner of garden tools and metal equipment from wheelbarrows to bicycles. He also did work for the lock trade as well as carrying out the traditional work on horse-shoeing and metalwork on harness and bridle.

In the course of time Joe married and raised a total of nine children. There were five sons: Harry (b.1876), George (b.1878), Joseph (b.1881), Albert John (Jack) (b.1885) and William (Billie) (b.1893) and four daughters: Lucy (b.1875), Lily (b.1884), Ethel (b.1888) and Daisy (b.1890).

Harry, the eldest son eventually joined his father in the business. He was quick to learn and was soon displaying considerable skills in designing and producing a wide range of special purpose machines and tools for use in the lock trade. In 1894 the business moved to Tempest Street near the centre of Wolverhampton and Harry was joined by his younger brother Joe Junior.

Later Joe Stevens acquired a small American built 'Mitchell' single cylinder four stroke petrol engine, presumably to provide power to blow the hearth. Whatever the reason, it aroused Harry's interest, who, not being overly impressed by either its quality or workmanship, set about to produce his own version. Rough castings were obtained from a firm in Derby. These together with the remaining internal parts were machined and assembled at the works by the two brothers during their spare time. Harry also managed to design and construct a suitable surface carburettor, by cleverly utilizing an old mustard tin. The engine was completed toward the end of 1897, having an approximate capacity of $1^{3}/_{4}$ h.p. and unlike the temperamental 'Mitchell' proved to be remarkably reliable and efficient.

Harry and his father were quick to recognize the huge potential that existed for the production of compact and efficient petrol engines to provide motive power for industry. With definite plans to form a new company for the manufacture of proprietary engines, further developments and experiments were undertaken to improve Harry's engine.

A new company was formed during the summer of 1899 under the title 'The Stevens Motor Manufacturing Company'. In order to finance the venture alongside the established J.Stevens & Co., it was agreed that George, Joe Junior and Jack would take on outside jobs, until Harry could get things established. As things turned out, the business got off to a good start and before long each brother in turn was recalled to the works.

It was around this time Harry turned his attention to road going vehicles. Powered transport of any description during this period was rare and attracted much attention and excitement. Harry's curiosity in such matters finally got the better of him. After reading an article on powered bicycles, he set about constructing a machine of his own. Using a B.S.A. bicycle that had been gathering dust at the works, Harry set about installing the 'Mitchell' engine into the frame. He had chosen to overlook the troublesome tendencies of this engine, in preference to using his own, on the basis of the rough and ready alterations which had been undertaken during its development. The compact 'Mitchell' was inclined forward in the frame between the steering head and the pedalling gear. A flat sided metal container was used to house the surface carburettor and petrol reservoir and was suspended beneath the cross bar. Two smaller

The four Stevens brothers with the Mitchell powered B.S.A. in 1900. Left to right: George, Joe Junior, Harry and Jack. *Photo: Joan Stevens.*

containers housing the trembler coil and battery were positioned below the leather saddle. A direct drive was employed using a round rawhide leather belt, in contact with a large diameter rim, supported from the spokes in the rear wheel. The drive also incorporated a rather neat adjustable jockey pulley arrangement to provide belt tension, but more importantly the device ensured an adequate 'wrap' of the belt around the engine pulley, thus preventing slip. Engine controls were in the form of two levers mounted forward of the petrol tank: one for controlling the mixture of air and petrol, whilst the other regulated the engine speed by advancing or retarding the spark.

Initial tests were to prove most promising apart from having to tolerate the temperamental nature of the 'Mitchell'. The machine was light, easy to control and attracted a great deal of attention. The four brothers set about tidying the machine prior to having their photograph taken with it at Jones Bros. Studios in Cherry Street. The resulting picture of the machine and the four proud brothers was taken in 1900, showing clearly how neat and compact the original configuration was.

Before long news of the Stevens machine came to the notice of William Clarke, Chairman of the Wearwell Motor Carriage Co. Ltd. The Wearwell name was already well known, for the Wearwell Cycle Co. Ltd. of Wolverhampton could trace their origins back to the very earliest days of the cycle industry. In fact, they used to claim that they were the oldest established cycle manufacturers in the world. They were also well established customers of the Stevens, who produced spokes and screws for them.

The Wearwell Motor Carriage Co. Ltd. however was a new concern, only being registered a year earlier on 26th October 1899. William Clarke was keen to enter the powered vehicle market. He had formed the Company and exhibited a four wheel powered vehicle at the Crystal Palace National Cycle Show during the same year. Motive power was by two 2¼ h.p. air cooled Butler engines, mounted side by side driving through a two speed gearbox. Due to its unorthodox tubular frame design, it was not

The Early Years

William Clarke, Chairman of the Wearwell Motor Carriage Co. Ltd.
Photo: Albert Clarke.

well received, as a result only a handful were made. Wearwell, now anxious to find the right product, were extremely impressed with the Stevens motor bicycle and immediately recognized that the concept represented at least 60% of what they already produced, namely the cycle parts. With this important factor in mind, Wearwell were keen to enter into an agreement. In due course a suitable contract was drawn up. The terms of the contract ensured the Stevens of a minimum quantity of engines of their own manufacture, to be delivered each week to the Wearwell Cycle Works in Pountney Street. It was further agreed that a settlement would be made each week following delivery. In due course Wearwell despatched a suitable heavy duty bicycle to Tempest Street and the Stevens Brothers set to work.

The first Wearwell-Stevens motor bicycle was to appear during the spring of 1901. It was fitted with a Stevens 2½ h.p. air cooled four stroke engine, with automatic inlet valve and mechanically operated side exhaust valve. This engine had internal flywheels and was set in a forward inclined position supported above the front down tube. The specification included accumulator ignition, surface carburettor and a direct belt drive. No provision was made for either clutch or gears. The complete machine

The first Wearwell–Stevens, of 1901.
Photo: Rick Howard collection.

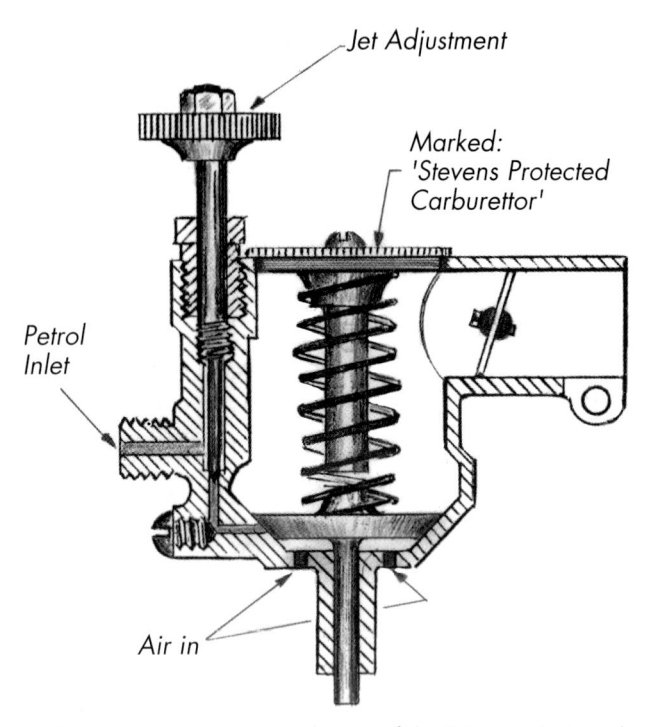

A sketch showing a sectional view of the 'Stevens Protected Carburettor'. Unfortunately this design did not prove very successful as the petrol supply was constant and therefore only suited to a constant speed set up, such as a stationary engine. With the variable speed of a road vehicle, the engine would be alternatively starved or flooded.
Sketch: Author.

Albert Clarke (son of William Clarke) and his wife Anne, pictured with their 1902 Wearwell in 1985. The machine is fitted with a 1910 Stevens engine having an external flywheel.
Photo: The Black Country Bugle.

tipped the scales around 80lbs and sold for forty two guineas (£44.10).

The machine proved to be extremely popular and remained unchanged until it was shown with a number of improvements at the National Cycle Show at Crystal Palace, in November 1902. The most significant improvement was the customers' option to choose either a Stevens surface or spray carburettor. The latter was listed under the heading of the 'Stevens Protected Carburettor'. Alterations were also made to the wheels and frame. During the exhibition, Wearwell invited a free trial or demonstration in the Palace grounds and this, coupled with a slightly reduced price of £40.0s.0d., led to a full order book.

During the early part of 1903, the brothers constructed their first complete motorcycle made entirely of their own products and proudly bearing the Stevens name. The machine, designed by Harry Stevens, had a modern appearance and was much more substantial than anything produced by Wearwell up to that time. The main frame was unusual in that it was of an open design and was ideally suited to the long skirts worn by female riders of the day. It consisted of twin down tubes that swept gracefully from a tall head stock tube, with a 2½ h.p. engine positioned almost vertically between them near the bottom bracket. A position that would become universally accepted for future motorcycles. The chaincase was fully enclosed and stretched from the pedals, situated immediately behind the crankcase, to the rear wheel. Petrol was carried in a triangle shape tank, secured between the sloping frame tubes above the engine. No clutch or gears were provided and final drive was by a twisted leather belt.

Lily, Harry's younger sister, was first to ride the Stevens machine on the roads of Wolverhampton. In so doing, she became the town's first woman motor cyclist. She was soon to be followed by her younger sisters Ethel and Daisy, who were both eager to test the machine. Whilst out riding the bike Ethel was stopped by a policeman in Darlington Street. Being only fourteen years of age at the time, she pretended to be her elder sister and later produced Lily's licence at the police station. Sadly the first Stevens machine never went into production and was later dismantled.

1903 brought changes to the Wearwell machines. The Stevens engine was driving the rear wheel by way of a 'Lincona' vee belt and

The Early Years

Joe Stevens Senior seated in the front of a 1903 Wearwell 'Motette', powered by a 2½ h.p. water cooled Stevens engine.
Photo: Joan Stevens.

This faded newspaper photograph shows Lily Stevens with the first Stevens motorcycle in 1903.
Photo: Express and Star.

1903 2½ h.p. Wearwell–Stevens as found in 1953. As number plates were not required in Wolverhampton until December 1903, the registration DA 44 must have been allotted fairly early in 1904.
Photo: Jim Boulton.

the earlier surface carburettors were discontinued in favour of the Stevens spray instrument.

Wearwell also introduced a forecar the 'Motette', which did much to increase the weekly production of the popular 2½ h.p. Stevens engine. The 'Motette' was really a lightweight tricycle based upon a modified version of the 2½ h.p. motor bicycle. A simple two wheeled axle now replaced the front wheel, onto which was mounted an attractively upholstered wicker passenger seat. Although the forecar put the passenger nearest the accident, they were not unpopular and certainly a big improvement over the earlier passenger trailers. The complete machine was listed at fifty three guineas (£55.65) and future lists were to include the fore carriage end as a conversion, complete with all necessary fittings for £16.5s.0d. (£16.25).

17

Above: DA 44 pictured after undergoing a full restoration. *Photo: Birmingham Museum of Science and Industry.*

Below: Jack Stevens (right) pictured in 1904 with specially adapted Wearwell machine. *Photo: John Waghorn.*

The Early Years

Quite apart from the success of their customers, the Stevens were fast earning a reputation for themselves. The Company had been busy developing a wide range of engines which included 1¾, 2½ and 3 h.p. air cooled designs, plus 2½ and 3 h.p. water cooled units. Carburettors, gearboxes, clutches and silencers were also offered. Demand for the Stevens products rapidly grew to such an extent, that a move to larger premises in Pelham Street was necessary during February 1904. Following the move, further engines were added to the existing range, including a 3½ h.p. unit which claimed a world record for travelling 49 miles 800 yards in one hour. The record had been achieved by a George A. Barnes of Lewisham, riding a cycle of his own make fitted with the Stevens engine at Canning Town Track on the 28th October 1904. Shortly after, and in complete contrast to this important feat, records show that Harry fitted one of his engines to a lawn mower belonging to an Osmond Evans of the Culwell Works. Quite possibly the first motor mower!

The move to Pelham Street had coincided with a redesigned Wearwell range offered under the name of 'Wolf'. These were much sturdier in appearance than the earlier models and were now fitted with Stevens air and water cooled engines up to a capacity of 3¼ h.p. The engine was positioned vertically near the bottom bracket and could be supplied with a clutch if required.

Toward the end of 1904, it was decided to form a Limited Company to encompass the interests of 'The Stevens Motor Manufacturing Company' and 'J. Stevens & Co.' under one title. The new Company was registered on 10th December 1904 (Reg. No. 10915), known as 'The Stevens Motor Manufacturing Co. Ltd.'

A maximum share capital of £5,000 (private) was made available, of which £2,000 was issued. The subscribers being: Joe Stevens Senior, W.Barnett (a partner with Joe Stevens in J.Stevens & Co.), H.Stevens, W.H.Haden (gentleman), G.Stevens, T.E.Lowe (accountant) and F.R.W.Hayward (solicitor). W.H.Haden, Joe Stevens Senior and W.Barnett were also Company Directors.

During the summer of 1905, the Company experienced financial difficulties due to a general slump in the motor industry. This did nothing to deter the brothers from continuing to develop new engines. These included a 4 h.p. single cylinder unit in both air and water cooled forms, 6, 7, 8 and 10 h.p. water cooled twin cylinder engines and 16 and 18 h.p. water cooled four cylinder units.

1905 Stevens 6 h.p. water cooled twin cylinder engine specially designed for use in forecars and light cars.
Photo: Rick Howard collection.

In view of the difficult trading conditions affecting the engine manufacturing side of the Company, it was decided to separate the screw, rivet and small turned parts side of the business. A new Company was formed to safeguard these interests early in 1906, under the title of 'The Stevens Screw Co.Ltd', with about half a dozen employees.

In the meantime the Stevens continued to produce engines for the 'Wolf' motorcycles and three wheel cars. The range had grown to include more than a dozen different models, each with a long list of specification options. The motorcycles, as opposed to the simple clip-on motor attachment types, were offered with 2½, 3¼ and 4 h.p. single cylinder engines, a 3 h.p. V-twin, plus 4½ and 5 h.p. vertical twin options. All could be supplied with a new revolutionary cork inserted clutch, designed by Harry Stevens, if required. Prices ranged between thirty seven (£38.85) and forty two guineas (£44.10). The three wheel cars were produced in passenger and commercial vehicle forms, with both lightweight and heavy duty models. The lightweight cars were a more modern version of the original 'Motette', but fitted with a larger 4½ or 5 h.p. water cooled vertical twin engine, coupled to a two speed gearbox with clutch. They retained handle bars and a leather saddle and were offered at seventy five guineas (£78.75). The heavier version gave the appearance of being much more like a car, as it was fitted with body panels and a steering wheel. A choice of 7 or 8 h.p. water cooled vertical twin engine was fitted, coupled to a three speed gearbox with clutch. A deeply upholstered seat was provided for the driver and prices ranged between one hundred (£105) and one hundred and five guineas (£110.25).

On top of this range, the tiny 'clip-on' engines fitted to the Wearwell bicycles were still proving popular and continued in 1½ and 2½ h.p. forms. They were now produced with outside flywheels positioned on the drive pulley side of the engine. This arrangement enabled a small compact crankcase to be used, allowing the engine to be fitted even closer to the front down tube. The smallest version, the 'Wolf' featherweight, was offered with a choice of accumulator or magneto ignition (Ruthardt magneto £4.10s.0d. (£4.50) extra). It weighed 60lbs complete and at only nineteen guineas (£19.95) with accumulator ignition, it was considered the cheapest motor bicycle on offer. The Wearwell Company also continued to sell the Stevens 1½ h.p. motor set complete with petrol tank and all necessary parts for £14.0s.0d., with a weight of 31lbs complete.

Unfortunately the motor business trade continued to decline. On 17th March 1907 T.E.Lowe was appointed receiver to manage the companies dealings with B.S.A. as a major debtor.

By taking outside jobs to supplement their income, the brothers struggled on until the revival of the motorcycle trade in 1908. They began to produce motorcycle frames as well as engines for their old customer Wearwell. To fully test and develop the machines, Joe Junior and Jack began to ride the 'Wolf' machines in reliability trials and speed events with considerable success. Many gold and silver medals were gained between May 1909 and August 1910. The brothers were firmly of the opinion that the experience they would gain from taking part in such endurance events, was the only way to develop their products. As history would later reveal this principle would stand them in good stead.

Later, during this period, the Stevens fortunes were about to change. They were to secure a very useful contract to produce motorcycle engines for a small Northamptonshire engineering concern based in the market town of Thrapston. The company was 'Clyno', later to become one of the best known makes of motor cycles and cars. It was run by two cousins, Frank and Ailwyn Smith, who were keen to break into the revitalized motorcycle market. This Company had earlier been involved in the trade by producing variable pulleys for belt driven motorcycles. It is thought the inclined faces of these pulleys inspired the 'Clyno' name.

The Stevens were to produce two engines for 'Clyno', a 2½ h.p. single and a 6 h.p. V-twin. The first 'Clyno' motorcycles were exhibited at the 1909 Stanley Show and were well received. This simple beginning was eventually to lead to a very happy and successful business relationship between the two companies.

Just as things were beginning to improve, the business arrangement between William Clarke and the Stevens family came to a sudden end, when an accounts wrangle came to light. Wearwell's Company secretary, a Mr. King, had for some time been using the Company's money to gamble at pool in a local public house. A great deal of money had been lost: so much that the Company was forced to close its doors and wind up its business. On learning the game was up, King had tried to commit suicide. William Clarke however, did not bring criminal charges against King, as he discovered that his brother was also involved.

Although shocked and saddened by the sudden closure of Wearwell, the brothers counted themselves fortunate in having been paid each week, under the terms of the original agreement struck with William Clarke. In view of these difficult circumstances, the Stevens brothers decided they should produce their own machines. With the light of their experience it seemed the right thing to do. Many saw the decision as an inevitable one and predicted a bright future.

To protect the existing name of their proprietary engines, it was thought necessary to introduce a new name for their motorcycles. After much deliberation, they chose to use initials only, as only one brother Jack had two Christian names (Albert John), the new marque was christened A.J.S.

Prior to the voluntary liquidation of the Wearwell concern, Joe Stevens Senior had secured premises in Retreat Street for the Stevens Screw Co. Ltd. This Company soon began to operate from the new address and was run by Joe Senior and two of his daughters, Lily and Daisy. Further freehold premises situated on the opposite side of the road, were acquired by the brothers for their new motorcycle venture.

In due course the brothers formed a new partnership under the title of A.J.Stevens & Co. Ltd.,

1910 A.J.S. 2½ h.p. single speed belt drive model 'A' machine.
Photo: Manufacturers catalogue.

1910 A.J.S. 2½ h.p. two speed chain drive model 'B' machine.
Photo: Manufacturers catalogue.

on 14th November 1909, (Reg. No. 12969). A share capital of £1,000 (private) was issued, with all shares held by the Directors: H.Stevens, G.Stevens, J.Stevens Junior and A.J.Stevens.

It fell to Harry Stevens to design the first two A.J.S. motorcycles, aptly named models 'A' and 'B'. Both were lightweight and shared the same 2½ h.p. single cylinder side valve engine, with a bore and stroke of 70mm. x 76mm. (292 c.c.). The more basic model 'A' was a single speed, direct drive, belt driven design, whereas the model 'B' had the luxury of a two speed gearbox, chaindrive and cork inserted clutch. Both were fitted with a forward mounted high tension magneto, Brown & Barlow carburettor and Brooks leather saddle and tool bag. Each was finished with four coats of black enamel on top of one special coat of rust preventative. The petrol tank was finished in aluminium with black panels, lined green, all bright parts being nickel plated. The model 'A' was listed at 110lbs in weight and offered at thirty seven guineas (£38.85), with model 'B' 120lbs and forty four guineas (£46.20) respectively.

The first machines were completed in August 1910. Production costs were largely met by Harry Stevens, from money paid to him by John Marston for designing a 2½ h.p. (349 c.c.) single cylinder side valve engine. This had a 75mm. x 79mm. bore and stroke and was destined for the first Sunbeam motorcycle.

Early A.J.S. frame and engine production was carried out at the Pelham Street Works, then despatched to the new Retreat Street premises to be assembled. About this time, the brothers were approached by a young man, Eric Williams, who had tried earlier unsuccessfully to obtain a fitters job at the Sunbeam Motor Car Works. He had decided to try his luck with the newly formed A.J.S. motorcycle company. Young Eric was no stranger to George Stevens, they had worked together at the Commercial Autocar Company based in Hereford. Eric had taken a brief apprenticeship with the Company after leaving school at an early age, whereas George had taken temporary employment there during the difficult trading period between 1906 and 1908. Eric was taken on and in so doing became the first employee outside the Stevens family.

By late autumn the brothers had decided to move their business down the road to Retreat Street, the Clyno concern was invited to take over the Pelham Street premises. This arrangement suited Frank and Ailwyn Smith well, it allowed them to be nearer to their engine suppliers, but equally important was the benefit of a high level of skilled labour that existed in the area.

Details of the new A.J.S. motorcycles were soon to be seen on the pages of the leading motorcycle journals. Without exception the new models received glowing reports, with particular praise given to design, performance and quality of finish. To the delight of the brothers the new machines were to receive further acclaim when they were exhibited at the 1910 Olympia Cycle Show in November. As well as displaying the 2½ h.p. models, Harry surprised everyone by including a 3½ h.p. 50° V-twin chain driven model, having a two speed gear-

The single speed model 'A' machine proved popular with lady riders of the day as seen here in 1911. *Photo: Rick Howard collection.*

Jack Stevens (left) and J. D. Corke on their specially adapted two speed model 'B' chain driven machines at the 1911 Isle of Man Junior T.T. race. *Photo: National Motor Museum.*

box. This machine was based on the earlier 3 h.p. V-twin 'Twin-Wolf' model, produced for Wearwell. It was primarily designed for sidecar work, but did not go into production. During the show the Stevens appointed H. Taylor & Co., 21a Store Street, Tottenham Court Road, as their sole London and district agents, an agreement that would span twenty one years.

The Olympia Show proved to be a great success, with the brothers receiving a steady flow of orders for their new machines. Further important recognition came when A.J.S. machines began winning many of the more important endurance trials. In light of later sporting achievements, Jack Stevens choice of 'Hoppit' for the Company's telegraphic address was to prove prophetic.

In 1911 it was announced by the Auto Cycle Union, that the Isle of Man Tourist Trophy races would be changed from the 15 mile 1430 yard short course, held since 1907, to a new 37½ mile 'Mountain Circuit'. In addition, it was decided to introduce a new Junior race alongside the established class for larger capacity engines. The brothers, realizing the importance of the sport to their trade, decided they would enter two carefully prepared machines very similar to the standard catalogue model 'B', except for polished engine internals and dropped handlebars. One would be ridden by Jack Stevens, the other by J.D. Corke a private owner.

The Junior class proved to be very popular with no fewer than thirty seven entries; twenty single and seventeen twin cylinder machines, representing sixteen different makes. Twin cylinder machines were given an advantage, being allowed a capacity of 340 c.c. as against 300 c.c. for the singles. The race was held on Friday 30th June, and was held over four laps totalling 150 miles.

Both machines were fitted with standard two speed countershaft gearboxes and all-chain drive. They proved extremely reliable and finished the gruelling race in fifteenth and sixteenth place. But for a 'tumble' when lying sixth, Jack Stevens would have certainly finished higher than his sixteenth place. The only single speed entries were of foreign manufacture.

The Company made a few changes to the catalogue for the 1912 season. Most important was the introduction of a new 5.h.p. 50° V-twin chain driven passenger machine, having 70mm. x 82mm. bore and stroke dimensions (631 c.c.) and listed as the model 'D'. It was fitted with a two speed gearbox designed on the lines of the 2½ h.p. unit, but much bigger and having ratios specially chosen for passenger work. A simple kick start lever was incorporated, which enabled the rider to start the engine from the

1912 2½ h.p. (315cc) model 'B'. *Photo: Author.*

Timing and drive side close-up of 1912 model 'B' engine. *Photo: Author.*

saddle. The complete machine weighing only 208lbs was offered at sixty guineas (£63.00). Models 'A' and 'B' had their engine strokes increased to 82mm. (315 c.c.) and were fitted with Amac multiple jet carburettors. The more expensive model 'B' was supplied with foot boards. Prices remained unchanged at thirty seven guineas (£38.85) and forty four guineas (£46.20) respectively. Due to popular demand, all three models featured specially designed frames, which were dropped at the rear allowing a much lower saddle height for the rider.

1912 was to prove a very busy year for A.J.S. A vast increase in sales, brought about by a successful Olympia Show in November, meant no further competition activities could be undertaken by the Company, due to its business commitments. However, this did not stop them featuring many of the sporting successes achieved by private owners, riding A.J.S. machines in their advertisements

By adopting a policy of continuous development, the Company was able to introduce further improvements and changes for 1913. These would include discontinuing the belt driven model 'A' and enlarging the side valve engine of the chain driven model 'B' to 349 c.c. (70mm. x 91mm.). A choice of two or three speed gearbox was included and each machine now had fully enclosed chain drive. Price in two speed form was forty six guineas (£48.30), with three speed offered at five guineas (£5.25) extra.

The model 'D' passenger machine was redesigned with a larger 6 h.p. V-twin engine

The Retreat Street works 1913. *Photo: Ray Jones.*

Retreat Street works interior 1913. The overall clad figure who can just be seen on the extreme left hand side of the picture, is thought to be Eric Williams. *Photo: Ray Jones.*

An interesting picture showing 6 h.p. model 'D' engines on test in 1913. Photo: Ray Jones.

having 74mm. x 81mm. bore and stroke dimensions (696 c.c.) and a three speed gearbox. Also featured for the first time was an internal – expanding rear wheel brake. Due to a longer wheel base of 4'9" and totally enclosed chaincases, the weight had risen to 255lbs and the price to sixty nine guineas (£72.45).

To accompany the model 'D', a coachbuilt sidecar complete with sprung tubular chassis was introduced. Although referred to as an A.J.S. sidecar, it was designed and manufactured by C.W.Hayward, based at that time in Church Street. The proprietor, Charles Hayward, later to become a step-brother in the Stevens family, had a year or so earlier made his first sidecar in a small upstairs room at the 'Sunbeam' works. Due to the close confines of the building, it was found necessary to dismantle the body in order to bring it downstairs. From this beginning, arrangements were made to supply both Sunbeam and A.J.S. with up to ten bodies each, per week.

During the early part of 1912, the A.C.U. had decided to make several changes to the existing rules governing engine capacity for the T.T. races. This was brought about by complaints regarding the unfair advantage given to twin cylinder machines, which led to the Junior event being raised to 350 c.c. for both single and twin machines alike. In spite of the new ruling, the 1912 races witnessed a walk-over for multi-cylinder machines, with the first six places in the Junior and first, third and fourth in the Senior going to twins. With total entries down to seventy four compared with one hundred and four for the previous year, the races proved rather disappointing.

The Stevens were again in the Isle of Man for the 1913 Junior event with two entries, ridden by Billy Heaton and Cyril Williams. To take advantage of the new A.C.U. capacity regulations, single cylinder A.J.S. engines were enlarged to 349 c.c. with dimensions of 74mm and 81mm. Both machines were fitted with two speed gearboxes and internal expanding rear wheel brakes, a new feature which would prove far superior to other braking systems. To avoid a reoccurrence of the disappointment that had surrounded the 1912 races, it was decided to extend both Junior and Senior events over two days. Each race was substantially increased in distance, resulting in six laps for the Junior (225

The Early Years

Billy Heaton No.42, closely followed by another competitor, takes his 2¾ h.p. A.J.S. round Bray Corner in the 1913 Isle of Man Junior T.T. race. *Photo: Rick Howard collection.*

miles) and seven laps for the Senior (262½ miles). Final entries were to exceed all expectations, with no fewer than forty four in the Junior and one hundred and four in the Senior. There was added interest for the spectators, with sixteen makes taking part in the Junior and thirty two makes in the Senior.

For the Junior event the riders were required to complete two laps during the morning of the first day, the Senior three in the afternoon. Both Junior and Senior races would then be run simultaneously for the remaining laps on the second day. To make things more interesting, the rules stated all machines would immediately come under A.C.U. custody. Following the first day's races, no work of any description would be allowed until the start of the second day. In order to be able to distinguish between them, the Junior entrants wore blue waistcoats, and the Senior riders red.

At the end of the first day Billy Heaton held 4th position, his machine being the only single cylinder in the first ten places. Cyril Williams was unfortunately dogged with mechanical problems and did not feature at all. During the second day, Billy Heaton moved into third place during his first lap, holding onto this position for a further two laps. On the last lap he suffered a succession of punctures, delaying him for a total of forty five minutes. Despite this he managed to finish a creditable ninth. With the exception of these misfortunes, the 1913 T.T. result had been encouraging, although no plans were made to take part in the following year. This decision was mainly due to financial reasons, the cost of developing and preparing the machines for the event had been high. The benefits of publicity surrounding a successful team, were now overshadowed by returning to a factory burdened by a lack of funds and an increasing backlog of overdue orders.

By far the largest sales growth for the A.J.S. concern, lay in their passenger machine market. The simple practicability of the sidecar had, during the ten years following its inception in 1903, established it as the most convenient method of converting a solo motorcycle, into a passenger carrying vehicle.

The new improved 6 h.p. three speed passenger combination proved so popular, the Company were unable to commit themselves to firm delivery dates. A large proportion of the sales could be attributed to the efforts of their London Agents, H.Taylor & Co., who later became increasingly concerned at the growing number of impatient customers visiting their showrooms. Although briefly eclipsed by the phenomenal sales of the model 'D' passenger

1913 6 h.p. model 'D' passenger machine. *Photo: Author.*

Drive and Timing side close-up of 1913 model 'D' engine. *Photo: Author.*

combination, the 2¾ h.p. single cylinder model 'B' continued to sell extremely well. As the end of 1913 drew near, it became obvious that the present struggles could not be allowed to continue, additional finances would have to be found in order to expand the business.

CHAPTER 2
1914... A Turning Point

Nineteen hundred and fourteen was destined to become an important milestone in both the Company's history and Britain as a whole. By February plans to float a public company had been put in hand, the brothers began to explore suitable premises to replace the cramped Retreat Street works. Meanwhile the A.C.U. had decided to reduce the distance of the T.T. races to five laps for the Junior (187½ miles) and six for the Senior (225 miles), with each race being run during one day only. Of importance was a rule governing the compulsory use of approved type crash helmets, following a fatality the previous year.

Barely two months before the T.T. races, the Stevens were approached by Bert Haddock and Cyril Williams, with a view to entering a team for the Junior race. After much persuasion it was agreed, the Company would have one last go for it and work immediately began to produce suitable machines. The A.J.S. entry consisted of five riders: Eric Williams, Billy Heaton, Cyril Williams (no relation to Eric), Billy Jones and Bert Haddock. Both Jones and Haddock were private entries.

The Junior race was held on 19th May and attracted an entry of forty nine compared with forty four for the previous year. A total of fourteen different makes were represented, comprising thirty four twin cylinder machines, against fifteen singles. The large Enfield and Douglas entries were principally responsible for the high number of twins. Favourite to win the race were the flat-twin Douglas's closely fol-

An historic line up showing the four Stevens brothers standing behind four of the five A.J.S. machines entered for the 1914 Junior T.T. race. They are from the left: (Standing) Jack, Harry, George and Joe Junior. (Riders) Billy Heaton, Cyril Williams, Eric Williams and Bert Haddock. Note the bulbous covers housing the twin chain gear arrangement. *Photo: Geoff Stevens.*

30

1914... A Turning Point

lowed by the V-twin Enfields. The most fancied singles were the new A.J.S.'s fitted with a revolutionary double primary chain drive and dog clutch arrangement giving four speeds.

Harry Stevens wrote his own account of the race and the events leading up to it, explaining the story in great detail. There can be no better tribute than quoting this verbatim:

"Until about seven weeks before the actual race we did not think of entering. We were so busy with our ordinary work, and our scheme for floating the new Company was mooted about that time. I really think the reason we did enter was because Mr. Heaton and C. Williams pressed us so hard. Mr. Heaton came over from Manchester, we had a meeting, and decided we would go for it, as we thought, for the last time. The question then arose, naturally, as to what type of machine we should use. The engine was, of course, the first consideration. We had been experimenting then for about nine months with a long stroke engine, 66½ x 100. This engine was made purely for speed work, and it turned out fairly fast, but we could not give the time to its development. I might mention that it seems now that this particular long-stroke engine is faster than that which won the T.T. Owing to the short time, and to a great extent the expense, we had to fall back on our standard.

Now perhaps a description of the actual T.T. engine would not be out of place. In so far as the usual parts were concerned, they were as far as possible standard. They were fitted with loose heads with large valve ports. This part of the engine was very carefully machined, and you would be surprised if you knew the time these heads took to prepare. They were polished like silver inside, the cylinder barrels were machined from practically a solid chunk of cast iron, and if the bore showed signs of being the least spongy, or porous, they were scrapped. The flywheels were slightly lighter than standard, the con rods were our standard rod lightened where necessary, and when finished were a beautiful piece of work. They weighed 10 ozs. each. Two rings were fitted to the top of the piston, which were of cast steel, and weighed 12 ozs. each complete. The valve timing was nearly standard, but a little overlap was allowed on both valves. The valves were 1¾ in. diameter across the heads, and had 7/32 in. lift, they were fitted with 65lb. valve springs. That is, it took a lifting strain of 65lb. to lift the valve off its seat. The compression ratio was six to one, but we eventually found this too high except for short blinds. The valve gear was our standard type, which, as no doubt you are aware, is simply a boat shaped bottomed tappet rod, working directly on to the cam, and I think if anything proved the reliability of this type of valve gear, the fact that it had to lift a valve fitted with a 65lb. spring, plus internal pressure did so. Plain bearings were used throughout, and here the efficiency and reliability of the plain bearings was again proved. The fact of our using plain bearings came as a great surprise to a lot of people. I do not wish to deny that for pure racing work ball or roller bearings would not be slightly more efficient than plain bearings, but in a race like the T.T. absolute reliability must take its place even in front of efficiency as it has been proved over and over again that it is not always the fastest machine that wins the race. Before going any further, I do not think I have mentioned the bore and stroke of the engine, this was 74mm. x 81mm.

I think I have now given you a good idea as to the general design of the engine as it was when fitted to the machines ready for despatch to the Isle of Man. Of course, when the engines were built there were still important details in connection with the machine that had to be discussed and designed. The frame and forks were exactly standard, not lightened in any way. To cut down machines for the sake of lightness, that are to be used for racing purposes, in our opinion is a great mistake. It is a policy that we do not agree with and never intend to adopt. They were fitted with carriers and tool bags exactly as standard. At this point, I might mention, those of you who saw the machines after the finish of the Tourist Trophy course will call to mind the dilapidated condition of the back of some of them, solely through designers doing away with the carrier for the sake of saving weight. It is all very well to design a machine for track work at Brooklands but it is a different matter when it comes to road racing for three or four hours together, at something like forty to fifty miles per hour, on roads that are none too smooth. I am inclined to think a lot of our success in this particular race was attained because we were determined to put on the road a machine as far as reliability was concerned, in which was embodied standard practice as far as possible. In the designing of the machines the rider's comfort was studied more than a little. From the very commencement, Billy Heaton and Cyril Williams spent a good deal of time in our works on this account, as we realized the success of a race like the Tourist Trophy depends largely on the comfort of the riders.

There is another important point that we did not overlook in designing the T.T. machines, and that was at least one good brake. The back hub was specially designed and was fitted with an internal expanding brake. No doubt most of you are conversant with the principle of this brake. They are most sensitive, and at the same time very powerful. The brake was operated through a heel-pedal by the right foot. Even this was specially designed and altered a number of times to give the rider just that position which he wanted, and I think the riders of the machine will bear me out when I say no trouble was too much for us to give them exactly what they required. The wheels, by the way, were shod with 26 in. x 2¼ in. Avon tyres.

Now comes what in my opinion was the most important feature of the whole machine. That is, the question of gearings. After looking carefully over the results of our experience in previous T.T. races we came to the conclusion that the more speeds the better, providing they could be operated simply and quickly. I might say that the question of a gear for the T.T. machines occupied my mind for some weeks, and at odd moments I designed a gear that could be used in conjunction with our two-speed gear box, that would give us four different speed ratios. The two-speed gear by itself, for a race like the T.T., considering the course, in my opinion is insufficient. The three-speed gear would be better, but four-speeds on the lines I will endeavour to explain, would be better still. One of the reasons why this special gearing was designed was this: as you know, it is both our ambition and that of other firms to get every ounce of power from the engine to the road wheels. On top gear with an ordinary two-speed gear box it makes very little difference whether the lay shaft is running in the gear box or taken out altogether. Consequently there is very little efficiency lost here. Immediately we commence to transmit our power by means of gear wheels a certain amount of efficiency is lost, owing to the friction set up by the gear wheels. I can illustrate this better I think by assuming the second gear of a motor car being too high. No doubt most of you have noticed if a car is too highly geared on second, it will do little more on an incline than it would on top gear. In consequence you have to fall down to third gear, and with this idea in mind I endeavour as far as possible to get a high top, or down hill gear without having to transmit power from gear wheels. Now so far as the transmission of power is concerned, I am a firm believer in the efficiency of a chain. Of course, I dare say there are those of you who doubt that a chain is any more efficient than a belt for transmitting the power from the engine to the road wheels. I do not think there are many of you who would care to push an ordinary bicycle fitted with a belt. I have never tried it myself, but imagining what it would be like, I never intend to.

My idea was to fit two chain wheels on the engine shaft of varying diameters, to get the necessary high second and normal gear. The two sprockets were fitted with internal dogs, and sliding between the two was a dog wheel with dog teeth on each side. This dog wheel fitted on a square that was an extension of the engine shaft. The shaft was slotted through and fitted with a key. In the centre of this key was screwed a spindle, on the end of which was a circular groove. When the sliding dog was placed between the dogs on the two chain wheels we got a free engine position. If it was pushed on either one

Close–up of one of the works 2¾ h.p. T.T. engines showing the ingenious four speed, twin chain gear arrangement.
Photo: Ray Jones.

side or the other it would engage the high top or a normal gear. This type of gear, of course, necessitates two chains. Both of these chains ran on the same clutch wheel, and the number of teeth in the clutch wheel and sprocket was so arranged that the length on the high and low gear was almost the same. The clutch was a standard pattern, but with two chain sprockets turned on it instead of one. The gears used were 4½, 5, 6¼ and 7¼. Now, I may say here, I have never been a believer in two chains running on one fixed centre. It is quite plain to anyone that the normal gear chain will stretch more than the low gear which is only used occasionally, and I would certainly not dream of using such a contraption for standard work. I had a set of gears made up and they were fitted to C. Williams' machine. The control was very crude and operated from the top tube. The machine was taken out one Sunday morning and the gear proved to work very well. I am so sure that we found a great increase in speed when the high-top gear was snicked in. The high-top seemed to score when a fairly steep descent was encountered, but you must understand that what we were after was not only increasing the speed, if possible, down the mountain, but the most important was to keep the number of engine revs constant.

1914... A Turning Point

This is an important point, as no matter how an engine is built or designed, it will not stand that "down the mountain" punishment for long. If it does you are very lucky. During the test of the gear it was used with one chain only, just to prove what power, if any, the extra chain was absorbing, and it did not seem to make the slightest difference whether one chain was used or two. That proved to me that to all intents and purposes we had two top gears that could be used on any part of the course when after tests they showed up to advantage. The gear was used in the following manner. To start up the rider would place the sliding dog on the engine shaft in the normal gear position, that is to engage the smallest chain sprocket, the gear box change speed lever is now placed in low gear, and he starts his engine up on the 7¼ to one gear. Changing into top in the gearbox gives him a five to one on top gear. On coming to a down grade he speeds up his engine until experience tells him that it is inclined to over-run the gear. He immediately slips into his high-top. This reduces the number of revs on his engine which, as I have pointed out before, is a very important point, and if the gradient is suitable to the gear it increases his speed. I may mention that in practice the 'boys' got very expert in using it, and continual practice gave them the positions on the course where the high gear change was advantageous or otherwise. The 7¼ gear was very seldom used, only in case they got baulked at a corner, or their engine began to labour unduly through under-lubrication or meeting a sudden gust of wind up the mountain. Before leaving the question of gearing, I should like to mention that although Cyril Williams handled the gear without a mistake, it occurred to us that the other boys, may not be so expert. It struck me then that it would be a fine thing if the extra gear could be operated from the handlebar. The idea was no sooner thought of than arrangements were made to fix up a simple apparatus on the handlebar, which controlled the gear on the top tube by means of Bowden cables. This proved to be a very useful fitment, as you

Details of the duplicate handle bar and tank mounted cable controls for operating the four speed arrangement. *Photo: Ray Jones.*

Billy Jones of Wrexham pictured with his 1913 standard three speed T.T. model machine in 1914. Note the large exhaust pipe. *Photo: Eric Stevens.*

will realize that at the time the high gear should be operated, the rider would probably be doing anything up to 65 miles per hour, and at this speed you will understand it is very dangerous to leave go of the handlebar with one hand for any reason whatever. With the gear change in the gear box things were different, as they would not change gear in the gear box unless the speed of the machine had dropped considerably. This would be perfectly safe. Engine lubrication was carried out by means of a hand-pump in the ordinary way. To operate this, of course, they would have to leave go of the handlebar, but here again they took care to lubricate when the machine was travelling at a reasonable and safe speed to steer with one hand. The extra gear on the engine shaft, of course, necessitated the shaft itself being made extra long, and in the event of a fall it would be dangerous for this extra length of shaft to be left unprotected. Consequently a large aluminium cover was designed, to bolt to the side of the crank case, and completely enclose the gear. The use of this cover also made it possible to simplify the operating mechanism in connection with the gear, at the same time protecting it in case they had a fall.

I might mention here that at about the time we decided to enter the T.T. race we made arrangements to enter two machines. As time went on Eric Williams made it plain to us that he would very much like to ride, and after due consideration we decided to enter him. Bert Haddock also made arrangements to enter with his standard touring machine, with the idea more especially of riding for his firm's tyres. But yet another who fancied his chance was determined to enter, and this was Mr.Jones of Wrexham. Mr.Jones, by the way, rode a standard T.T. model machine, with a three-speed bottom bracket gear. The other four we decided to put on T.T. machines to which the four-speed gear arrangement was fitted. This was a good thing, as other events which happened in the Isle of Man will prove. I may say that building these special machines cost us a good deal of money, as from start to finish they had to be very carefully watched, and only the very best men were allowed to do anything on them at all. As for myself, I should think for quite three weeks before the race I did nothing else but supervise the building of the machines and also I did a considerable amount of the most particular fittings myself. I hardly think you can possibly realize what these weeks were like to us. As the machines were finished they were taken in and out of the shop for test runs, to see what difference the various little adjustments we made to them from time to time had made, and all this, mark you, in the busiest part of the season.

As the machines gradually began to look like motor bicycles, it was all the more necessary that every attention should be given to them, and any special part or alteration should be made with the least possible delay. To prove to you how thoroughly we try to do a thing when once we make a start, the output of our works dropped down to something like about one half, and during the last few days previous to going over to the Island, T.T. stuff was put before anything. The whole works was bitten by the bug. Speaking personally, the last few days were like a nightmare, and more than once I ran up to my father's place in the afternoon feeling worn out, and my father often said to me, "Why on earth are you letting this job worry you so, I should let it go" but, of course, I simply had to tell him it was impossible. We had put our hand to the plough and we were going to see it through. Little did he think what a proud man he would be in the course of a few days.

It was a strange thing considering that although all these machines were built practically to the micrometer in every part, you would be astonished at the varied results we got when we took them on the road, as each one was ready. Cyril, I might say, did most of the donkey work with regard to taking the machines out and giving them a run. He would take them sometimes for as much as 100 miles at a stretch. I can assure you it was a very anxious time we had waiting for his report on his return. We could usually tell by the look on his face, if the machine was not going as well as it should, he took it to heart just as much as we did ourselves, and to give you any idea of the little things, artful dodges, small adjustments that were continually necessary before the machines could leave for the Isle of Man, would be absolutely impossible.

Eventually, we got them all finished, and a fine little lot they looked indeed. On Friday morning, May 8th, we started for the Isle of Man. The machines were taken up to Liverpool by my brother Jack by train, and got safely on to the boat. It happened that quite a lot of T.T. enthusiasts were travelling by the same boat, and I am proud to think of the many favourable comments that were made at various times on the machines. If they could have seen them a few days later on I have no doubt that they would have been staggered. However, I will refer to this later on.

On arriving at the Quay in the Island, we were, of course, inundated by enquiries from numerous 'touts' that stand about this particular spot, as to whether we wanted the machines taken off the boat. I may say, however, that we had made up our minds not to have any.

With the help of Cyril, Bert and Eric, whom we met all smiles on our arrival, we soon hoisted the T.T. machines safely on terra firma. 'Pratts' people were there to meet the boat, so we didn't have much difficulty in getting petrol to enable the machines to be driven out to Greeba, which was our depot during our stay.

1914... A Turning Point

On Saturday morning Eric, Cyril, Bert and Billy Heaton were up early and each man took his actual T.T. machine to Quarter Bridge, and registered them for their practice lap, and I may mention in this practice run they all qualified. My brother Jack and myself waited very anxiously for their arrival at the depot. After a run round, with the exception of one, that was Cyril, they were all dissatisfied with their machine, and then the fun began. Bert Haddock's language started to make the trees bow their heads, but we very soon shut him up on telling him to get his jacket off and start to work, and when you mention work to Bert Haddock it almost breaks his heart. Cyril was fairly well satisfied with his machine. Eric, although we could see by the look on his face, was far from satisfied, he was not the chap to grumble. He knew the game, and forthwith started to remove his cylinder, and carry out any little idea that occurred to him, or on our instructions.

What each one told us of the experience round the course, proved pretty conclusively that the compression was too high, and strange to say, the machines did not show up nearly so well as they did in Wolverhampton. I have heard quite a lot of T.T. riders say exactly the same thing, that immediately they get their machines over to the Isle of Man they are not the same. Why this is I don't know. One of the cylinders, I forget now which machine it was, we found to be scored very badly apparently through under-lubrication. This we replaced with a new one. To lower compression we fitted a suitable number of cooperite washers underneath the foot of the cylinders. This reduced it to about five to one. Various other adjustments were made, and the machines got ready for the following Monday morning when they were taken out again. On arrival at the depot, we again listened carefully to their experiences round the course. They had all stuck up about three times at different places on the mountain. Cyril again had done the best. Why this was so we could not explain. Eric in his usual quiet way started to remove his cylinder and make an examination. Bert very reluctantly started to do the same thing. Apparently the trees were getting used to Bert, but the fowls who usually ran about the lawn would not come out of their nests. I think they must have been mind readers, for I did not hear Bert use any bad language that morning. Billy Heaton was very disappointed with this machine. We found on removing his cylinder the big end had gone, and the piston end was quite blue. Now this was very disheartening, as although the other engines were built and lubricated in exactly the same way, we had this trouble with one of them. I do not think for a minute it was because he had not used sufficient oil, as the oil tank was practically empty. Why the big end should have gone, at the time, was a mystery, as practically the whole of the oil that went to the engine was forced through the big end by means of oil-ways through the centre of the shaft, up-web in the flywheel and through into the crankpin itself. I may mention here that the engines were fitted with very large relief pipes, and in the top of the relief pipe was a large ball valve, but to this I will refer later on. Of course, Heaton's engine had to be taken completely out of the frame, re-bushed, and put together again.

In the meantime the other boys had done what they thought was necessary to their machines, and put them on one side for the following morning's practice. Bert's machine was fitted with a 'Senspray' carburettor. Cyril had a 1912 type large 'Amac', Eric and Heaton had an 'Amac' also, but of the 1914 pattern. Various adjustments had been made to these carburettors with varying results, and we could not see how the carburettors could affect the running of the machine, or the lubrication of the engine. However, Haddock swore by his 'Senspray' carburettor, and one after the other, the others tried it, and came to the conclusion that they got better results. In consequence Bert went over to Douglas and arranged to get three 'Senspray' carburettors. One was fitted to Heaton's machine, and one to Eric's but Cyril would stick to his old 'Amac'. I am inclined to believe now that the carburettors had very little to do with it, but as I said before, whatever the men suggested we endeavoured to get them, if they thought it would be better. They fancied the 'Senspray' carburettor, and, of course, they had it.

On the Tuesday morning we decided to try some cast iron pistons, which we had brought with us. They all thought that cast iron pistons would be better. I think you will see that from the time we started, things, if anything, were getting a little better. First the carburettor seemed to improve things, lowering the compression seemed another slight improvement, and the cast iron pistons were better still.

On Wednesday they started off as usual. Eric and Cyril came in, Cyril highly delighted with the way his machine was running, Eric reported that his was doing fairly well, and thought it would get better. Billy Heaton and Bert had not turned up, and after a good deal of waiting we could not think where they had got to. At a time like this I think you will realize that the strain was very great, not having got any news of them for about an hour after the others had come in. Eventually I took my machine towards Douglas to see if I could see anything of them. I came upon them discussing the fall of a rider. I think he rode an 'Ariel'. From what I could gather his front tyre had blown off, and he came down on his head. His helmet proved this, as the one side was knocked in, and if it had not been for the foresight of the A.C.U. in providing these helmets, the man would undoubtedly have been killed. In fear and trembling I asked them both how they were going. "Not so bad," they said, "I think they are a little better." I went on in front and left Bert and Heaton to come on behind. I should think they came in in about ten minutes. On their arrival I noticed Bert Haddock hanging on to the carrier of Billy's machine. Now the first thing I said was, "You will see what that soft game will do for you one of these mornings," and the trees for miles around again bowed their heads. "It's all very well, but my bloody con-rod has gone." As he turned the engine round I could hear something happening inside. Even before the cylinder was taken off I had in my mind that it was not the con-rod that had broken, and in this I proved to be correct. It was not the con-rod, but the crankpin. Now here was a sight, but it happened we had some spare crankpins. Of course, Bert didn't grumble at all or swear a bit, at least not much. He doffed his jacket and commenced to remove his engine. Billy Heaton in the meantime had been up and down the road with this machine when we noticed him coming up the road pushing it. All eyes were on Billy. "What's the matter, Billy?" "I think the piston has gone," he said, and he was right. With this I think you will begin to realize that we were almost heartbroken. At any rate the cast iron pistons were not trustworthy, and would have to be removed. We afterwards found that the metal, although the caster had endeavoured to put the very best iron in them, was not suitable for the purpose. They had no more strength when broken, than so much cardboard. Now the lubrication with the cast iron pistons seemed a little better. In consequence we turned our attention to better lubrication for the cylinders, as these pistons had to be replaced by the steel ones. This was carried out by fitting oil scoops to the baffle plates on the edge of the crankcase, and this little idea proved to be a good thing. I may say fitting these took a good deal of time, and this had to be done by the lights of acetylene lamps. Now even though we were looking after the lubrication of the cylinders it occurred to me that oil was being used in plenty, the oil tank of each machine proved this, and after a test that was made, which took some time to carry out, we found that a lot of the oil was being lost through the relief valve, and after various experiments we adopted a simple and plain relief pipe, which was fitted to the gear side of the engine underneath the footrests, and tied to them by insulating tape. Now from what I have explained you will see what was going on in the depot during Wednesday. On Thursday, the men turned out as usual, and their experience after their arrival after the practice run gave us more heart. The lubrication idea had apparently got over a lot of our trouble. Cyril and Billy Heaton complained of their valves stretching, as they had had to stop on various parts of the course and adjust the tappets. Now this is a thing we had never had happen before in all our experience. As a matter of fact we have never known one of our valves stretch or break for years. After a good deal of argument we came to the conclusion that instead of the valve stretching, it was the cooperite washers underneath the cylinder that were sinking. These we replaced by cardboard washers which we cut from Hans Renold chainboxes. I may mention here that Cyril appeared to be satisfied with his so he did not disturb them, and I think subsequent events will prove that he is sorry for it up to this day.

On Thursday Billy reported that he had made a very fast lap, and was delighted with the way his engine was running. Nothing had been altered, but he was using the 'Senspray' carburettor, and I noticed that when he came in his machine was absolutely smothered with oil, and the gauze box on the carburettor was simply teeming with lubricating oil. Where it had come from I do not know. Now I had heard that a lot of fellows were using oil in their petrol and they either found it, or thought it was a good thing, and I thought it would not be a bad idea to try a small quantity of lubricating oil in the petrol. This we tried on Thursday afternoon. I remember Billy going towards St. John's to have a test. He was away some little time, and the cry went up, "Where has Billy got to," what had happened to him. When he came back he was being towed behind a Douglas Cyclecar, which was driven by Billy Douglas. "What's the matter, Billy?" " I think the connecting rod has gone." I think you will begin to realize that at this stage we were all about fed up with the whole thing. Everybody was disgusted and disappointed. Billy Douglas tried to cheer us up by telling us that they were all having the same trouble. He told us that their boys were having an enormous amount of trouble, and from the time of their arrival in the Isle of Man they had nothing but breakages. He ended up by inviting and insisting that the whole gang went into the pub and had a drink with him. I suppose this cheered us up a bit.

In the meantime Bob Shakespeare had removed Billy's cylinder, and found it was not the con-rod but the crankpin. This was two that had gone. Now it began to dawn on my mind that there was something wrong with these crankpins. We have never had crankpins go before, and to prevent, as far as possible, anything occurring in the Isle of Man, they were made from the finest steel we could get. On taking the engine apart we found that not only had the crankpin broken, but it had broken the side of the flywheel. This meant either one or a pair of flywheels. Flywheels you will understand are things that you don't think of taking as spares. What were we going to do. I know, Bert Haddock's practice machine. The idea was no sooner thought of than the engine from Haddock's practice machine was taken out, and flywheels removed. Whilst Shakespeare was preparing another crankpin he noticed that the shank end, that is the part that is pulled in the flywheels, was cracked. We had half a dozen of these crankpins with us, and everyone showed either one or more cracks in the very same place. Of course, every member of the little gang had their eyes on these crankpins. "Are those safe that are already in the engines?" No, they were not. It happened about this time that brother Joe had arrived at Greeba, and after a good deal of argument and discussion, it was decided that the engines should be removed from the frames, and that Joe should visit Douglas, and see if he could either get some firm or repairer to make us half a dozen crankpins, or make them himself, if he could not find a man capable. These he must insist upon being made from ordinary common mild steel. It was arranged also that if he was successful in getting a firm to make them, he should get a supply of prussiate of potash, which we should use for flash-hardening them. I believe on his way to Douglas he met brother George, who had come over to see how things were going. When he told him what was happening I can quite understand he must have felt sick.

All he could see when he arrived at Greeba was a number of frames without their engines. Every single engine had been taken out, and taken to pieces waiting the arrival of the new crankpins. These we had some difficulty in getting, but eventually Joe found a place, and had a promise of crankpins at 4 o'clock on Friday afternoon. In the meantime I had experimented with a piece of steel he brought back, and found it excellent. All day Friday we anxiously waited the arrival of the crankpins, but it was not until mid-day on Saturday that we got them. I want you here to understand, if you can, the position of things up to Saturday mid-day. All the engines were in pieces in boxes, and on the Tuesday following they had to try their hand at winning the T.T.

We eventually got the crankpins and flash-hardened them ready for fitting to the flywheels. Now this job was one that could only be tackled by an expert, so you will see as our facilities in the shed in which we worked were very limited, even if it had been possible for the other boys to help they could not have done so. There was only one very frail bench and a vice. However, Bob Shakespeare worked like a brick all the afternoon. After tea a few of us went to Douglas for a breather, and on our arrival back at the depot, which was about 11 o'clock, Bob was trying to true the flywheels by the aid of acetylene lamps. All were thoroughly downhearted, with the exception of Bob Shakespeare, who kept telling us that we should win the T.T. All our trouble is over when this job is done. Little did we think that his words would come true. I can tell you he was about beat, and for the life of him he could not true those flywheels. If I remember right, I insisted that the work should cease forthwith, and every man be up early on Sunday morning.

This we did, and on Sunday morning I was up myself about 6 o'clock. I trued two pairs of flywheels in a very short time, not but what Shakespeare could have done so, but because he was worn out. After breakfast things went along with a swing, and on Sunday afternoon the machines began to look like their old selves. Now I should like you to carry your mind over the incidents that happened during the few hours previous, and try to imagine what all this meant. Our efforts to put up a good show I can assure you were almost superhuman, and after all when success eventually came to us we looked back on these very anxious times and without exception everyone could only say "It was worth it". On Monday morning they took their machines out again, and the report was very favourable indeed. The short time we had at our disposal between the time they had finished practising and the time they had to be at Douglas to be examined was all too short, but eventually we got to Douglas in good time. The machines were weighed, examined and fitted up with their proper numbers and safely housed in the A.C.U. tent. You can imagine what was running through everyone's mind from the time this was done to the time to start on Tuesday. I expect if I could have read the minds of them all it was a case of what will be our fate tomorrow?

On Tuesday morning, May 19th, all the chaps were up looking very fit for the fray. After loading up the sidecar machines in which we were going to put the necessary oil and petrol fillers, also the boys, you may depend we had a fairly large load to take up to Douglas. When the Junior competitors began to assemble in the enclosure at the top of Bray Hill the sky was rather over-cast, but the day eventually turned out ideal. At 9 o'clock the competitors were lined up in the gangway between the stands and the pits, and a quarter of an hour later one by one they paraded in front of the stand and took up their positions in pairs on the starting line. In the meantime myself and the other boys whose duty it was to fill their men up on their arrival, had taken up our positions in the pits allotted to us. My duty was to look after Eric, Jack had charge of Billy Heaton and Joe had to put up with Bert Haddock. Cyril was helped by Bob Shakespeare and W.Jones was filled up by a friend of his, and very well he did it too. Promptly at 9.30 Hugh Mason, last year's winner, was sent away, and received a very hearty cheer, and one by one the other competitors were despatched, with 40 seconds interval. W.Jones was the last man of our team to leave. Our old friend Mr.Travers took up his position immediately behind our pits, and with his watch ready we waited very anxiously for our boys to come round. At exactly 18 minutes to 10 o'clock news came that three riders had passed Ballacraine in their starting order, then came Billy Heaton. He had picked up a few places. Sailors at the top of Bray Hill now took up their positions with very powerful telescopes to watch for the vanguard. Heaton was going very well on the first lap. Poor Walker, who rode an Enfield, was leading. His time for the first lap was 47 min. 57 secs., a record at that time. Eric Williams was second, 48 min. 42 secs. None of our other riders on this lap were in the first six. They were all going very steady, and apparently had had no trouble. As each one passed the depot we gave them a rousing cheer.

Seperate oil tank fitted to the works T.T. machines.
Photo: Ray Jones.

On the second lap the intervals between the riders increased, and men began to drop out. Eric's second lap was a very fast one, and was only 28 secs. behind Walker. The Douglas riders were pressing them very hard. At times it seemed as if the race was developing into a three-cornered fight between Enfield, A.J.S. and Douglas riders. Practically all the riders stopped to fill up, and it was a surprising thing to me how leisurely this most important thing was done by some of the riders. The filling up part of the business we had again thought of. Their tanks were filled with petrol by means of a large can specially made with a valve in the bottom. This was given to the riders immediately on their arrival, and all they had to do was to lift up the filler cap, which was held down by a spring, place the mouth of the filler in the opening and pull down the valve. The petrol simply fell into the tank which was full in next to no time. Whilst this was being done the oil tank was filled by a large open top can. This we could tip up without it overrunning, and the oil went into the tank in prac-

tically one gulp. I think a lot of valuable time was saved our men in the way they were filled up.

Bert Haddock, of course, on the second lap must overshoot the mark at the top of Bray Hill, but he did not get far - there was a telegraph pole waiting for him. He scrambled back again at a good pace, and pulled up about 200 yards further down than he ought to have done. Back he came like a roaring bull. When he did arrive at the official filling up place the air for yards around was so thick you couldn't breath. As a matter of fact, the grandstand began to rock and a few of the ladies, who were almost within touching distance thereof, seemed to be very uncomfortable. He complained that his bloody brake was no good, but after the race we noticed that his tyre had the appearance of a hexagon nut. At any rate off he went again, everyone wishing him good-luck. I believe if we had offered him a bottle of beer he wouldn't have stopped for it. I think I should mention here that the second lap was the fastest ever made in any Junior T.T. race. It was made by Eric in 47 mins. 18 secs. On the third lap all our men again passed the grandstand. Eric on this lap assumed the leading position, his time for the three laps being 2 hours 24 mins. 47 secs. Billy Heaton came next - 2 hours 28 mins. 22 secs. Fifth in the line came Cyril - 2 hours 34 mins. 21 secs.; sixth Bert Haddock - 2 hours 35 mins. 49 secs. By the time Ramsey was reached on the fourth round the A.J.S. team further established themselves among the vanguard. In position, Heaton led, with Eric and Cyril coming next. The times for the fourth lap were as follows: Eric 3 hours 14 mins. 15 secs., Heaton 3 hours 16 mins. 3 secs., Cyril 3 hours 22 mins. 22 secs. and W.Jones 3 hours 28 mins. 24 secs. On the fifth lap Billy Heaton was going strong and a likely winner. Eric on his final lap was the leader of the band and although Eric started later, he managed to retain his position by, I am told, the smart way he was filled up on the fourth lap. Cyril arrived a few minutes later.

Then news came that Heaton had passed Ramsey. The field now was thinning very considerably. The strain of that last lap every one of our little band in the pens will never forget. It was simply awful. You can understand what our feelings were, when, not only was the trophy within our grasp but our machines were lying in the fifth lap, first, second, third, fourth and sixth. We could hardly realize it, and I shall be very much surprised if a performance like this is ever equalled again, but, as quoted by the 'Motor Cycle', "There is many a slip, etc." Jack was anxiously waiting for Billy Heaton, who had passed Ramsey, only about 7½ miles from the finish. After this no news was heard of Heaton for some time. In the meantime, the seconds seemed like hours whilst waiting for Eric. At last the megaphone made it quite clear to us

Eric Williams No. 27, crosses the finishing line to win the 1914 Junior T.T. race. *Photo: Keig collection.*

that Eric Williams, No. 27, had passed Hillberry. It was only a matter of a few seconds then before the winner of the Junior T.T. hoved in sight round the corner on the top of Bray Hill. Those few moments I shall never forget.

The scene in our camp was indescribable, and amidst the cheers of the onlookers he was carried shoulder high to the back of the grandstand, whilst I gladly pushed his machine into the A.C.U. official tent for the purpose of having the cylinders measured. I forgot to mention that almost at the same time, practically on Eric's heels, came Cyril. F.J. Walker was the next man to come in sight at the top of Bray Hill, but, as we all know, this poor chap either lost his head, or misjudged the speed at which he was travelling, and instead of turning the corner he ran straight on and crashed into a telegraph pole that was placed there as a barrier. Poor Walker the following day died in Douglas Infirmary. The next man to finish was E. Barker, who rode a Zenith and following close on his heels came Bert Haddock. After seeing all our machines safely in we got through into the paddock where an extraordinary scene met our view. Eric was simply surrounded by about thirty photographers, who were anxious to get a snapshot. W. Jones, who finished fourth, had a nasty spill almost in sight of the finish, and knocked his thumb about pretty badly. So far as Bert Haddock was concerned, they say the

An exhausted Eric Williams is helped by Jack Stevens (left) and Joe Stevens Junior after the race. *Photo: Geoff Stevens.*

The victors of the 1914 Junior T.T. are held aloft by Jack and Joe Stevens Junior. Harry Stevens is pictured far left, while George can be seen far right. Photo: Joan Stevens.

devil looks after his own. I believe the only real trouble that was encountered was reported by Cyril, who said he had to stop on the last two laps three or four times to adjust his tappets, and if you will remember I said that Cyril was so satisfied with his machine that he did not trouble to take the Cooperite washers from underneath the foot of the cylinders, and replace them by cardboard ones, and, after examining the engine we found that the Cooperite washers were simply being pressed out by the pressure of the cylinder bridge, and I am afraid if he had had to go another lap, the packing would have come clean away.

After a few drinks and a chat together, Jack and myself had a look inside the official tent where the cylinders were being examined by the officials, who were to check the capacity of the engines. All this was done very quietly and hardly a word spoken. I believe Archibald Sharp, whose task it was to measure them, looked across at the Rev. Greenhill, who was present. What he meant by that look I don't know, but you can understand what I was thinking about. Jack also went very white. At any rate Jack asked Mr. Sharp if everything was all right, and his words were, "Yes, quite in order Mr Stevens." That finished it. At about this time we heard a shout from the roadway that W. Heaton had again started, coming home very slowly with a badly buckled front wheel. This was the first news we had had about him for some time, notwithstanding all our enquiries of other competitors, none had seemed to notice him on the course. In about ten minutes a very dejected looking object came round the top of Bray Hill, riding very slowly, with the front wheel scraping the sides of the forks. He was knocked about pretty badly, but everyone who was near gave a rousing cheer. His first words were, "I am very sorry. I have done my best, but I think my luck is out. I was determined to finish." I do not think poor old Billy just at that moment realised what he had lost, but subsequent incidents proved that he took it very much to heart, as if you will remember last year he had the trophy within his grasp. Still I think it was some consolation to Billy to wish him better luck next time.

I have now endeavoured, as far as my memory serves, to describe to you how we won the T.T., and all that remained to be done afterwards was to celebrate it. This, of course, meant 'getting up the pole', buying flags, and doing other daft things. Towards evening we all sailed down to the Sefton, only to be inundated with congratulations on every hand. I did manage to get into the smoke room eventually, and

Eric Williams, the youngest ever T.T. winner poses for the camera astride his oil streaked winning A.J.S. *Photo: Keig collection.*

everybody was asking me what I was going to have to drink, but unfortunately for me they all seemed to ask at the same time and it ended in a gigantic farce as eventually I had to pay for my own. I remember George coming up to me, to give me what he thought was some brotherly advice, but it proved to be a case of 'Do as I say, but not as I do'. He said, "Harry, go steady, the night's young." After a time we all made our creepings to Greeba. I think about two motor cars accompanied us, and if I remember rightly, they had on board about half a dozen cases of champagne. This was unloaded at Greeba, and the boxes opened one after the other, by means of anything handy. Champagne was cheap that night. We did not buy any, but I know one or two, who shall be nameless, who knew all about it the next morning. I think I was about the only one sober in the whole crowd. Toward the finish, after I had gone to bed, I believe they were drinking champagne out of pint pots. I should not like to cause any ill-feeling, but Joe had about as much as he could carry away by 8 o'clock. Eric, like a sensible chap, cleared off. The following morning brought many headaches, but none of them grumbled, all they could say was, "Well it was worth it."

I think I have told you about as much as I can remember, and I think I can safely say that when I look back from the time we started until we finished up, everyone agreed the fruits of success well repaid all our little troubles and anxieties.

Harry Stevens.

The race was a sweeping victory for the Wolverhampton concern, with A.J.S. machines gaining first, second, fourth, sixth and twenty ninth places. Eric Williams was the eventual winner with a record race speed of 45.58 m.p.h. He also managed the fastest time with second lap speed of 47.57 m.p.h. and a time of 47 minutes 18 seconds. Oddly enough he had chosen to ride in the event without the aid of goggles. In those days riders had to carry and finish with a tool roll; Eric had left his at Greeba where he changed a plug. However, Bob Shakespeare managed to produce a substitute before the officials had time to check. Having celebrated his twentieth birthday during practice week, Eric Williams went on record as the youngest ever T.T. winner. No team deserved victory more,

The large crowd gathered outside Wolverhampton (High Level) Station to welcome home the A.J.S. team. *Photo: Geoff Stevens.*

Cyril Williams astride the 2¾ h.p. A.J.S. which took him to second place in the 1914 Junior T.T. race. Using this same machine less than a month later he went on to win the 'Brooklands' Junior T.T. *Photo: Charles Williams.*

The front entrance of Graiseley House. Photo: Geoff Stevens.

they had triumphed over tremendous odds since arriving on the island ten days earlier.

On returning home, the team were given a rousing welcome by a large crowd gathered at Wolverhampton (High Level) Station. After posing for press photographers amid loud cheers and blowing of horns, Eric and Cyril Williams were placed in a position of prominence in the procession of gaily decorated motor vehicles which proceeded to the A.J.S. works in Retreat Street. Here a large and enthusiastic crowd had assembled, who cheered and hoisted the winners to shoulder height carrying them into the works. The procession returned to the Kings Hall Restaurant, headquarters of the Wolverhampton Motor Cycling Club, of which both riders were members, where another reception awaited the victors.

The following month witnessed another great A.J.S. victory, with Cyril Williams winning the 'Brooklands Junior T.T.' on 13th June at an average speed of 53.93 m.p.h. Cyril's machine, the same as he had ridden earlier in the Isle of Man Junior T.T., was the only A.J.S. entered and had easily won after taking the lead on the first lap.

The result of the 1914 Junior T.T. race was seen as the turning point for A.J.S. Overnight, demand for the '2¾ h.p. T.T. Sporting Model', as ridden by Billy Jones more than doubled. In response, a new public company was formed to take over the interests of A.J.Stevens & Co. Ltd., registered on 18th July 1914 (Reg.No. 137062), with the title 'A.J.Stevens & Co,. (1914) Ltd'. Nominal share capital £50,000 (public) issued £30,000. Directors were: H.Stevens, G.Stevens, J.Stevens Junior, A.J.Stevens, E.E.Lamb (Stock broker) and E.L.Morcom (Engineer). The registered office was at Retreat Street.

With the increased demand for A.J.S. machines, new manufacturing premises were urgently sought. Enquiries were to reveal details of a country estate situated close to the existing works on the outskirts of the town. Known as 'Graiseley House', it included an impressive mansion once part-owned by Sir Rowland Hill, originator of the 'Penny Post' in 1840.

The brothers wasted no time, purchasing the estate from Richard Evans Willoughby Berrington, a civil engineer who emigrated to Australia after the sale. Following the purchase of Graiseley House, plans were drawn up and work began to erect a single factory building measuring 260 feet x 80 feet.

Back at Retreat Street, the four brothers could hardly believe their new found success,

1914 6 h.p. model 'D' passenger combination. *Photo: Manufacturers catalogue.*

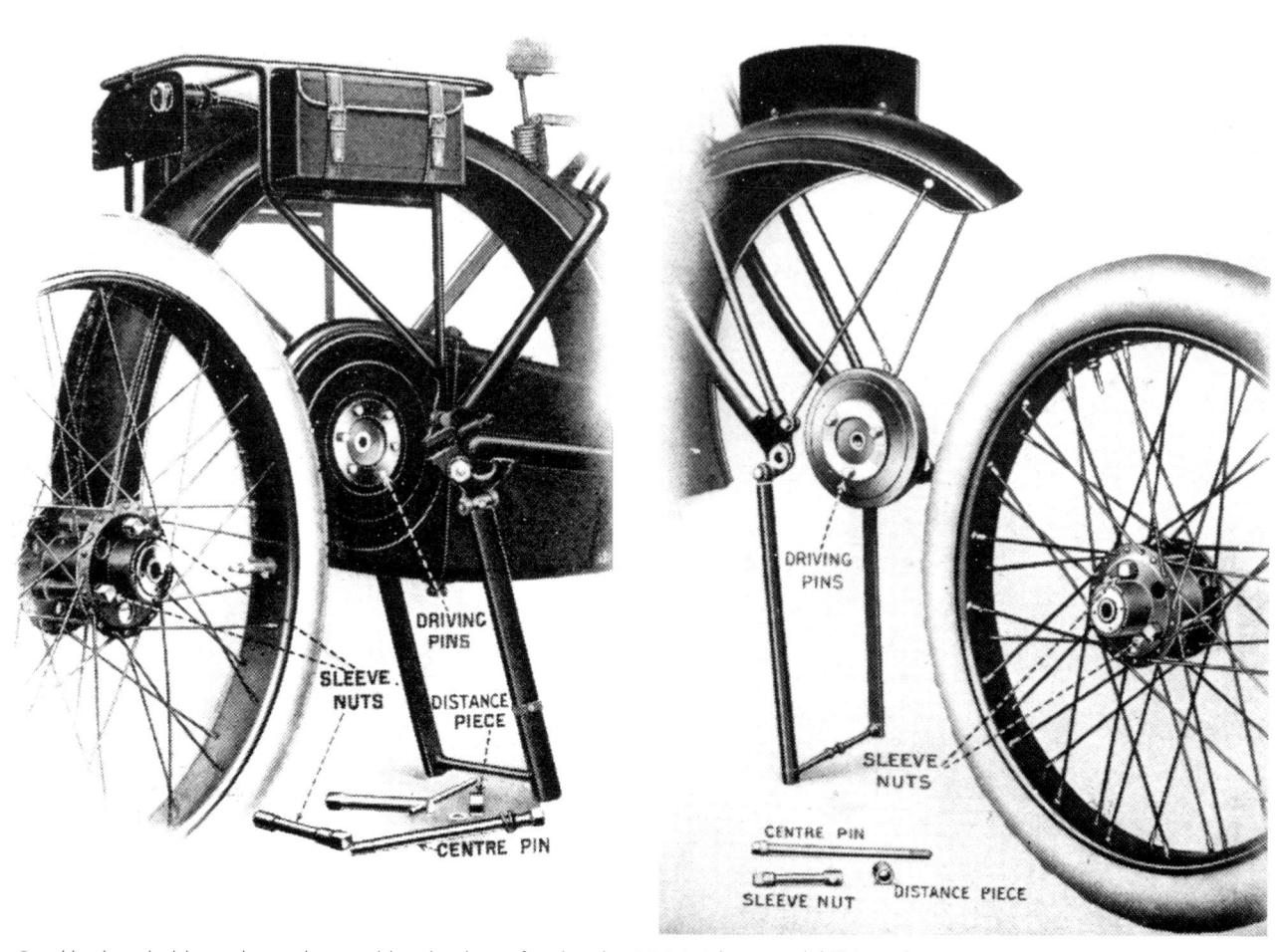

Quickly detachable and interchangeable wheels, as fitted to the 1914 6 h.p. model 'D' machines.
Photo: Manufacturers catalogue.

demand for A.J.S. machines had never been so great. As a gesture of loyalty and goodwill, it was decided from the beginning each brother would successively take over the position of Managing Director for one year.

Popularity for the 6 h.p. V-twin model 'D' passenger combination, received a further boost with the introduction of quickly detachable and interchangeable wheels. So well received was this feature, the company offered conversions for 1913 and early 1914 models. At this time, the A.J.S. sidecar manufactured by C.W.Hayward took on a more luxurious appearance, beautifully upholstered in 'Crocketts' leather, it could be supplied with folding weatherproof hood, side curtains, windscreen and Axminster floor covering at additional cost.

The Wedding of Lily Stevens To Jabez Wood, 1914. This photograph was taken outside the motorcycle works in Retreat Street, just prior to the Company going public as A.J. Stevens & Co. (1914) Ltd.
Main members of the Stevens family can be seen as follows:

1. Harry Stevens. 2. Ethel Stevens. 3. Lucy Stevens. 4. Billie Stevens. 5. Lily Stevens. 6. Joe Stevens Senior. 7. Daisy Stevens. 8. Mrs. Joe Stevens Senior. 9. Jack Stevens. 10. George Stevens. 11. Joe Stevens Junior.

Photo: Susan Taylor.

CHAPTER 3
1915-1919 Ideas on Hold

Hardly had the brothers set foot on the Graiseley estate, when the Kaiser's War broke on the world. At first production at Retreat Street continued unaffected, but eventually the Company had to accept War Office contracts, involving the production of aircraft components and munitions.

The War Office was not slow to realize the potential of the motorcycle in war and appealed for volunteers to become despatch riders. This prompted Eric Williams, who at this time was chief tester and tuner at the works and William, the fifth and youngest of the Stevens brothers, known to the others as 'Young Billie' to join up. 'Billie' had played only a minor role in the motorcycle business, usually working with his father Joe Senior and his sisters in the Stevens Screw Company, on the opposite side of the road to the A.J.S. factory in Retreat Street. Like so many of the enthusiastic volunteers of the time, Eric and 'Billie' had jumped at the opportunity to serve 'King and Country'. 'Billie' later saw service in Salonika and the Dardanelles, whereas Eric was awarded the Distinguished Conduct Medal at Neuve Chapelle before being badly wounded, following the Battle of the Somme in 1916 and invalided out of the army the following year.

The Company was now working full out on War Office work, but the brothers still managed to design and complete a new range of motorcycles for the 1915 season. These were introduced early in November 1914 and consisted of four models. The most striking feature of the new machines was an entirely new style of frame, comprising a straight sloping top tube. This style replaced the curved dropped frame which had been introduced for the 1912 season. The new frame necessitated the fitting of a wedge shaped petrol tank, incorporating an engine oil compartment and a new Best & Lloyd semi-automatic drip feed unit. This was fitted with a sight feed on top of the pump. American made 'Splitdorf' magnetos replaced the earlier German 'U.H.' instruments on the V-twin models, whilst Thompson-Bennett D.D.M. magnetos were used on the 2¾ h.p. single cylinder models. All engines were again fitted with

'Young Billie' photographed while serving 'King and Country', 1916.
Photo: Jim Stevens.

improved Amac carburettors. The new models were designed with wide front mudguards, which meant the forks had to pass through the detachable valances. Most interesting of the new machines, the model 'A', was described in the catalogue as 'Double-Purpose'. It was suitable as a solo mount or could be attached to a sidecar. The model 'A' was fitted with a 4 h.p. 50° V-twin engine (550 c.c.), having a 65mm. x 83mm. bore and stroke. An improved design three speed bottom bracket gearbox was

1915 - 1919 Ideas on Hold.

Drive side view of a well used 1915-16 6 h.p. model 'D' passenger machine, as captured by the camera in 1965. Note the spring seat pillar offered as an extra on this model for £1.13s.0d (£1.65).
Photo: Mark Baker.

Joe Stevens Junior and his wife Lucy pictured with their 6 h.p. model 'D' passenger outfit at Old Wyche Cutting near Malvern, in 1915 while taking part in a reliability trial.
Photo: Geoff Stevens.

1915 2¾ h.p. two speed model 'B' touring machine.
Photo: Author.

employed, which was operated by a gate change-speed lever as patented by George Stevens in 1913. An enclosed, internal expanding, foot operated, rear brake was included. Fully enclosed weatherproof chaincases were supplied, having hinged inspection doors rather than the sliding type fitted to the earlier 1914 model 'D'. Having a wheelbase of 4'7", the model scaled 236lbs. solo or 376lbs. as a complete passenger combination. Prices were sixty six guineas (£69.30) or eighty one guineas (£85.05) when fitted with the specially designed sidecar.

The 6.h.p. model 'D' was a larger version of the model 'A' previously described, having the same 748 c.c. V-twin engine of the previous year with 74mm. x 87mm. bore and stroke. This model turned the scales at 280lbs. or 430lbs. as a combination. Wheelbase was 2" longer than the model 'A'. The model 'D' was priced at seventy two guineas (£75.60) or eighty eight guineas (£92.40) with sidecar. A Lucas dynamo lighting outfit was available as an extra on this model only, at fourteen guineas (£14.70).

As in 1914, the 2¾ h.p. model 'B' was produced in two forms, either as a tourer or a sporting model. In both cases a choice of two or three speed gearbox was available. The sporting model was fitted with footrests, extra large exhaust pipe with detachable fish-tail silencer, cutaway rear chainguard and T.T. style racing handlebars. It was also supplied with two additional engine sprockets to provide alternative gear ratios for competition work. The touring version had footboards, expansion chamber type exhaust system, totally enclosed weatherproof chaincase and high position handlebars. Both weighed 160lbs. and were priced in accordance with gearbox specification. Fifty guineas (£52.50) for the three speed, whereas the two speed cost forty seven guineas (£49.35).

Timing side close-up of model 'B' engine.
Photo: Author.

The finish of the 1915 models was the usual four coats of finest black enamel, with the petrol tank painted aluminium and a single black panel on each side lined green. The A.J.S. letters were now positioned closer to the front of the petrol tank. This year also saw the first appearance of the Company shield transfer, displayed on the frame headstock, removable clutch cover and sidecar door.

To promote the new 1915 models, it was arranged to have a special A.J.S. London exhibition at the showrooms of their sole London and district agents, H. Taylor & Co. Ltd. This took place from 30th November until 5th December and proved to be most successful.

Motorcycle production was switched to the new factory building at Graiseley Hill, following its completion in 1915. The Retreat Street premises were retained and used as offices and a repair department until 5th November 1917, when the registered office address was changed to Graiseley House.

Because of a shortage of material and labour, the Company announced late in 1915 that the 2¾ h.p. model 'B' would be cancelled until further notice. A note was attached inside the cover of the 1916 catalogue explaining the difficulties facing the Company, due to the effect of the war. These years, although very difficult, were not wasted, as valuable experience was gained by the Stevens Brothers, particularly in the field of heat treatments and working with light alloys connected with the aircraft industry. When time permitted a certain amount of motorcycle development work was undertaken. With increased fuel prices and scarcity of petrol, the factory began to utilise coal gas as a fuel for bench testing their engines prior to despatch.

For 1916 the model 'A' and 'D' V-twins remained very much the same as in the previous year. The 'Splitdorf' magnetos were however superseded by 'Dixie' type M.2 instruments. The 4 h.p. model 'A' price was increased to £76.0s.0d., or £93.17s.0d. (£93.85) when offered as a passenger combination. Prices for the 6 h.p. model 'D' were also increased, to £84.0s.0d and £102.18s.0d (£102.90) respectively. Lucas dynamo lighting was available as an extra on model 'D' only.

During the middle of 1916 Jack Stevens, then aged 31, received a serious setback which ended his motorcycling days. Following a shooting trip he received a thorough soaking. Continuing to wear his wet clothing, he contracted polio. The severe illness that followed eventually left poor Jack without the use of his legs and only able to walk with the aid of sticks.

1916 4 h.p. 'Double-Purpose' model 'A' machine.
Photo: Author.

Drive side close-up of model 'A' engine.
Photo: Author.

The Ministry of Munitions issued an order on 3rd November 1916 prohibiting the manufacture of motorcycles, except those required for war duty. This action was tantamount to preventing A.J.S. from continuing its development of civilian machines.

Earlier in the year Russia had decided to mechanize part of its army. They realized it would be able to move faster than the horse and would not have to rely on fixed railways. In July they gave their shopping list to the Ministry of Munitions, who were responsible for military buying in Britain. The order nearly caused wholesale panic, as the Russian requirements for 1917 would involve much of the available vehicle production in Britain and slow down shell manufacture. The problem was partially solved by subcontracting a large portion of the order to Fiat and various North American manufacturers. One section of the order that could be met by the home industry was motorcycles. The number required for 1917 was 8,394 of which 4,344 would be motorcycle combinations to serve as machine gun carriers, light ambulances and ammunition carriers. The Ministry allocated the contract thus:-

Delivery Dates		Feb	March	April	May	June	Total
A.J.S.	6h.p.	-	200	275	300	325	1100
Clyno	8h.p.+S/C	-	180	250	350	364	1144
	5h.p.	-	100	-	-	-	100
Enfield	8h.p.+S/C	60	85	85	85	85	400
	6h.p.	90	125	125	125	135	600
James	6h.p.	-	66	150	180	204	600
Matchless	8h.p.+S/C	-	50	140	275	285	750
New Imperial	8h.p.+S/C	-	50	140	275	285	750
Norton	6h.p.	-	100	150	150	150	550
Rover	6h.p.	-	150	150	150	150	600
Royal Ruby	8h.p.+S/C	-	50	80	160	160	450
Sunbeam	8h.p.+S/C	250	150	150	150	150	850
	5h.p.	-	100	130	130	140	500

The 6 h.p. A.J.S. military machines ordered by the War Office, retained many of the earlier features that had made them popular during peacetime, of which the most practical and endearing were the renowned A.J.S. interchangeable and quickly detachable wheels, now highly favoured by the Ministry. One important change had to be accommodated to satisfy military specification, this was the position of the magneto. It was moved from in front of the engine and mounted high up on an adjustable platform situated behind the saddle down tube. The modification necessitated a much longer cast aluminium chaincase, stretching rearward to enclose the chaindrive. Other changes included a specially designed saddle type petrol / oil tank to accommodate the sloping top frame tube. This was supported from beneath on brackets brazed to the lower frame tube.

In April 1917 the Tsar was deposed and a council of Soviets was established under the socialist, Korenski, who endeavoured to continue the war. However, the situation slowly degenerated towards the Bolshevik revolution and the war seemed less and less important. During that summer, Britain and France ceased to have any confidence in the Russians and an embargo was placed on further supplies of mechanical vehicles. Production continued under contract and A.J.S. along with the other manufacturers were paid, since the Treasury had raised a massive loan to cover the deal.

At long last the war was drawing to a close. Harry Stevens resumed his work on engine development, while brothers Joe Junior, Jack and George managed the general running of the works. Harry's main interest lay in an overhead valve design, with similar features to those employed on an early Peugeot racing car engine.

1915 - 1919 Ideas on Hold.

Graiseley machine shop about 1917-18.
Photo: Geoff Stevens.

Graiseley House, prior to the office conversion in 1919.
Photo: Geoff Stevens.

With the signing of the Armistice on 11th November 1918 hostilities finally ceased. The brothers lost little time before arranging to have plans drawn for the erection of additional buildings at Graiseley. Three new buildings were commenced early in 1919, having the same floor dimensions (260 feet x 80 feet) as the one completed in 1915. Work was undertaken on Graiseley House to convert the residence into offices. In 1917 the offices and repair department at Retreat Street had been moved to Graiseley: the old premises, still owned by the four brothers, were handed over to Joe Stevens Senior and used as additional premises for the Stevens Screw Co. Ltd.

The end of the war brought with it a huge demand for new vehicles. Earlier, machines that had been despatched to dealers prior to the Ministry of Munitions Order in 1916, had been swallowed up in the record 152,960 machines registered in Britain in 1916. The shortage eventually led to prices reaching astronomical heights, following a free for all after the Ministry finally gave the green light to the industry in January 1919.

A new era of motorcycle design was heralded at the 1919 Olympia Show held in November. Due to the enforced gap of five years, a variety of remarkable new ideas, many resulting from technical advances achieved for war purposes, were to be seen. A.J.S. on Stand 31, had decided to concentrate their efforts on the passenger machine market, by displaying an entirely new 6 h.p. three speed combination, listed as their 1919/1920 model 'D'. The standard specification of this motorcycle included a new style saddle tank, A.J.S. interchangeable and quick detachable wheels, a specially designed sprung seat pillar for added comfort (originally introduced as an extra in 1915) and new style, deep moulded rubber footboards. A novel innovation was a superbly engineered, patent folding, lever operated, rear stand, enabling the rider to lift the complete outfit onto the rear stand, with the minimum of effort. Particular emphasis was paid to quiet running, with the introduction of a large cast aluminium silencer, transversely mounted in front of the engine.

The V-twin engine retained its previous 1916 dimensions of 74mm. x 87mm. (748 c.c.), but

6 h.p. model 'D' machines under construction in the main fitting and assembly shop at Graiseley, 1919.
Photo: Geoff Stevens.

1915 - 1919 Ideas on Hold.

1920 6 h.p. model 'D' passenger machine, fitted with 'Tan-Sad' pillion seat.
Photo: Author.

Drive side close-up of model 'D' engine.
Photo: Author.

was now fitted with detachable cylinder heads. An improved Amac multi-jet carburettor was again chosen, and parallel type valve springs replaced the earlier conical pattern. A Thompson Bennett magneto was carried in front of the engine, incorporating a very neat vernier timing arrangement that allowed minute timing adjustments to be made. The three speed gearbox remained almost identical to the 1916 pattern, except for an improved clutch mechanism. Lucas dynamo lighting was offered as an extra.

The single seater sidecar was a handsome piece of work, constructed of steel panelling and beautifully upholstered. Standard equipment included, a hinged dash carrying the windscreen, storm proof apron, folding hood, hood cover, side curtains, luggage grid, tool locker and spare wheel, mounted at the rear. The latter was instantly detachable and interchangeable with the wheels of the motorcycle. During the brief period of inflation which followed the introduction of the combination in March 1919, prices ranged from £142.0s.0d to £200.0s.0d.

After returning home from the war, 'Young Billie' was given a hero's welcome by the rest of the family. A visit to Graiseley House and a tour of the new works quickly confirmed the huge changes that had taken place during his absence. 'Billie's' father immediately appointed him as a director of the Stevens Screw Company, whilst his brothers offered him a manager's position at Graiseley, to take charge of spares and the newly formed export department. This he gratefully accepted.

Much of the brothers' time was now spent organising and equipping the works at Graiseley. Production at the factory now centred on the 6 h.p. sidecar combination 'De-Luxe', with a weekly output totalling sixty five finished units per week.

The factory area, including various basement stores, now totalled 109,600 square feet. Each main building was formed into six gabled bays with north light roofing, the floor area was divided into specific departments, each arranged to allow the materials used during manufacture to work through from the goods receiving and issuing stores on the north Graiseley Hill side and finish as complete motorcycles on the south side. During construction of the main buildings, temporary corrugated iron sheeting was employed on the south side wall of each building, to simplify future extension work.

The factory comprised of sixteen main departments:

a) Receiving and Issuing Stores
b) Frame Building Department
c) Press Shop
d) Brazing Department
e) Wheel Department
f) Enamelling Shop
g) Heat Treatment Shop
h) Machine Shop
i) Engine Erecting Shop
j) Gearbox Fitting Shop
k) Engine Test Department
l) Toolroom
m) Main Fitting & Assembly Shop
n) Final Assembly Shop
o) Repair Department
p) Despatch Department

The machine shop occupied the whole of the original building erected in 1915. Power for the machine tools, was almost exclusively operated from groups of overhead line shafting.

CHAPTER 4
1920-1925 The Golden Years

Following the end of the war, Harry Stevens had been busily engaged with the design and development of his latest creation, an advanced single cylinder 2¾ h.p. overhead valve engine. Although Harry socialised with his brothers, it was difficult for him to separate his work from his hobbies. He was never happier than when, after work, he returned to his workshop at the rear of 25 Oaklands Road. Because of the day to day pressures at Graiseley, most of the work on the engine had been carried out unnoticed in his workshop. He would work through the night until the early hours, rather than leave something unfinished, before snatching a few hours sleep.

The new overhead valve engine, primarily designed to defend their 1914 Junior T.T. title, was finally completed in February 1920. Following a series of encouraging tests at the works, it was decided to build a number of machines using the engine, to compete in the first post-war T.T. races to be held in June.

Harry had decided to retain the earlier engine dimensions of 74mm. x 81mm. bore and stroke (349 c.c.) and stipulated the use of steel flywheels. A light steel piston was employed, carrying two rings at the top, and a series of oil grooves, with the lower part of the piston skirt heavily drilled. A detachable cast iron cylinder head, having a hemispherical shaped combus-

Howard R. Davies astride his 1920 six speed 2¾ h.p. overhead valve T.T. A.J.S.
Photo: Geoff Stevens.

Members of the 1920 Isle of Man team. From the left: Cyril Williams, Howard R. Davies, Harry Stevens, Eric Williams (sitting), H.F. Harris, Arthur Curran and Bob Shakespeare.
Photo: Robert Cordon Champ.

tion chamber carried two inclined valves set at 90° apart. These were operated by very tall inclined push rods through rockers, carried on bolted steel brackets. The vertically finned head and cast iron cylinder barrel was held down by a flexible steel strap, passing over the top and tightened down by screwed turnbuckles, situated on either side of the crankcase. A Thompson-Bennett magneto, positioned in front of the engine provided the ignition, with an Amac carburettor feeding the engine. Transmission from the engine shaft, to a three speed countershaft gearbox, was a logical development of the 1914 arrangement to provide six speeds. By using a simple, cable operated lever, situated on the right handlebar, a choice of high or low gears could be selected, by engaging either of the two engine sprockets.

Although standard frames and forks were used, a split pattern, two gallon, saddle tank was employed which bolted together. Oil was carried in a separate tank mounted behind the saddle tube, with its filler passing through the petrol tank, to make the task of refilling much easier during a pit stop. An internal expanding rear brake was fitted, the one chosen for the front being the universally accepted stirrup pattern. Subsequent road testing of the new machines, led the team to have high hopes of victory for the race.

The first post-war T.T. Junior race was held on Tuesday 15th June 1920 in brilliant sunshine. Due to several course changes the lap distance now stood at 37¾ miles.

Compared to the last Junior event in 1914, entries were down from forty nine to thirty two. This total would have been fewer but for the inclusion of a new lightweight class, (run concurrently with 350 c.c. Juniors) to encourage machines up to 250 c.c. Although the number taking part was disappointing, no one had expected a large entry due to the disruptions caused by the war. The Junior entry which included seven lightweights, was supported by ten different makes. A.J.S. were favourites to win the race with six works and two private entries. The works team included Cyril Williams, H.R. Davies, Eric Williams, Ossie

Wade, H.F. Harris (father of the famous sidecar racer) and Tom Sheard.

During the first lap, the brothers had every justification for their early optimism, as A.J.S. machines filled the first three places. Eric Williams led, Howard Davies was second and H.F. Harris was third, although news came that Ossie Wade and Tom Sheard had been forced to retire. During the second lap the positions of the first three remained unchanged. Cyril Williams had now moved into fifth place behind R.O. Clark on his 2¼ h.p. Levis. On the third lap came a big surprise; one by one all three leading A.J.S. machines had broken down. This resulted from a lack of team discipline, with the trio indulging in a dog fight among themselves. Meanwhile, Cyril Williams on the lone works A.J.S. managed to pass R.O. Clark on the remarkably quick Levis, and he now led the race. Cyril increased his lead to over 15 minutes on the fourth lap and looked comfortably set to take the trophy. However, on the last lap near Kepple Gate, with less than four miles to the finish, the drive dogs in the gear change failed; after coasting down to Hillberry Corner, he was forced to push for the remainder of the way. Such was his lead at the time of the incident, that he still won by a margin of over nine minutes. Only one other A.J.S. finished, that of private entrant H.V. Prescott, who apparently caused much amusement in the grandstand by taking a full five minutes luncheon interval in the pit during the race. Due to his push to the finish, Cyril Williams's race average of 40.74 m.p.h. was nearly five miles an hour slower than the 1914 race. However, Eric Williams before retiring on lap three, had managed to raise his previous lap record set in 1914 to 51.36 m.p.h., with a time of forty four minutes, six seconds.

The Stevens brothers, delighted with their second T.T. victory, presented Cyril with a magnificent 72 oz engraved silver rose bowl, to commemorate his win and to show their deep appreciation and gratitude for his special efforts in securing victory.

Quite apart from the remarkable T.T. victory, 1920 turned out to be a good sporting year for the Company. A.J.S. machines gaining no less than fifteen challenge cups; eighty six gold, thirty nine silver, and twenty six bronze medals; plus ninety firsts, fifty one seconds and twenty one thirds in reliability trials and speed events. In addition, Howard Davies became the

An exhausted Cyril Williams paddles his crippled A.J.S. to victory in the 1920 Junior T.T. race.
Photo: Geoff Stevens.

The magnificent 72oz. silver rose bowl, presented to Cyril Williams by the Stevens Brothers to commemorate his remarkable 1920 Junior T.T. Victory.
Photo: Author.

Howard R. Davies aboard the remarkable record breaking 2¾ h.p. experimental overhead valve A.J.S. at Brooklands October 1920. *Photo: Ray Carter.*

first rider to achieve 80 m.p.h. on a 2¾ h.p. machine, when he rode an experimental o.h.v. model at Brooklands on 19th October 1920, covering the flying kilometre in 27.8 seconds, equalling a speed of 80.47 m.p.h. He also captured no fewer than twelve class and eight international records.

For the 1921 season, A.J.S. again chose to concentrate solely on the passenger machine market, by introducing a new, enlarged 7 h.p. version of their popular model 'D' combination. This was given an increased engine capacity of 799 c.c. with bore and stroke dimensions of 74mm. x 93 mm. Large, interchangeable valves and detachable cylinder heads were retained, but the cooling fins were considerably deeper than on the previous 6 h.p. model. Roller type big end bearings replaced the earlier plain type. Another refinement was the ingenious patent gearbox adjuster, for correctly maintaining primary chain tension. This was carried out by a simple draw bolt method of sliding the gearbox back and forth in slots, carried in the bottom bracket. A new 'Brooks' B600, laminated leaf spring saddle, replaced the earlier sprung seat pillar type and was cantilevered from the rear carrier frame. The old handlebar lever operated, front 'stirrup' brake, was finally superseded by an internally expanding type, operated by a right foot pedal through a stout Bowden cable arrangement. A large capacity, steel silencer replaced the previous cast aluminium type. Apart from minor alterations to the lift up dash, position of the door, and an additional locker situated at the rear, the A.J.S. sidecar remained much the same as for the previous model.

At the Olympia show held from 29th November to 4th December 1920, A.J.S. on Stand 119, listed the new 7 h.p. model with sidecar at £215.0s.0d, or £159.10s.0d (£159.50) in solo form. Due to fluctuating costs and high inflation, no prices were printed in the 1921 advance sales catalogue.

Despite rising prices, 1920 had been a busy year for the motorcycle industry, with machine registrations increasing to nearly 279,000 com-

1921 7 h.p. model 'D' passenger combination reg. CL 4481, as discovered in 1992. Note the 'Brooks' B600 cantilevered leaf spring saddle. Photo: David Hawtin.

pared to almost 115,000 for the previous year. Demand for the A.J.S. passenger machines had never been greater, so steps were taken to increase output by constructing further factory buildings on the Graiseley site.

During the early part of 1921, finishing touches were put to a prototype A.J.S. three wheel car. With two wheels at the front and one at the rear, it was nicknamed the 'Pterodactyl' by Jack Stevens. Although the patented design showed considerable promise, it never entered production and the vehicle was eventually sold to an employee.

Following their second T.T. success, the Company came under increasing pressure to re-introduce a 2¾ h.p. model alongside the new 7 h.p. model. This action was mainly to satisfy an avalanche of requests from prospective buyers, it also seemed pointless to enter competitions with 2¾ h.p. machines, when the Company did not list one in their catalogue.

A new three speed touring machine, listed as the model 'B' was introduced in March 1921, incorporating many refinements over the previous model last produced in 1915. It was fitted with a 349 c.c. single cylinder side valve engine having a bore and stroke of 74mm. x 81 mm. and a roller bearing, big end assembly. Adjustment of the gearbox to tension the primary chain followed the same draw bolt method employed on the new 7 h.p. model. A simple, coil spring shock absorber was fitted to the engine shaft. The frame was a neat and sturdy piece of work, perfectly proportioned, with the top frame tube being slightly sloped and dropped at the rear. A 'Brooks' saddle was pivoted on the top tube and supported from the carrier frame. The quick detachable rear wheel was fitted, being a somewhat unusual feature on a lightweight machine. Contrary to the saddle pattern tank fitted to the 7 h.p. model, a wedge shaped tank was supported between the top and bottom frame tubes. The rear brake was of the internal expanding type, while the front was the usual stirrup pattern. Druid pattern forks were chosen, and front and rear mudguards were sensibly proportioned to match the rest of the machine. Deep treaded rubber pads were fitted over the footboards and a large efficient steel silencer, was transversely mounted in front of the engine.

In the light of previous experience, redesign work had begun on the 2¾ h.p. racing machine as early as midsummer 1920, to rectify the mechanical problems that dogged the team during that year's T.T. races. Preparations were also put in hand to improve road holding. To begin with, a new frame fitted with Druid forks was designed to enable a lower riding position to be adopted. The earlier split pattern saddle tank was replaced by a wedge shaped design similar to that fitted to the new 2¾ h.p. model 'B' road machine.

Although there were a number of important modifications carried out to the overhead valve engine, the fundamental bore and stroke dimen-

1921 three speed 2¾ h.p. model 'B' touring machine.
Photo: Author.

Drive and Timing side close–up of 2¾ h.p. model 'B' engine.
Photo: Author.

sions of 74mm. x 81mm. were retained. A new, cast iron cylinder head with improved cooling carried two identical, hollow, nickel-chrome steel valves, trumpet shaped and set 80° apart. Separate cams directly operated the adjustable tappets, providing a lift of 5/16" and the following timing : Inlet valve opened 15° before t.d.c. and closed 58° after b.d.c.; exhaust valve opened 50° before b.d.c. and closed 25° after t.d.c.; which gave an overlap of 40°. Each valve covered a port diameter of 1 9/16" and was carried in separate cast iron guides, pressed into the cylinder head casting, each having six cooling ribs machined on the exposed surface. Conical valve springs were used, secured by sturdy but light spring cups and plain cotter fixings. Light gauge push rods measuring 7/16" diameter connected the rockers with the tappets, using ball and socket locations. The inlet and exhaust rockers were interconnected by a powerful tension spring. A chain driven Lucas magneto, replaced the earlier Thompson Bennett unit and provided a spark, 13mm. before top dead centre at full advance.

Because of the previous difficulties in obtaining a perfect compression joint between the cast iron cylinder and cylinder head, considerable time and attention was given to perfecting a suitable method. The problem was eventually solved using a copper asbestos washer, pinched between a flat face on the cylinder head and a corresponding tapered face location on the top of the cylinder barrel. The whole assembly was held down on the crankcase, by the proven method of using a flexible steel strap and turnbuckles.

A light steel piston having a liberally drilled skirt to reduce weight and friction, carried four, narrow, cast iron rings at the top and provided a compression ratio of 5.5:1. The length of the piston was slightly less than its diameter, and when complete with its hollow gudgeon pin, weighed no more than 12 oz. 7" diameter steel fly wheels were supported by 13/16" diameter shafts, carried in long, plain bronze bearings. The big end bearing was made up of a twin row of 5/16" diameter rollers, running directly on the surface of the crankpin. The outer race taking the form of a hardened steel ring pressed into the connecting rod.

The temperamental six speed, twin chain arrangement which had proved fragile and unpopular with the riders was scrapped in favour of a conventional three speed, close ratio unit, providing ratios of 4.88, 6.00 and 9.25:1. Transmission was carried out by 'Renold' ½" x ¼" chain throughout, driven via a multiple plate, cork inserted clutch. The primary drive was interesting; it used a new experimental 'Renold' roller-less chain, having the advantage of enabling larger bearing surfaces to be employed and providing greater lateral rigidity.

An unusual amount of care was exercised during the design and manufacture of the cylinder barrel. It had cooling fins 1" in depth and 9/16" in pitch, extending fully from top to bottom. Harry Stevens had insisted both the cylinder and the head be copper plated before 'blacking', in an attempt to improve cooling. To improve the rider's control, a foot operated oil pump was fitted which delivered oil direct to the crankcase. Finally the machine was shod with 26" x 2¼" tyres and due to careful weight saving the machine weighed only 188 lbs.

The early design work, started during the summer of 1920, enabled the new machines to progress carefully and unhurriedly through each production stage at the works. Final completion took place in February 1921, allowing sufficient time for testing and sorting out teething problems. During tests the machines proved to be very reliable and showed a remarkable turn of speed. At Brooklands on 24th May, H.R. Davies riding a stripped version of the new machine, succeeded in capturing both the one hour (66.09 m.p.h.) and two hour Class 'B' records (65.30 m.p.h.). He was also successful in lowering the class times for a 350 c.c. machine over fifty miles (45 minutes 6.8 seconds - 66.49 m.p.h.) and one hundred miles (92 minutes 45.6 seconds - 64.68 m.p.h.). These feats were made even more remarkable with the piston in Davies's machine being damaged by a valve breakage the previous day.

There was much excitement the following month in the Isle of Man, with overall entries more than double those of the previous year. The Junior race had attracted sixty five entries, of which twenty one were in the new Lightweight class, with no fewer than twenty three makes (fifteen Junior, eight Lightweight). Sixty eight took part in the Senior race, comprising fifteen makes of machine.

For the second year running, A.J.S. were firm favourites to retain their Junior title, with the factory putting forward seven entries. The riders included Eric Williams, H.R. Davies, H.F. Harris, Tom Sheard, Ossie Wade, George Kelly and V. Olsson.

The Junior race was staged on Tuesday 14th June, a tolerably fine day. The two favourites to win the race, Eric Williams No.52 and H.R.Davies No.59, were late starters. Following the departure of the last man, No.66, some amusement was created in the grandstand, by the appearance of a Post Office official clutching a telegram and calling loudly and repeatedly for Eric Williams; who by this time was nearing Kirk Michael. He was advised to run quickly if he wanted to catch him!

From the start Davies set off at full bore and at the end of the first lap had broken the record at 54.6 m.p.h. The first six lap leaders were Davies and Harris (A.J.S.), Whalley (Massey Arran), Kelly, Williams and Sheard (A.J.S.). The first report of trouble involved V.Olsson (A.J.S.), who had fallen at Sulby Bridge and twisted his front forks, after his front stirrup brake caught in the spokes and threw him. Fortunately he managed to escape with nothing more than a severe shaking. Davies, when leading his team mate Harris, took a puncture whilst on the mountain section. This cost him over twelve minutes and relegated him to eleventh place at the end of the second lap. Harris was now in the lead, with Whalley in second place, Williams third, Kelly fourth and Sheard fifth. Eric Williams, one of the favourites to win the race, had been lapping very consistently, despite suffering from chronic rheumatism. Due to his condition, he had spent the previous day in bed and had chosen to ride in the event with both arms heavily swathed in Thermogene wool. Nevertheless, by the end of lap four he had taken the lead, to the relief of the A.J.S. camp. He went on to win the race at an average of 52.11 m.p.h. from Howard Davies and Tom Sheard.

The result was a wonderful achievement for the Stevens brothers, with A.J.S. machines finishing in first, second, third, fourth, sixth and eighth places and Howard Davies setting the fastest lap at 55.15 m.p.h. (41 minutes 4 seconds).

Attention now focused on the 'Blue Riband' event, the Senior, to be held on Thursday 16th June. Of the sixty eight entries, Norton was at the head of the list with fifteen machines, followed by Triumph and Sunbeam with nine: next came Scott and B.S.A. with six. A.J.S. had two machines, both 350's to be ridden by H.R.Davies and H.F.Harris. To give some indication of the difficult course conditions during this time, Harry Stevens had, following the Junior event, given strict instructions that both Davies's and Harris's engines be transferred to new frames for the Senior race. He held grave doubts that the original cycle parts could withstand the punishment of two gruelling races, totalling eleven laps

The Senior began in glorious weather with last year's winner, Tommy de la Hay, first away on his Sunbeam. By the end of the first lap,

Eric Williams, winner of the 1921 Junior T.T. Here he is pictured on his three speed winning A.J.S. Considering the advanced technical specifications of the 1921 works machines, it is rather surprising that the factory continued to fit a stirrup type front brake. Photo: Keig collection.

Freddie Dixon led on his very quick Indian, followed by Howard Davies on the little A.J.S. only a second behind. Freddie Edmond on a Triumph was third and George Dance fourth on a Sunbeam. On lap two, Dixon started to drop back with Edmond taking the lead, closely followed by Davies second, and Dance third. George Dance managed to find something extra on lap three and took the lead, but still Davies held on to second place. The positions changed again for the fourth lap after Dance fell at Glen Helen. Alec Bennett (Sunbeam), now took the lead, closely followed by Davies ten seconds behind. Further excitement followed during lap five with Davies finally passing Bennett and leading the race for the first time, one second ahead. Edmond now lay third almost two minutes adrift. Davies, full of confidence and determined to taste victory following his ill luck in the Junior, dug his heels in and won the race at 54.49 m.p.h. some 2¼ minutes ahead of Freddie Dixon on the Indian. Bert le Vack on another Indian was third, and the A.J.S. of H.F. 'Curly' Harris finished fourteenth.

1920-1925 The Golden Years

Howard Davies had achieved the impossible, a 350 had beaten the best of the 500's in a unique Senior win. The crowds in the grandstand, sensing a great moment, rose as one to cheer him over the line. The achievement was made even more remarkable, as it was later revealed Davies's engine had not only completed both Junior and Senior races, but had been the very same that had been used to capture the records at Brooklands a few weeks earlier.

A civic reception awaited the jubilant A.J.S. team when they arrived at Wolverhampton station. A large band led a joyful procession that marched through streets brightly decorated with flags and streamers and lined with cheering crowds to welcome home the triumphant victors.

Further successes were to follow as Howard Davies added both five mile (74.5 m.p.h.) and ten mile (72 m.p.h.) records, set at Brooklands on 350 c.c. machines. Other A.J.S. riders added numerous medals, including gold, in British and International speed and reliability trials.

Owing to the enormous growth in motorcycling during 1921, the trade had never been busier, new machine registrations rising above 373,000, which represented a 33% increase on the previous year. With all the publicity surrounding the A.J.S. sporting successes, the Company was riding high; almost six hundred people were now employed on motorcycle pro-

Howard R. Davies and the remarkable 349 c.c. machine he used to win the 1921 Senior T.T. race at 54.49 m.p.h. *Photo: Keig collection.*

Frank Giles in action on his 7 h.p. A.J.S. outfit, at the start of an acceleration test during the Matchless Cup Trial in October 1921. *Photo: Mary Robinson.*

63

duction at Graiseley. To meet demand, new buildings began to spring up all over the Graiseley site, just as fast as Wolverhampton Corporation could pass the plans. With demand for passenger machines reaching a peak during this period, the sidecar and chassis works at Stewart Street were at full stretch. As a result, Charles Hayward was appointed to the main A.J.S. board on 23rd November 1921.

Meanwhile, the brothers decided to 'cash-in' on their double T.T. success, by introducing two new 2¾ h.p. sporting models, alongside the existing 2¾ h.p. touring and 7.h.p. passenger machines for the 1922 season. The new models were quoted as special machines in the 1922 advance sales lists, comprising of a three speed, standard, sporting machine listed as the model 'B1' and a 'stripped' version listed as the model 'B2'. In the case of the 'B1', the general equipment was similar to that used on the existing 'B' touring machines. Differences included T.T. pattern handlebars replacing high level touring type and footrests replaced footboards. The 'B2' stripped version conformed more closely to the 'Tourist Trophy' specification, having no kickstarter, lighter chaincases and no side valance to the front mudguard. All three models were fitted with larger capacity petrol tanks and the hand operated gear lever was tilted forward to clear the knees of a longer legged rider. Unlike the actual T.T. machines, none of the 2¾ h.p. models was fitted with overhead valve engines. Each used the well proven 74 mm. x 81 mm. bore and stroke (348 c.c.) side valve engine, with the sporting models having a higher compression ratio, high lift cams and long sports exhaust pipe, incorporating an aluminium expansion box and detachable fish-tail. Amac two lever carburettors were fitted as standard. These engines were fitted with a specially designed shock absorber mounted on the engine shaft. This comprised a floating sprocket prevented from rotating by a face cam

The Stevens brothers seated outside Graiseley House in 1921. From the left: George, Jack, Harry and Joe Junior.
Photo: Jim Stevens.

splined onto the crankshaft and held in engagement by a powerful coil spring.

The latest type 'Druid' forks were used with springs carried between the fork blades; both front and rear brakes were internal, expanding type and the rear wheel was quickly detachable without disturbing the brake or chain. A very simple but ingenious method of adjustment was provided for the footrests, the boss was machined to provide an eight pointed, star shaped hole, which could be mounted in a number of different positions, without any fear of slip, on a square ended cross-bar. Each model shared identical gearbox ratios of 5.5, 9.3 and 14.0:1, with the Company claiming a top speed performance of over 60 m.p.h. for the 'stripped' sporting version. All three models were priced at £85.0s.0d.

In addition the Company introduced a new, coachbuilt, lightweight sidecar and chassis for use with the 2¾ h.p. touring model. Having a length of 5' 4" and with a width of 1' 8½" it weighed 170lbs complete. The price of the sidecar complete with stormproof apron was £25.0s.0d.

Except for a few details, the 7 h.p., model 'D', passenger machine continued unchanged. The front mudguard was reduced in width and made to pass between the front fork members, to allow a greater air flow to the cylinders. A larger version of the face cam type shock absorber fitted to the 2¾ h.p. machines was used and larger exhaust pipes were fitted, secured by external clamping nuts. The price for a complete combination was £175.0s.0d.

During the Olympia Show held from 25th November to 3rd December 1921, A.J.S. on Stand 127 came in for much criticism. Although the new models were good and exciting, it was generally thought the Company should have offered an overhead valve model. After all, surely the T.T. series in the Isle of Man were intended to prove the worth of catalogued models offered to the buying public. Who could argue? A.J.S.. had always claimed their machines were competition bred. However, despite the criticism, the Company did rather well and came away from the show with a full order book.

By 1922, A.J.S. had come a long way. Barely eight years after going public, their growth and achievements during this time had been nothing short of remarkable. Following an eight month overseas tour by George Stevens, covering some 42,000 miles, the Company's export sales had risen dramatically; A.J.S. now boasting agents in most towns in India, Africa, Australia and New Zealand. Disappointing however was the fact that no market penetration had been achieved in the U.S.A., this being put down to trade tariffs.

On the sporting scene, the A.J.S. racing team came under considerable pressure, they were expected to match their sensational 1921 achievements. Outwardly the 1922 racing machines prepared for the Isle of Man Junior T.T. appeared much the same as for the previous year, except the factory now fitted internally expanding brakes to front and rear wheels, these being interconnected and simultaneously applied by the foot pedal. In addition to this feature, the front brake could also be operated independently from the handlebar lever. The overhead valve engine carried a number of modifications, the most significant, a redesigned cylinder head fitted with modified rocker gear and a slightly larger exhaust valve and port; the exhaust pipe having no less than 2⅝" internal diameter. On account of the compact nature of the rest of the machine, the pipe appeared even larger than it actually was, its proportions eventually leading to the 'Big Port' nickname. Much larger cams were employed, the radius of the profiles being equal to the radius of the gear wheel which carried them; while a slightly higher compression ration of 5.7:1 was chosen. Steel flywheels were retained, although a single row roller bearing big end replaced the earlier double row type.

Although the Tourist Trophy races were proving increasingly popular among spectators, competitors and manufacturers alike, all was not well between the Auto Cycle Union and the Manx authorities. There were many who considered the larger capacity machines would prove too fast for the course. The fact that Howard Davies had gained victory in the 1921 Senior event, while riding a Junior machine further reinforced the argument for the Senior capacity to be reduced to 350 c.c. The dispute rumbled on until it seemed the 1922 races might be staged in Belgium. To their everlasting credit, the Auto Cycle Union resisted the proposed changes. The rules remaining as they were, except the smaller 250 c.c. Lightweight class would be separately recognised with a trophy all of its own, although the machines would still have to be run with the 350's. Happily with all the differences eventually ironed out, the Isle of Man continued to host the world's greatest road races. The Junior event attracted forty eight entries, with A.J.S. seen as clear favourites to win their fourth consecutive victory. Seven A.J.S. machines took part, all being works entries. Among the riders were H.R.Davies,

Frank Longman, H.F.Harris and Tom Sheard. Although A.J.S. were not the only manufacturers to use overhead valve engines in the Junior, they were recognized as leading the way in this field, their engines proving by far the most advanced and reliable. Blackburne and J.A.P. also featured this layout. Practice revealed the A.J.S. machines to be extremely fast; H.R.Davies putting up the fastest Junior class time, but there was strong competition from Bert le Vack on his New Imperial - J.A.P. The interconnected brakes on the A.J.S. machines were not favoured by the riders and were soon abandoned by the team early during practising.

Tuesday 30th May saw the stands filling up in brilliant warm sunshine. At 10 a.m. the race began, Green number plates (250 c.c.) 1 to 32 being sent off first; then Blue numbers (350 c.c.) 33 to 70 following at half minute intervals. Once again it was an anxious time for team manager Joe Stevens Junior, as le Vack on the New Imperial led for the first lap, closely followed by Harris on the A.J.S. just three seconds behind, with Davies on another A.J.S. following one second later. By lap two le Vack had increased his lead over Harris and Davies, who were falling back. Lap three saw le Vack still leading, but Tom Sheard coming through to take second place with team mates Longman, Grinton and Harris holding third, fourth and fifth places respectively. On lap four le Vack's New Imperial expired and Joe Stevens Junior was able to breath a sigh of relief once more as Sheard now led his team mate George Grinton by over ten minutes, with third place Cyril Pullin on the Douglas some five minutes behind. Tom Sheard became the first Manxman to win a T.T., the race duration being some ten minutes less than in 1921, with Sheard's race average being 54.75 m.p.h. Scottish team mate George Grinton was second followed by Cyril Pullin on the Douglas. The A.J.S. camp were delighted, their fourth consecutive Junior victory won in record time; however the race had been no walkover for the Wolverhampton concern, the only other A.J.S. to finish coming home in 14th place, ridden by Herbie Chambers.

In the hope of repeating their remarkable 1921 T.T. double, the A.J.S. team entered three of their 350 c.c. machines in the Senior event; the riders were the previous year's victor Howard Davies, plus Ossie Wade and George Kelly. The race turned out to be a disappointment for the team, Davies and Kelly retiring while Ossie Wade could do no better than twelfth place. Alec Bennett was the eventual winner on a Sunbeam, marking their second Senior T.T. victory.

As might be expected following the earlier criticism that no overhead valve A.J.S. had been available on the open market, the Company announced a sports version based on their winning T.T. machine. Known as the '2¾ h.p. Three Speed Overhead Valve T.T. Model', it was introduced at the 1922 Olympia show in readiness for the following season. The machine was priced at £87.0s.0d and eventually became known as the immortal 'Big Port'.

By the Autumn of 1922, the Graiseley works had increased in size, some 57,140 square feet being added to bring the total area to almost 167,000 square feet. Unfortunately, it was not possible to extend the C.W.Hayward sidecar works at Stewart Street. Owing to its cramped production facilities the Company was forced to turn down a number of lucrative contracts to produce additional sidecars for Ariel, Norton, Levis and New Imperial, plus an opportunity to expand the coachbuilt car body side of the business. It became obvious that in order to take advantage of the increased demand, the business would have to move to larger premises. By strange coincidence, earlier that year the Briton Motor Company Ltd., once the occupier of the Stewart Street premises, had been forced into liquidation. Its name, manufacturing rights and stock had been bought by Charles Aaron Weight, owner of the Staffordshire Engineering and Boiler Covering Company Ltd (SEBCO) and moved to premises at Chillington Fields, leaving the large Lower Walsall Street factory still owned by Briton vacant. Set in approximately 3.6 acres of land running alongside the London and North Western Railway line between Horseley Fields and Lower Walsall Street the factory was ideally suited. Following negotiations with Briton's receiver and liquidators, a deal was struck to purchase the freehold for a sum of £7,000.0s.0d., legal ownership being transferred to A.J.S. on 3rd October 1922. Following completion, steps were quickly taken to rehouse the existing Stewart Street works.

In 1923 the Company chose to enter the rapidly expanding wireless market, the main driving force behind this business was Harry Stevens. Harry, a keen amateur for many years, had been quick to recognise the tremendous market potential following the formation of the British Broadcasting Company at the end of 1922; as a result wireless manufacture commenced at the Lower Walsall Street works under the title of 'A.J.S. Wireless and Scientific

Instruments'. From the outset, it was decided the business should aim towards the quality end of the market, the Company producing a superb range of two, three and four valve receivers with prices ranging from £17.10s.0d. (£17.50) to thirty guineas (£31.50). The business soon became well established with A.J.S. wireless products gaining an enviable reputation for quality and performance.

The Isle of Man T.T. races in June saw the Junior and Lightweight classes being run separately over six laps (226½ miles), the same distance as for the Senior. The Junior race attracted no fewer than seventy two entries, nine of which were A.J.S. machines. Stanley Woods was the eventual winner on a Cotton at 55.73 m.p.h., while the A.J.S. of H.F. Harris was second at 55.16 m.p.h., Jimmy Simpson on another A.J.S. making the fastest lap at 59.59 m.p.h. With just a few minutes separating the first two places, Harry Harris may well have won had he not stopped at the pits to secure a loose rear stand during the closing stages of the race. While in the pits, Harry Stevens removed one of his boot laces which he threw to Harris enabling him to tie the stand up.

1923 was also the year which marked the beginning of the team's international road racing programme; Frank Longman appearing on the Continent as a late entry in the 350 c.c. class of the French Grand Prix, held at the Circuit de Touraine near Tours on 24th June. Longman was successful in winning his class in the sixteen lap 227.2 mile race, at an average speed of 56.4 m.p.h. as well as making the fastest lap at 60.79 m.p.h. Following a disappointing Belgian Grand Prix a month later in which Frank Longman and Billy Hollowell both retired, the team again tasted victory in September when Ernesto Gnesa won the Italian Grand Prix of Nations at Monza in front of 40,000 spectators.

In October, A.J.S. attended the Olympia Show and exhibited their latest seven model range on Stand 59. Sales forecasts were good, as the earlier high inflation period which had seen prices soar to ridiculously high levels was now under control. In addition to the top of the range 7 h.p. model 'D' De Luxe passenger combination, now attractively priced at £130.0s.0d., the Company offered a much cheaper 'no frills' version at £95.0s.0d. Listed as the 'D1' this model was devoid of electric lighting and featured less elaborate mudguarding and chaincases; the sidecar also being shorn of the usual windscreen and hood. To support their established model 'B' and 'B1' 2¾ h.p., sidevalve models priced at £62.0s.0d., a lighter sporting 'B5' machine was added at £52.0s.0d. To complete the line up, two 2¾ h.p., overhead valve mod-

Members of the racing team, Isle of Man 1923. From the left: N. Black, Arthur Barnett, L.R. Cohen, —?—, Clarrie Wise, G. Kelly, Arthur Cowan, Joe Stevens Junior, Frank Longman, Ossie Wade, Jimmy Simpson, Bob Shakespeare, George Rowley, Hanford Stevens, Charlie Hough, Arthur Curran and J.W. Hollowell. *Photo: Mary Robinson.*

A confident looking Frank Giles pilots his 4.98 h.p. A.J.S. outfit, during the 1923 Scottish Six Days Trial. Photo: Mary Robinson.

els were included, these being the 'B3', which replaced the original 'T.T.' sports model and the 'B4', a racing machine stripped of a rear carrier and supplied with a high compression piston and polished engine internals. Both these models were offered at £65.0s.0d. each.

1924 was to prove an exceptionally good year for the Company with orders for motorcycles far exceeding supply, particularly from overseas markets. The A.J.S. wireless made at Lower Walsall Street had been well received, resulting in strong sales. Between May and December a further 62,500 square feet of factory buildings were added at Graiseley Hill, bringing the total manufacturing area to almost 230,000 square feet, while Lower Walsall Street had grown to over 150,000 square feet, the latter now employing a total of 1,300 people on sidecar, wireless and car body production.

Although both factories were operating practically full out, the brothers never lost sight of the fact that much of the Company's success had been brought about through its sporting achievements. To this end, work on the 1924 racing machines continued unabated. As a result completely new engines were produced incorporating several interesting features, not least the use of dry sump lubrication; two Rotoplunge pumps, one larger than the other, driven off the crankshaft. The smaller pump drew oil from a tank mounted on the saddle tube of the frame and delivered it to a trough situated beneath the flywheels. A 'dipper' on one flywheel splash fed oil to the piston and bearings, with the surplus draining into a sump from which it was returned by the second larger pump to the oil tank. A 6:1 compression ratio was obtained using a flat topped, aluminium piston, cut away for valve clearance. In complete contrast to any previous motorcycle engine design, A.J.S. fitted an inlet valve larger than the exhaust, the combustion chamber having an increased valve angle and the port diameters measuring $1^{11}/_{16}$" for the inlet and $1\frac{1}{2}$" for the exhaust. Each valve was fitted with two concentric springs and had a lift of $^{5}/_{16}$"; the overlap being 40°. Light tubular push rods were operated by tappets acting directly on the cams, no cam levers being employed. The overhead rocker arms were splined to graphite impregnated bearing tubes, while a special, two jet Binks carburettor was screwed directly into the cylinder head, so eliminating the usual inlet stub. Gear ratios of 5.27, 6.47 and 9.91:1 were chosen, the centre clutch plate and gearbox sprocket being produced in light alloy. The normal A.J.S. practice of mounting the magneto in front of the crankcase was dropped, this

1924 7 h.p. model 'D' passenger machine.
Photo: Author.

Timing side close–up of model 'D' engine.
Photo: Author.

now being repositioned behind the engine. Bolted twinfuel tanks having a combined capacity of three gallons were used, gripping specially located frame lugs between the points of attachment. The total weight of the machine complete with fuel and oil scaled 230lbs.

At the Isle of Man T.T. races, the Junior event held on Monday 23rd June attracted no less than fifty nine entries, A.J.S. machines topping the list with ten, six of which were works entries. Practising led the team to have high hopes for the race, the latest engines proving fast and reliable. However during the race things turned out rather differently with seven out of the ten A.J.S. machines retiring with mechanical failure. There was some consolation in the A.J.S. camp however, with Jimmy Simpson being the first rider to lap the course at over 60 m.p.h. and South African rider, I.H.R. Scott, bringing one of the works machines home in third place. Jimmy Simpson also set the fastest lap of the race before retiring, at 64.54 m.p.h., completing the course in 35 minutes 5 seconds. Not only was this a Junior record but it also exceeded the new Senior record set by Freddie Dixon on a Douglas, his time being almost half a minute slower. Not to be outdone, the A.J.S. team pressed on with its overseas racing programme, gaining resounding victories in the 350 c.c. classes of the French Grand Prix and the Speed Championship of Europe to name just two. In reliability trials, 350 c.c. and 799 c.c. A.J.S. machines were successful in the A.C.U. English Six Days 1,000 Miles Stock Machine Trial, winning three gold medals, the special team prize and the best sidecar performance. In the Scottish Six Days Reliability Trial, A.J.S. won the Manufacturers Sidecar Team Prize for the second year in succession, also gaining five silver cups and two silver medals.

With the motorcycle now firmly established as a popular means of transport among all classes of society, the total number of machines registered in 1924 exceeding half a million, the A.J.S. board had every reason to feel optimistic about the 1925 season.

In order to make future machine identification easier and to assist the process of dealing with spares and export orders, the Company adopted a new prefix letter code system for its motorcycles, beginning with the letter 'E' for 1925. In addition, all models appearing in the 1925 catalogue were given a different horsepower classification; the previous 2¾ h.p. (349 c.c.) side valve and overhead models now being listed as 3.49 h.p. and the 7 h.p. (799 c.c.) V-twin passenger machines altered to 7.99 h.p. As for the previous year, two models of the V-twin passenger combination were listed, the De Luxe 'E1' and the Standard 'E2' priced at £115.0s.0d. and £90.0s.0d. respectively; the former representing a real luxury passenger outfit, standard specification including Lucas 'Magdyno' electric lighting, Brooks 'Supple Seat' saddle and totally enclosed transmission chains. The steel panelled sidecar was fitted with glass windscreen, celluloid sidescreens and stormproof apron. Turning to the 3.49 h.p. solo models, a very comprehensive range was included, the tourist being catered for by the 'E3' De Luxe Touring machine priced at £57.0s.0d., while the sporting rider had the choice of three machines, these being the 'E4' De Luxe Sporting at £57.0s.0d, the 'E5' Standard Sporting model at £49.10s.0d. (£49.50) and the Overhead Valve 'E6' priced at £60.0s.0d.

In preparation for the racing season, the A.J.S. team decided to revert back to a total loss lubrication system for their engines, the advanced, dry sump system being temporarily shelved in favour of the simple, foot operated oil pump, that had been previously employed on the 1921 works machines. Other modifications included the use of equal sized inlet and exhaust valves operated by valve rockers constructed from duralumin. In addition to the usual 349 c.c. capacity racing machines, the team sprung a surprise; the factory having produced for the first time a five hundred engine having bore and stroke dimensions of 84 mm. x 90 mm. (498 c.c.). Apart from relatively minor differences this complete machine was built along the same lines as its smaller brother, making it extremely compact and light for a five hundred.

A.J.S. machines numbered five among a field of fifty two for the Isle of Man Junior T.T. race. The best placed was that ridden by Jimmy Simpson who finished third followed by Charles Hough who was fourth. The three other A.J.S. machines ridden by Frank Longman, George Rowley and S.M.Williams were all forced to retire. George Rowley, whose father was in charge of the machine shop at the Graiseley works, had been given his first T.T. ride after taking over from an injured rider. George would later emerge as one of the sport's great all rounders, excelling in road racing, trials, hill climbs, sprints and even motorcycle football, all while riding A.J.S. machines.

Among forty eight starters for the Senior event, A.J.S. machines numbered four; three of which were the new 498 c.c. works machines making their debut in the capable hands of Jimmy Simpson, Charlie Hough and Frank Longman. The remaining A.J.S. being a 348 c.c. engined machine ridden by S.M.Williams.

After an early tussle, Howard Davies went on to win on a machine bearing his own initials with Frank Longman some four minutes behind in second place. True to form, after puncturing on his first lap, Jimmy Simpson went round the island on his next lap in 32 minutes 50 seconds recording the fastest ever lap at 68.97 m.p.h. before retiring with clutch trouble at Ballacraine; the A.J.S. machines of Hough and Williams were also forced to retire.

The T.T. sidecar race, only the third to be held on the island, concluded the week's racing and was held over four laps (151 miles). A.J.S., keen to promote their latest range of lightweight sports sidecars, entered two 348 c.c. overhead valve machines fitted with special streamlined aluminium sidecars. Each tubular chassis had a four point attachment to the motorcycle and was substantially reinforced where possible by inserting two 'D' shaped tubes 'back to back' inside the main frame tubes. To assist cornering, a loop frame was carried over the sidecar and padded cushions fitted to the top of the mudguard covering the sidecar wheel allowing the passenger to lean well out on left hand bends. Frank Longman and Jimmy Simpson were chosen to ride the outfits, their intrepid respective passengers being Leo Davenport and George Rowley. Although there were only eighteen entries, ten makes were represented, Norton and Douglas topping the list with four each. Following a race which had developed into a duel between the Douglas and Norton teams, Len Parker was the eventual winner on a Douglas in 2 hours 44 minutes (55.22 m.p.h.), followed by the Nortons of Bert Taylor and George Grinton in second and third places. To everyone's amazement the little A.J.S. outfits, giving almost 250 c.c. away to most of the other machines, finished in fourth and fifth places, Frank Longman and Leo Davenport crossing the line first.

Although the sidecar T.T. races had proved popular, it would be 1954 before the next event was held on the island, this being staged on the short Clypse Circuit until 1960 when it was changed back to the classic Mountain Circuit again.

A.J.S. workshop, Douglas Isle of Man 1925. Back three from the left: Arthur Barnett, Cyril Greenwood, Arthur Curran. Front five from the left: Joe Stevens Junior, Clarrie Wise, George Rowley, Jimmy Simpson and Bob Shakespeare.
Photo: Doug Hough.

Jimmy Simpson No. 46 at the start of the 1925 Senior T.T.
Photo: Ivan Rhodes.

On the international racing scene, the A.J.S. team entered three machines for the 350 c.c class and one for the 500 c.c. class at the French Grand Prix, held at Montlhéry on Saturday 18th July, 1925; the riders taking part in the 350 c.c. event being Frank Longman, Hanford Stevens (son of George Stevens) and Billy Hollowell, who at the time was engaged to be married to Hanford's sister Millie. Jimmy Simpson was chosen to ride the 500 c.c. It was the first race meeting to be held on the combined 'Piste de Vitesse' road circuit, the new road section having just been completed with fifteen major corners and varying gradients. The twenty eight lap race (217 miles) was won by Hanford Stevens with Billy Hollowell second and Frank Longman fourth. Hanford however was far from happy with the result, he was certain there had been a mix up and that he had been credited with one lap too many. After sportingly bringing the matter to the attention of the organisers, considerable effort was spent checking the official time sheets. Following the organisers' decision not to change the result, the matter was communicated to 'The Motor Cycle' who eventually brought it to the attention of the official responsible for the race, Georges Longuemare, vice president of the Union Motorcyclist de France and Charles Fourreau, the general secretary of the U.M.F. When interviewed Georges Longuemare had expressed great surprise that the matter should have been brought to public attention and pointed out that according to the rules, a protest should have been filed in writing within twenty four hours of the end of the race accompanied by a fee of fifty francs. M.Longuemare however, not wishing to hide behind the cloak of officialdom, personally went over the time-keepers' sheets himself before announcing that no mistake could be found and as such the result would stand.

The 500 c.c. race was run over thirty two laps (248 miles) and saw sixteen starters. Jimmy Simpson was the winner, comfortably bringing his A.J.S. home in front of second place man Joe Craig on a Norton, while Jim Whalley was third on a Douglas.

The A.J.S. team took part in the Belgian Grand Prix a month later at Spa-Francorchamps, Frank Longman and Billy

Hollowell both competing in the 350 c.c. class, while Jimmy Simpson was entered for the 500 c.c. event. The race was marred by the fatal crash of Billy Hollowell on lap five whilst lying in third place. This came as a very sad blow to the Stevens family, especially because of Billy's engagement to Millie. As a result Frank Longman was pulled up on lap eight and Jimmy Simpson withdrawn from the 500 c.c. event.

In reliability trials, A.J.S. continued its winning ways with highlights coming in the form of the A.C.U. Six Days 1,000 Mile Stock Machine Trial staged from 27th April to 2nd May. A.J.S. machines ridden by Frank Giles, George Rowley and Jimmy Simpson winning three gold medals plus the best team and sidecar performances.

In the Scottish Six Days Trial held 27th July to 1st August, A.J.S. won the manufacturers' team prize for the third year in succession for the best performance by a team of three sidecar machines; Frank Giles and A.F. Downie each receiving silver cups (highest awards), while A.L. Downie received a silver medal. This was followed by the International Six Days Reliability Trial held from 17th to 22nd August over a distance of 1,150 miles, in which A.J.S. machines swept the board; the 3.49 h.p. solos of J.H. Simpson, G.E. Rowley and S.M. Williams each gaining gold medals, as well as winning the 350 c.c. team prize and the A.C.U. exhibition medal. Three gold medals were also awarded to riders of 4.98 h.p. A.J.S. machines; one solo ridden by A.G. Stratford and two sidecar machines ridden by Frank Giles and A.W. Gregory. Frank Giles accompanied by his wife Adelaide as passenger also went on to achieve the best sidecar performance, being the only sidecar to complete the trial without the loss of marks, and the only sidecar to climb the notorious Alms Hill near Henley-on-Thames, having a reputed gradient of 1 in 2.9. Frank, along with B. Kershaw (346 c.c. New Hudson) and G.S. Carter (499 c.c. James) made up the Great Britain 'A' team which won The International Trophy and The International Silver Vase.

To round off the 1925 sporting season, Charlie Hough came second in the 500 c.c. class of the Brooklands British Motor Cycle Racing Club 200 mile race held on 15th August, riding one of the works 4.98 h.p. machines at an average of 82.67 m.p.h.; while Frank Longman won the 500 c.c. class of the French Grand Prix on 4th October at Linas, Montlhéry at an average speed of 66.59 m.p.h. He also recorded the fastest lap of the race at 68.42 m.p.h

A new milestone was reached in September when the Company introduced its first production 500 c.c. overhead valve model in readiness for the 1926 season. Listed as the model 'G8', the machine was featured as a dual purpose sports model suitable for solo or sidecar use. It had a 498 c.c. (84 mm. x 90 mm. bore and stroke) engine developed from the successful works machines, which had proven their worth

A jubilant Frank and Adelaide Giles on their 4.98 h.p. A.J.S. during the 1925 international Six Days Trial. Photo: Mary Robinson.

A.J.S. of WOLVERHAMPTON

PLAN of WORKS LOWER WALSALL STREET WOLVERHAMPTON
BELONGING TO
MESSRS. A. J. STEVENS & Co. (1914) LTD

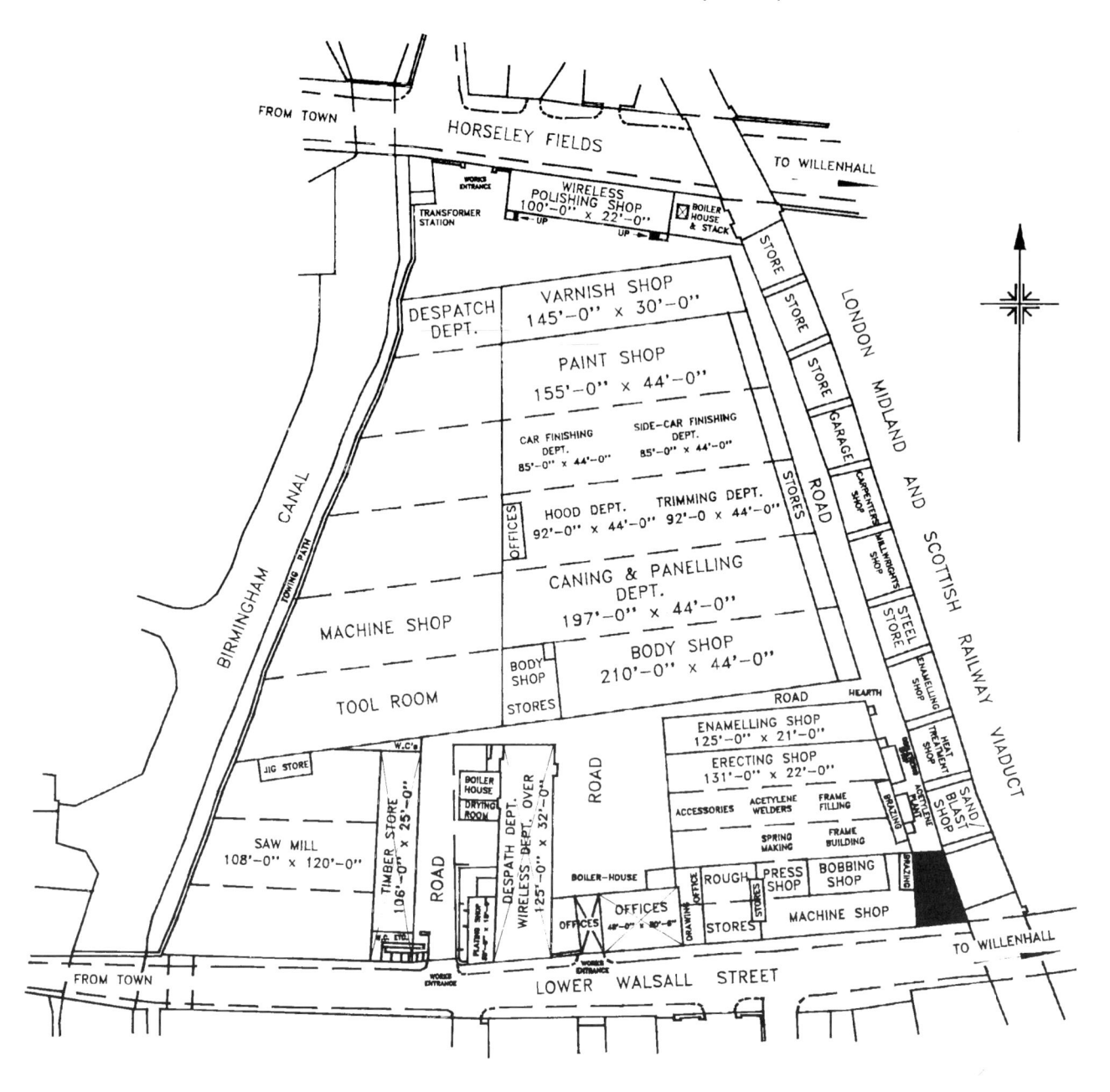

Floor Space – 150 000 Superficial Feet.
Number Of Tools – 200.
Number Of Employees – 1300.
Power – Electric 480 Horse Power.
Lighting – Electric.
Gas For Heat Treatment – Enamelling & Brazing.
Telephones – G.P.O. No. 30 Pair.
Telephones – Internal Private Wires No. 30.
Heating – Low Pressure Hot Water Installation.

Plan of Lower Walsall Street works, in 1925.
Drawing: Ron Bubb.

1920-1925 The Golden Years

in speed and reliability events during the year. The production engines were fitted with slightly larger valves than the experimental works engines, $1^{11}/_{16}$" diameter as compared to $1^{5}/_{8}$". These were inclined at an included angle of 82° and fitted with double coil springs, being operated by duralumin rockers in a heavily ribbed, detachable cylinder head held down by a substantial bridge piece and two long studs tightened from the bottom by sleeve nuts with left and right hand threads of the turnbuckle type. All the valve gear with the exception of the valves themselves were interchangeable with those of the smaller 349 c.c. overhead valve production engines. A shallow domed, aluminium piston was employed having four rings, three at the top and one at the bottom acting as a scraper; the compression ratio being 5.5:1. Plain, phosphor bronze bushes were used to support the mainshaft, while a double row roller bearing was used in the big end. Lubrication was provided by the usual tank mounted hand pump, although a Pilgrim mechanical pump was available at extra cost. Transmission was through a three speed gearbox providing standard ratios of 4.6, 8.3 and 15:1; while the hand change quadrant was altered and placed towards the forward end of the petrol tank. The exhaust pipe carried a large, fish-tailed silencer and was secured to the port casting by means of a castellated nut; while the petrol tank was of the usual A.J.S. design and finish holding 1⅝ gallons of petrol and three pints of oil. The frame was exceptionally sturdy with a view to sidecar attachment, providing a wheel base of 4'8" and a saddle height of 28". Other items of the specification included Druid type forks, a twist grip operated Binks carburettor and Terry saddle. The total weight of the machine scaled 274lbs. and was priced at £62.10s.0d. (£62.50).

In the meantime, the A.J.S. wireless business had gone from strength to strength, the number of Broadcast Licence holders having risen to over one and a half million. As a result additional labour was recruited and manufacturing facilities made available at Stewart Street to increase the output of wireless cabinets. In addition, new prestigious offices and salesrooms were opened at 122-124 Charing Cross Road, London in October 1925.

With the A.J.S. workforce now exceeding 3,000, steps were taken to organise various social outings. These activities became extremely popular and eventually led to the formation of the A.J.S. Social and Sports Club Ltd., during the autumn of 1925. The club premises were situated close to the Graiseley Hill works on land at Woodfield Avenue, with a main driveway entrance leading from Penn Road. The Club was financed by deducting a small contribution from the wage of each of its members and quickly grew to include a licensed bar, tennis courts, bowling green, shooting range, large snooker and table tennis rooms and a large pavilion which was used for weekly dances. Further land in Pinfold Lane was used to stage hockey matches by the ladies' and men's hockey teams, as well as regular games of motorcycle football. Millie Stevens was captain of the ladies hockey team, she also played an important role on the main committee, organising many of the Club's activities. Over the years Millie had gained a reputation as a 'game for anything' dare devil, often to be seen roaring around the Wolverhampton area on her 'Big Port', with Mick, her faithful pet dog, crouched on the petrol tank. In reality she was an extremely kind person given to acts of generosity toward those less fortunate than herself. On one occasion Millie wrote to the schools in the Wolverhampton area, asking teachers to invite children from the neediest families to attend a Christmas Party she had organised at the Company's motorcycle despatch department on Marston Road. Some of the children who attended came from such humble backgrounds that they sat throughout the party reluctant to remove their coats for fear that someone might take them!

By and large, the post war years had been good for the motorcycle industry. Although it had been a commercially unstable period, it was nevertheless a remarkable one which had witnessed some of the most brilliant ideas and designs yet seen. For the Stevens brothers and the A.J.S. concern it was without doubt their greatest period of achievement.

Many employers were finding unrest on the shop floor at this period, culminating in the General Strike of 1926. The Stevens, possibly remembering their own humble origin, tended to reward their employees for loyalty and a closer family atmosphere reigned. Such benevolence as the Social Club fostered this. However, the golden era of the Company was about to close and things at A.J.S. would never be quite the same again.

Members of the A.J.S. Ladies Hockey Team, with Millie Stevens (Captain) seated in the centre of the front row.
Photo: Pat Craddock.

'Ajess Artistes' dance and drama group.
Photo: Susan Taylor.

CHAPTER 5
1926-1930 Times of Change

With only a few detailed improvements and the introduction of the new 4.98 h.p. overhead valve production model, the latest model 'G' range remained practically unchanged from the previous year. Prices however were reduced on average by approximately 11%.

On the sporting scene there were many outstanding A.J.S. performances in open competition. George Rowley, riding a 3.49 h.p. machine in the Victory Cup Trial held in March, made the best performance of any motorcycle, as well as winning the 'Henley Cup' and a gold medal for the best solo performance of a machine not exceeding 350 c.c. In the same competition S.Jackson was awarded the 'Turner Cup' and a gold medal riding another 3.49 h.p. A.J.S.; while a further two gold and three silver medals were gained by other riders of A.J.S. machines during the trial. In the London - Lands End Trial, A.J.S. machines won no less than nine gold and two silver medals, whilst also gaining three gold and two silver medals in the Colmore Cup Trial. Other notable performances saw 3.49 h.p. and 4.98 h.p. A.J.S. machines taking the 'Premier Award' for the best performances of the day at the Travers Trophy Trial, Manville Trophy Trial, Western Centre Open Reliability Trial and the ACE. M.C. Midland Daily Telegraph Reliability Trial. At the Scottish Six Days Trial two A.J.S. sidecar machines were awarded silver cups (highest awards), while in the International Six Days Trial all four A.J.S. machines entered (three solo and one sidecar) gained gold medals.

On the racing scene, Jimmy Simpson brought his A.J.S. home in second place in the Isle of Man Junior T.T. race, then became the first man to lap the circuit at over 70 m.p.h. in the Senior event, raising the existing record to 70.43 m.p.h. on his second lap before retiring with engine trouble. During the following month the A.J.S. team won both the 350 c.c. and 500 c.c. classes of the Belgian Grand Prix at Spa-Francorchamps. Frank Longman won the twenty four lap (222 miles) 350 c.c. race at an average speed of 61.06 m.p.h., while Jimmy Simpson took the 500 c.c. event held over twenty eight laps (259 miles) at an average speed of

Frank and Adelaide Giles pictured during the 1926 Scottish Six Days Trial.
Photo: Mary Robinson.

1926 3.49 h.p. model 'G5'.
Photo: Author.

Drive and Timing side close-up of model 'G5' engine.
Photo: Author.

The A.J.S. board of directors pictured outside Graiseley House, in 1926.
Standing from the left: Frank Hill, Edgar L. Morcom, Edgar E. Lamb (Chairman), Charles W. Hayward and Jabez Wood (Company Secretary).
Stevens brothers, seated from the left: Harry, George, Joe Junior, and Jack.
Photo: Geoff Stevens.

67.98 m.p.h. The latter's run of success continued when he won the 350 c.c. class of the German Grand Prix in August, also recording the fastest lap in all classes at 85.24 m.p.h.

After a promising start, the A.J.S. wireless business found itself facing increased competition from foreign manufacturers and the home built market alike. To make matters worse, there had been a gradual movement away from the early conventional type of design adopted by A.J.S. which had exposed valves and complicated controls, as a result sales had fallen. With the market now demanding sets with fully enclosed workings and simplified controls, A.J.S. were forced to completely redesign its entire wireless range or face the consequences. As a result, a new range of two, three, five and seven valve models were shown at the first National Radio Exhibition held at Olympia. The new models were marketed under the title of 'Symphony Range' and were based on the new 'Superhet' principle, which gave increased power and the ability to separate stations in an already crowded waveband simply at the twist of a knob. The new sets were well received and for a time the Company enjoyed an upturn in sales. The market however had become fickle with sales becoming increasingly seasonal. As a consequence, many of the workforce were laid off during slack periods and the Company forced to adopt mass production techniques in order to reduce its manufacturing costs.

In readiness for the forthcoming 1927 motor-cycle season, A.J.S. offered no fewer than eight production machines and a choice of eight side-cars in their new series 'H' catalogue. These comprised two 7.99 h.p. passenger combinations listed as the 'H1' De-Luxe priced at £95.0s.0d. and a cheaper 'H2' Standard model at £80.0s.0d. Also included were four 3.49 h.p. machines, three with side valve and one overhead valve. The side valve machines were listed as the 'H3' De-Luxe Touring and the 'H4' De-Luxe Sporting, both priced at £48.10s.0d. (£48.50), while a cheaper 'H5' Standard Sporting model was available at £44.0s.0d. The overhead valve sporting machine was designated as the 'H6', priced at £53.0s.0d. The remaining two machines in the line up were both 4.98 h.p. models; an overhead valve model listed as the 'H8' priced at £62.10s.0d. (£62.50) and a completely new 'H9' De-Luxe Touring side valve machine offered at £56.0s.0d. Racing editions of the 3.49 h.p. and 4.98 h.p. overhead valve were available (models 'H7' and 'H10') but not catalogued. The choice of sidecars ranged from a large, coachbuilt, two seater measuring 6'6" in length, with its seats arranged tandem fashion, to a specially constructed, aluminium, streamlined, racing model, identical to those used by the A.J.S. team in the 1925 sidecar T.T. race.

The new motorcycle range incorporated many detailed improvements over the previous years' models. The engines were fitted with roller bearings to the main shafts and with the exception of the model 'H5' which was fitted with semi-automatic hand pump lubrication, each employed a sight feed 'Pilgrim' mechanical oil pump plus an auxiliary hand pump mounted on the tank. In addition, each of the models carried improved cylinder heads, incorporating additional cooling fins around threaded exhaust ports, enabling the exhaust pipes to be retained by ring nuts. Other important changes included improved, clutch operating mechanisms; larger diameter ball races fitted to the steering head; strengthened front forks; larger diameter, friction shock absorbers; enclosed exhaust lifter mechanisms, and an improved, gate change quadrant and gear lever. A simple but ingenious device that was included in the tool kit of the latest models was a patented, rear wheel alignment gauge designed by Harry Stevens. This comprised a small clip fixed to the chain stay and a shaped plate corresponding to the cross sectional profile of the wheel rim. When the rear wheel was correctly aligned, the edge of the plate attached to the rim was made to just clear the straight edge of the clip on the stay.

Since making its first appearance in 1920, the overhead valve, push rod racing engine had undergone a systematic programme of development to yield more power. Unfortunately in doing so the engine had become increasingly less reliable. Steps were taken in 1926 to produce a new overhead camshaft design, resulting in two entirely new racing machines making their debut in the spring of 1927. These

Road Test Department, Graiseley Hill 1927.
Photo: Doug Hough.

Frame Building Department, Graiseley Hill 1927.
Photo: Geoff Stevens.

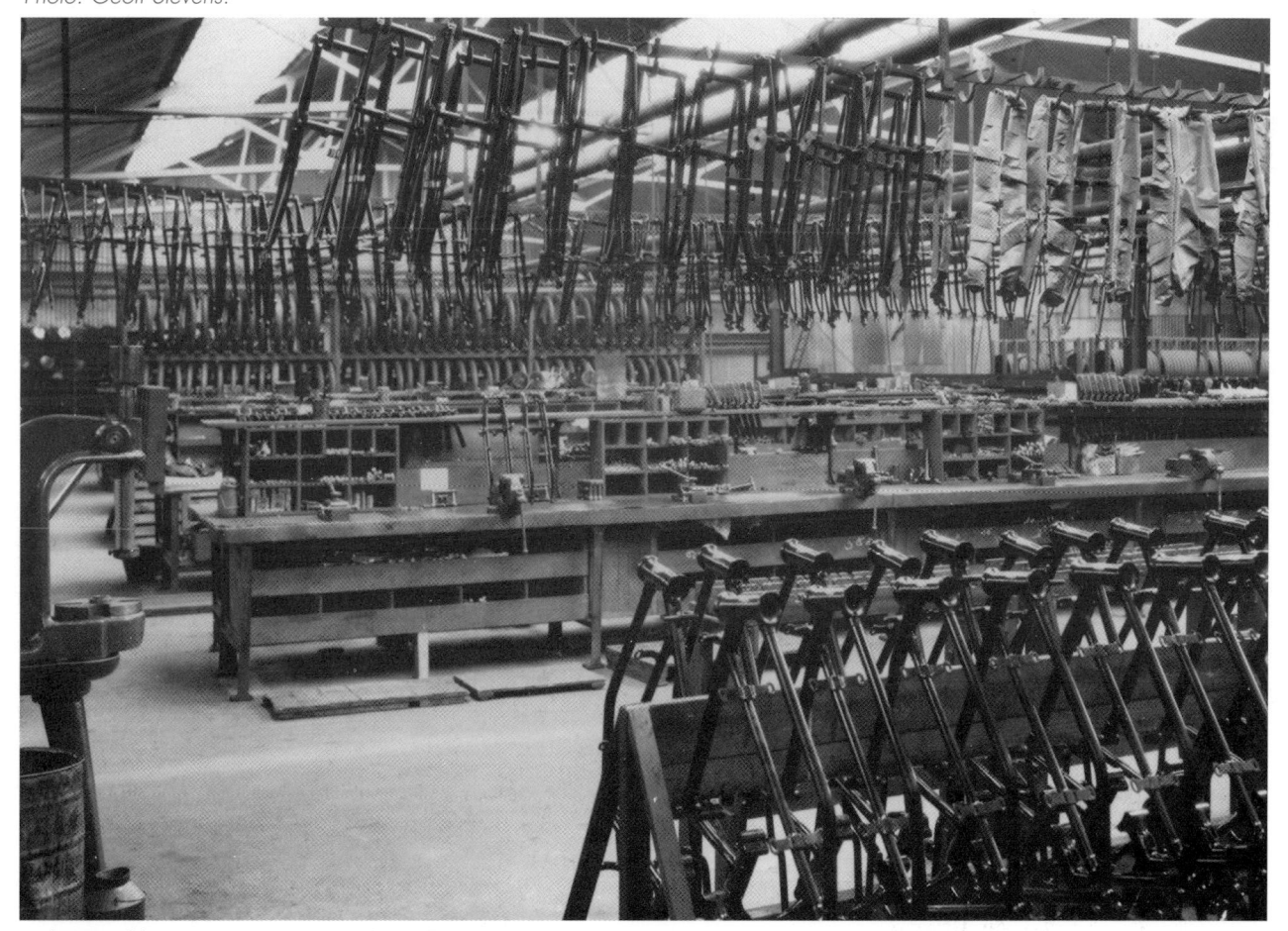

Fork Assembling Department, Graiseley Hill 1927.
Photo: Geoff Stevens.

Wheel and Brake Department, Graiseley Hill 1927.
Photo: Geoff Stevens.

Engine Test House, Graiseley Hill 1927.
Photo: Geoff Stevens.

A.J.S. testers leave the Graiseley Hill works in 1927, led by Bill Huxtable on a 4.98 h.p. model 'H9' De Luxe touring machine. Photo: Doug Hough.

machines retained the same bore and stroke dimensions as the relegated push rod designs (74 mm. x 81 mm. / 84 mm. x 90 mm.), having capacities of 349 c.c. and 498 c.c. However, instead of employing the usual method of vertical shaft and bevels to drive the camshaft, the A.J.S. design cleverly incorporated a chain-drive; the tension being controlled automatically by a Weller patented, spring leaf tensioner. A return to dry sump lubrication was made and a four speed, close ratio gearbox replaced the earlier three speed unit, something of a rarity for the time. Before undergoing final preparations for the Isle of Man T.T. races, the new machines were tested at Brooklands by Jimmy Simpson. Although only minor difficulties were encountered by the team during practising, serious lubrication problems arose during the actual races, with only four out of the nine Junior and five of the eight Senior machines managing to complete the course; Jimmy Simpson being the best placed A.J.S. rider with third place in the Junior event. Most of the main difficulties were soon overcome however, the new machines achieving success in the Grand Prix d'Europe, Belgian, Swiss and Austrian Grand Prix during July and August. Back in the British Isles, 3.49 h.p. A.J.S. machines won the Brooklands Grand Prix as well as taking second and fourth places in the Ulster Grand Prix.

A.J.S. continued their winning ways in many reliability trials during 1927, gaining three first class awards and the team prize in the A.C.U. Six Days Stock Trial; Frank Giles riding a 4.98 h.p. A.J.S. combination representing Great Britain for the sixth year in succession. This also being the third occasion an A.J.S. had assisted Great Britain to victory. Other notable successes came in the London - Edinburgh Trial, Travers Trophy Trial, Kickham Memorial Trial, Victory Cup Trial, London - Lands End Trial, Colmore Cup Trial and the Scottish Six Days Trial in which the three A.J.S. combinations entered, all finished and became the only sidecar team to complete the course without loss of a single mark on condition at the finish.

While the Company's impressive sporting achievements continued to grow, sadly its motorcycle, sidecar and wireless trade began to feel the effects of a deepening recession following the General Strike of 1926. As a result, the first of the Company's difficulties became apparent when it failed to declare a dividend to its shareholders.

It was generally thought the answer to restoring full production lay in diversification. As a result of a growing interest in passenger vehicles at this time, a decision was taken by the

A.J.S. board to produce commercial vehicles. This coincided with a contract secured between C.W.Hayward and The Clyno Engineering Co. (1922) Ltd., for the Lower Walsall Street works to produce bodies for the new Clyno 'Nine' motor car, following the latter's move to their new factory at Bushbury earlier in the year. In order to accommodate additional manufacturing facilities alongside existing sidecar body and chassis production, the Company decided to re-house the ailing wireless business at the Stewart Street works.

In accordance with their traditional policy of offering the public what they raced, A.J.S. broke the news in October 1927, that two overhead camshaft racing models would be included in their 1928 series 'K' catalogue. Listed as the 'K7' (349 c.c.) and 'K10' (498 c.c.), the new camshaft models replaced the earlier uncatalogued 'H7' and 'H10' push rod racing machines and together with a new 248 c.c. lightweight model listed as the 'K12' formed an impressive eleven model line up. The ever popular 7.99 h.p. V-twin passenger combination continued to be offered in De Luxe ('K1') and Standard ('K2') forms priced respectively at £95.0s.0d. and £80.0s.0d. In response to a growing number of enquiries, the Company also offered its big twins in solo form priced at £76.10s.0d (£76.50) and £66.0s.0d. Five 3.49 h.p. machines were catalogued for 1928; three sidevalve models comprising the 'K3' De Luxe Touring and the 'K4' De Luxe Sporting each priced at £47.0s.0d., plus the 'K5' Standard Sporting machine listed at £43.10s.0d. (£43.50). For the more serious sportsman, the 'K6' Overhead Valve model was available at £50.0s.0d., while the new advanced 'K7' Overhead Camshaft machine incorporating dry sump lubrication was offered at the remarkably low price of £62.0s.0d. Three 4.98 h.p. machines were included in the catalogue, each featuring a different method of valve operation. The first, an overhead valve, push rod machine listed as the 'K8' was priced at £59.10s.0d. (£59.50), followed by the 'K9' De Luxe Touring model having side valve layout and priced at £55.0s.0d., plus the new 'K10' Overhead Camshaft machine listed at £73.0s.0d. Finally to complete the range, the Company offered a new 2.48 h.p. lightweight side valve model listed as the 'K12' priced at £39.17s.6d. (£39.87½). Although the external appearances of the new 'K' models did not differ very markedly from the earlier 'H' series, they had in fact been re-designed. The old familiar method of using a bridge piece and tie rods to retain the cylinder head and barrel was abandoned in favour of studs and nuts, while new cylinder heads and barrels for all the established models were

1928 7.99 h.p. model 'K1' passenger machine, fitted with acetylene lighting set.
Photo: Jim Davies.

Clyno car body production at Lower Walsall Street 1927.
Photo: Geoff Stevens.

made more robust with larger cooling fins. On the overhead and side valve models, the cylinder head setpins were extended to protrude above the cooling fins, making them more easily accessible. Following the use of needle rollers in the big end bearings of the camshaft racing engines used in the T.T. races, this practice was adopted for all the new models, although with the exception of the model 'K7' and 'K10' machines, plain bearings were used to support the engine mainshafts, this being considered the most satisfactory method for ordinary use. To prevent oil leakage, new, two piece, oil tight tappets were used on the overhead and side valve engines, the former also having modified rocker gear incorporating wider bridge plates to provide improved support and better cooling facilities. Although the gearbox and transmission components remained largely unchanged, the line of the final drive was altered to allow larger section tyres to be fitted.

Terry spring top saddles were fitted as standard equipment to the whole A.J.S. range. To allow a lower riding position, each saddle was hinged at its peak, being bolted through the down swept top tube at a point just above the rear end of the petrol tank; a special strengthening lug being fitted over this point to prevent the frame from being weakened. The lower tank rail was then effectively extended rearwards with a tubular cross piece forming a tee, to which the rear springs of the saddle were attached.

Without exception all the standard A.J.S. sidecars and those produced for the trade by C.W.Hayward were fabric covered for 1928. The decision to adopt this type of construction followed considerable use of fabric coachwork on the contract to produce car bodies for Clyno; fabric covered body panels enjoying a vogue at this time. The sidecars were impressive: no less than fourteen different types being offered. These included five commercial and nine passenger bodied versions, with prices ranging from £11.10s.0d (£11.50) for a single seater semi touring model listed as the Universal type 'K02', to £28.5s.0d. (£28.25) for the Special Racing type 'KD2' having a reinforced tubular chassis.

Even with such an impressive range the Company was unable to improve on its home market position with sales continuing to decline, due to the widening recession. However, on a brighter note, exports were up, with overseas demand for A.J.S. motorcycles increased by over 2,000 machines; the painstaking groundwork covered by George Stevens a few years earlier was now paying dividends.

Although the lubrication problems, which had beset the camshaft racing machines during the 1927 Isle of Man T.T. races, had now been overcome, the performance of the engine was found to be lacking. As a result the team chose to revert back to using push rod engines for much of 1928. As in 1924, the latest pushrod engines featured dry sump lubrication, although the new system featured a special double Pilgrim pump, the oil supply being taken to the timing gear, big end bearing and the base of the cylinder; this last feature being a point of difference from the system employed on the 1927 camshaft engines. Another important change was the reversion to a three speed gearbox replacing the previous four speed unit, while an entirely new design of bottom link fork was used working against a centrally mounted compression spring positioned directly in front of the headstock. A deeper than usual fuel tank, giving the impression of being a saddle type design, carried 3½ gallons of fuel and was supported between the top and bottom frame tubes, while a separate oil tank containing engine oil was mounted on the saddle tube and incorporated an adjustable drip feed supply to the primary chain. The brakes, 6" diameter front and 7" diameter rear were both foot operated, allowing the rider greater freedom to manipulate the remaining controls.

In the Isle of Man T.T. races, the Junior event proved to be a disaster for the A.J.S. team. In a race dominated by the Velocettes of Alec Bennett and Harold Willis, all six A.J.S. machines ridden by Jimmy Simpson, Tommy Spann, George Rowley, J.E.Wade, L.R.Cohen and Ronnie Parkinson being forced to retire due to engine failure. The crux of the problem affecting five of the six machines lay in a last minute decision by the Company to fit valve springs supplied by an alternative manufacturer. These springs which had not been properly finished off, had draw marks in the surface finish of the wire, which eventually led to breakages during the race. A.J.S. reverted back to their usual supplier for their Senior machines, and despite their poor showing during the Junior event, practice form pointed towards the prospect of an exciting Senior race between A.J.S. and Sunbeam. As it turned out the weather ruled otherwise with the race turn-

Members of the 1928 racing team enjoy a promenade stroll, Douglas, Isle of Man. From the left: George Rowley, Charlie Hough, Ronnie Parkinson, Tommy Spann, Len Cohen and Jimmy Simpson.
Photo: Susan Taylor.

1926-1930 Times of Change

Frame, Carrier and Saddle Assembling Department, Graiseley Hill 1927.
Photo: Geoff Stevens.

Finishing Department, Graiseley Hill 1927.
Photo: Geoff Stevens.

Experimental Department, Graiseley Hill 1927.
Photo: Geoff Stevens.

ing out to be one of wettest T.T.'s on record. Despite the dreadful conditions Jimmy Simpson took off like a rocket to lead the race for the first two laps, setting the fastest time of the day in the process at 33 minutes 20 seconds (67.94 m.p.h.), before being side lined with engine trouble on lap three. After picking up places on his Sunbeam, Charlie Dodson found himself in the lead before eventually being overtaken on lap six by the Rudge of Graham Walker who then went on to build his advantage to over three minutes. However, with only thirteen miles to go to the finish, Walker's Rudge struck trouble and he was forced to retire with mechanical problems. Dodson went on to win his first ever T.T. by a margin of eight minutes over second place man George Rowley; this being George's best ever Island placing, while Tommy Hatch riding a Scott was third. Tommy Spann riding the only other A.J.S. machine to finish came home in thirteenth place.

At the Dutch T.T. held at Assen in June, Jimmy Simpson, set to ride the overhead camshaft models in both 350 c.c. and 500 c.c. classes, declared himself a non starter claiming the machines were too slow. Jimmy never rode for A.J.S. again, his entries being taken over by Charlie Hough and Tommy Spann, both men choosing to race push rod engined machines. Although Charlie Hough retired on lap ten of the 350 c.c. event, Tommy Spann went on to finish second in the 500 c.c. race. Further successes followed at the Czechoslovakian Grand Prix in July with George Rowley winning the 350 c.c. event as well as recording the fastest lap in record time; while at the Austrian Grand Prix held near Vienna in September, Wal Handley won the 350 c.c. class and George Rowley the 500 c.c. class riding overhead camshaft machines. In Ireland, Leo Davenport, riding a privately entered camshaft machine, came second in the 350 c.c. Ulster Grand Prix.

Further important successes in reliability were achieved by the Company during 1928, A.J.S. riders gaining no fewer than five gold medals in the London - Exeter Trial; three gold and three silver medals in the Colmore Cup Trial, plus three gold medals and the team prize in the Six Days Stock Machine Trial. In the Victory Cup Trial, two gold and three silver medals were gained plus the 'Olia Cup'; while in the Scottish Six Days Trial, A.J.S. gained the special merit award, plus silver cup and gold medal. In the International Six Days Trial, no fewer than five gold medals were gained, A.J.S. also being a member of the winning International Silver Vase Team. Cups and medals were also gained in the Leicester - Cardiff, London - Land's End, London - Edinburgh, Cork 'Twenty' Reliability and Kickham Memorial Trials.

Although A.J.S. motorcycles continued to enjoy many successful achievements, it was an altogether different story for the wireless business which had been going through a particularly difficult time. Despite the earlier introduction of its new 'Symphony' range of receivers, sales had continued to fall and as a consequence a decision was taken during the summer of 1928 to close the business down and put the Stewart Street factory on the market.

A.J.S. suffered further financial difficulties when its lucrative contract to produce car bodies for the Clyno 'Nine' motor car ran into serious cash problems. The difficulties followed Clyno's unsuccessful introduction of their new cut price 'Century' model during a price war with their much larger rivals Austin and Morris. Clyno had hoped to sell three hundred a week, but despite the incredibly low price of £112.10s.0d. (£112.50), the expected sales of the 'Century' never materialized and Clyno found itself with mounting debts and difficulty in meeting its financial commitments.

About this time, Charles Hayward left A.J.S. to pursue a new career in London as a stockbroker and industrialist. His position of overall responsibility at Lower Walsall Street being taken over by Joe Stevens Junior; who, in view of the worsening crisis at Clyno, stepped up development work on the new commercial vehicle venture.

Despite difficult trading conditions the A.J.S. management stood firm in their belief that the development of their products should not be neglected whatever the circumstances. In addition to the development of their standard range of motorcycles, a few unusual designs were considered. One of which, an in-line four cylinder overhead valve push rod machine was

George Rowley, Charlie Hough and Clarrie Wise in Edinburgh, during the 1928 Scottish Six Days Trial.
Photo: Doug Hough.

developed. Although not all the precise details of this design are known, the engine had a capacity of 660 c.c. and was air cooled. A three bearing crankshaft was employed supported in plain white-metal bearings; similar bearings being used for the big ends. The push rods were operated from a three bearing camshaft, chain driven from the front end of the crankshaft, while a skew gear fitted to the rear end of the camshaft served to drive a distributor and a gear type oil pump. Oil taken from the sump being delivered under pressure to the main bearings and big ends through the crankshaft, while an external pipe carried oil to the rocker box. Oil leaving the pump passed through a simple four tube external oil cooler mounted in front of the engine, while a tank mounted oil gauge was used to monitor pressure. The rear end of the crankshaft carried a car type clutch and flywheel assembly, the drive being taken through a splined shaft into a three speed unit construction gearbox, where it was transferred through right angles by bevel gears to a final drive gearbox sprocket; the final drive being by chain. The cylinders were produced in a single, cast iron block having a detachable, cast iron cylinder head, each piston floating on a fixed gudgeon pin held in the small end of the connecting rod by a set pin. Lucas coil ignition was employed, a DS4 distributor serving to supply an unorthodox 1, 2, 4, 3 firing order; the two middle pistons rising, as the two outer ones descended. The engine was slung in a special, long wheelbase, duplex frame from two long bolts rubber bushed at each end to discourage vibration. Although this particular design never got the green light, it is known that one of the experimental prototypes registered in 1928 belonged to George Stevens.

Completely new machines were announced by the Company for 1929. Realizing their existing models were appearing to look somewhat dated alongside their competitors' machines, the A.J.S. designers had been extremely busy. Everything it would appear that could be changed had been, fashion it would seem dictating all. Gone was the unmistakable black and gold, slim line, flat tank look, replaced by a heavier, chunkier, saddle tank design emblazoned with magenta coloured, side transfer panels edged in black and gold and carrying revised lettering inset. The new A.J.S. 'M' range as it was called was extremely comprehensive, offering no less than eleven catalogued models and thirteen, sidecar body options. Quite apart from the obvious cosmetic changes, particular attention had been paid to improve weather protection for the mechanisms of the machines and produce engines which on the whole were cleaner, quieter and more flexible in use. As such the new models featured a number of important refinements; the most significant being the standardization of dry sump lubrication. Other changes included new frames, redesigned with a straight top tube to accommodate the new style saddle tanks, and a carrier mounted nearer to the saddle to improve weight distribution and comfort, especially when carrying a passenger. New spring forks having tubular, triangulated fork blades were

One of the 1928 experimental in-line four cylinder machines.
Photo: Geoff Strevens.

fitted, with a single, barrel type compression spring mounted vertically between; the lower links incorporated shock absorbers, while a steering damper was built in at the base of the steering column, controlled by a simple, aluminium handwheel at the top. All but the smallest machine now had a flush mounted speedometer set in the top of the petrol tank positioned opposite the filler cap. Although the three speed, countershaft gearbox fitted to the new models remained largely unchanged, the kickstart quadrant was placed between the clutch and gearbox sprocket rather than on the outside of the clutch face as hitherto. The outer cover of the gearbox was also altered to accommodate the speedometer drive. Where possible valve operating mechanisms were enclosed or shielded, and for added comfort the position of the handlebars could be adjusted.

As was customary, V-twin machines headed the new catalogue. Listed as the model 'M1' De Luxe and 'M2' Standard, each was fitted with a larger 996 c.c. capacity, side valve engine (84 mm. x 90 mm. bore and stroke). Described by A.J.S. as possessing "an enormous reserve of power coupled with flexibility, docility at low speeds and silence". Each was recommended as an ideal sidecar machine or equally as a fascinating solo mount. The 'M1', tipping the scales at 385lbs., was priced at £76.10s.0d. (£76.50) while the cheaper 'M2' weighing 40lbs. less was offered at £66.0s.0d. As with the previous 'K' series models, five 3.49 h.p. models were available for 1929; three side valve machines comprising the popular 'M3' De Luxe Touring and 'M4' De Luxe Sporting models priced at £48.10s.0d. (£48.50) and the 'M5' Standard Sporting model representing outstanding value at £45.0s.0d. The 'M6' Overhead Valve model had been considerably improved in design, the push rods and rocker gear now enclosed with adjustment provided at the exposed rocker ends in contact with the valve stems, rendering it unnecessary to remove an inspection plate situated at the upper ends of the push rods. Lubrication of the push rod ends was now carried out through a grease nipple situated at the centre point of the inspection plate, grease being distributed to each end through an aluminium tee piece. The model was offered with an option of single or twin port cylinder head, the single port costing £52.0s.0d., while the twin port an extra £2.10s.0d. (£2.50). The 'M7' Overhead Camshaft model featured much the same technical specification as for the previous year, except a choice of wide or close gear ratios was available. Price was unaltered from the previous year at £62.0s.0d. As in the previous catalogue, the Company listed three 4.98 h.p. models; these being the 'M8' Overhead Valve model, which like its smaller 'M6' brother was offered with a choice of single or twin ported cylinder head, priced at £59.10s.0d. (£59.50) and £62.0s.0d. respectively. This was followed by the 'M9' side valve De Luxe Touring model at £54.0s.0d. and the 'M10' Overhead Camshaft model at £72.0s.0d. Finally the smallest A.J.S. the 2.48 h.p. side valve Lightweight model 'M12' weighing under 200lbs., was offered at £39.17s.6d. (£39.87½).

With dirt track racing increasing in popularity during this period, many well known manufacturers recognized the potential for good sales in this field and offered specially modified models from their ranges. A.J.S. were no exception offering adaptations of their 'M6' 'M7' 'M8' and 'M10' machines for this purpose. Their overhead camshaft models proved extremely fast in the hands of such notable riders as Billy Lamont, Frank Arthur and Cecil Brown. Sadly A.J.S. never gained lasting fame for their speedway machines, that honour falling to Douglas and Rudge. However, even they had to move over eventually when J.A.P. came along and offered a competitively priced engine specially designed for the job. Many specialized firms took up this design and assembled the engine into frames of their own manufacture. Eventually all speedway machines came to look alike.

Having managed to raise further capital, Clyno struggled on. However, as is so often the case, they chose to ignore their immediate problems in favour of developing a new 22 h.p. straight eight cylinder design and as a result the company again slipped heavily into debt. In consequence a receiver was appointed in February 1929. The subsequent loss of Clyno body production at its Lower Walsall Street works hit A.J.S. hard, as the Company had come to rely heavily on the work to provide additional funds to develop its commercial vehicle business. As a result a decision was taken by A.J.S. to produce its own light car and a successful approach was made to the designer of the original Clyno 'Nine', Arthur G.Booth, to join the Company and take overall responsibility for the project.

By coincidence, the appointment of the receiver at Clyno came at the same time as A.J.S. announced its first commercial vehicle chassis, the 'Pilot'. Initially designed as a normal control vehicle with the driver seated behind the engine, the 'Pilot' chassis was intended as a high speed, long distance coach capable of carrying twenty people. Soon after, a further version was introduced with forward control, the driver now seated alongside the engine in a separate cab; this new configuration providing additional space behind the driver in which to include a further two seats. The chosen power unit was a Henry Meadows, 6 ERC, six cylinder engine having overhead valves and a capacity of 3800 c.c. The engine developed 54 b.h.p. at 2000 r.p.m. and was coupled to a four speed gearbox. Priced at £685.0s.0d. for normal control and £705.0s.0d. for forward control, the 'Pilot' soon established itself in the six cylinder market, appealing mainly to small independent operators.

Following its early success, work was undertaken to produce a new, larger, forward control, designed chassis capable of carrying a thirty two seat body. Built along the same lines as the later forward control version of the 'Pilot', the Company announced the 'Commodore' model in October 1929. The power source chosen being a six cylinder, Coventry Climax, L6, side valve engine having a capacity of 5748 c.c. and developing 75 b.h.p. at 2000 r.p.m. Although the 'Commodore' faced much competition within its class, at just £850.0s.0d. it was one of the lowest priced six cylinder chassis on the market. The 'Commodore' quickly gained a reputation for reliability and performance, and like the 'Pilot' became popular with the small operator.

In the motor cycle department after undergoing further development, the overhead camshaft engine was reinstated into the Company's racing programme for 1929. Considerable success followed the A.J.S. team in the classic races, which included Wal Handley finishing second in the Isle of Man Junior T.T., while George Rowley won the 350 c.c. class of the Austrian Grand Prix. In September A.J.S. enjoyed a first and second in the 350 c.c. Ulster Grand Prix, Leo Davenport crossing the line ahead of George Rowley, while during the following month both riders were to finish in the same order in the 350 c.c. European Grand Prix held in Spain.

A.J.S. machines again featured well in many of the important reliability trials during the year, the trio of George Rowley, Leo Davenport and Clarrie Wise riding 3.49 h.p. solo machines in the Scottish Six Days Trial held from 6th to 11th May, gaining silver cups for their special first class awards, as well as gaining the manufacturers' team prize for the best performance in their class. The same victorious team also accomplished similar successes in the International Six Days Trial starting in Munich and finishing in Geneva, a distance of 1030 miles. George Rowley on this occasion served as a member of the successful Great Britain International Trophy Team.

In addition to its usual road racing and trials activities, A.J.S. turned its attention to track racing and record breaking. Their entry into this field led principally by the partnership of R.M.N. Spring and A.Denly, two very experienced men who had built up enviable reputations racing Norton machinery. While Nigel Spring took charge of machine preparation, Bert Denly rode them; each wasting little time in establishing the A.J.S. name to the forefront, breaking no less than one hundred and seventeen records during a period between 6th April and 28th September 1929.

Although elated by the recent A.J.S. speed achievements, Jack Stevens was of the opinion that one record in particular would eclipse all others - the world's motorcycle land speed record. Such was Jack's enthusiasm for the project, that by the summer of 1929, the first important steps to produce a suitable design had been taken. Under Jack Steven's supervision, a very special machine emerged, the engine of which had a capacity of 990 c.c. and basically comprised a pair of the latest 495 c.c. (79 mm. x 101 mm. bore and stroke), 'R10', overhead camshaft singles mounted on a common crankcase and forming a 50° V-twin configuration. The engine and three speed gearbox were housed in a huge, duplex frame of immense strength, having a 60" wheelbase and weighing 426lbs. Once completed the mighty twin was found to produce almost 70 b.h.p. and was thought to be capable of attaining a speed of 150 m.p.h., some fifteen miles per hour greater than the existing record held by Germany's Ernst Henne on his supercharged 743 c.c. B.M.W. at 134.75 m.p.h. Owing to an unfortunate clash between oil sponsors, Bert Denly, the man chosen to capture the record for A.J.S., had to withdraw, his position being taken over by another experienced record man Captain Oliver M.Baldwin. After adapting the machine to suit his own requirements, Baldwin appeared at Brooklands in July 1930 with the object of running the engine in at a speed of between 90 and 100 m.p.h. while carrying out final adjustments, prior to travelling to Arpajon in August to make an attempt on the record. While early tests had been encouraging, the actual record attempt proved disappointing with Baldwin just managing to achieve 130

Bert Denly pictured with Nigel Spring, after winning the 350 c.c. class of the 200 Miles Solo Race at Brooklands at 89.20 m.p.h. on 27th May 1929.
Photo: Dr. Joseph Bayley collection.

m.p.h. before a piston seizure in the rear cylinder brought the attempt to an end.

Amid mounting financial difficulties and poor trading conditions, A.J.S. boldly introduced a redesigned motor cycle range for 1930. Listed as the 'R' series, the Company offered a reduced seven model range, its overhead camshaft machines ('R7' and 'R10') no longer appearing as catalogued models. Only one twin cylinder machine was available, this being the 9.96 h.p., side valve, V-twin model 'R2' priced at £63.0s.0d. Three 3.49 h.p. models were listed; the De Luxe Side Valve model 'R4' at £44.10s.0d. (£44.50), a Standard Lightweight model 'R5' at £40.0s.0d. and the Overhead Valve model 'R6' having a twin port head at £53.0s.0d. Just two 4.98 h.p. models were listed, these were the overhead valve, De Luxe, Two Port model 'R8', at £59.10s.0d. (£59.50) and the De Luxe Side Valve model 'R9' priced at £52.10s.0d (£52.50). Finally completing the range was a very neat 2.48 h.p., overhead valve machine listed as the Two Port model 'R12' at £40.0s.0d.

The most striking feature of the new range was the appearance of forward inclined engines within new, semi-cradle type frames on the side valve and overhead valve 'R4', 'R6', 'R8' and 'R9' models; the magnetos on these types being mounted on an adjustable tilting platform to the rear of the cylinder, chain driven from the inlet cam wheel.

Generally, many of the internal and structural changes which had been incorporated in the new models, were as a result of lessons learnt from recent track and record breaking experiences. Although only small alterations were carried out to the dry sump lubrication system, the engines now benefited from stiffer flywheel assemblies and crankcases, double row roller big ends being carried in duralumin cages, while ball bearings were employed on both crank axles; two races being fitted on the drive side separated by a white metal, oil retaining ring. In the top half of the engines, thicker cylinder

Captain Oliver Baldwin and the mighty twin at Members Bridge, Brooklands, July 1930.
Photo: Geoffrey St. John.

heads and relieved aluminium pistons were used, the heads modified to accept flange fitting, 'Amal', needle jet carburettors. All overhead valve engines were fitted with twin port heads and larger diameter, duralumin push rods, while on the side valve models the cylinder head finning now followed a horizontal pattern. On the transmission side, entirely new, three speed gearboxes were used, incorporating enclosed, kickstarter mechanisms and shock absorbers; while a redesigned, tank side, gearbox gate control was repositioned further forward and attached to the frame rather than the tank itself.

The new semi-cradle frames fitted to the inclined engine models were constructed with duplex chain stays, vertical seat pillars and 1½" diameter top and front down tubes. Huge engine and gearbox cradle plates were used, the bottom bracket and rear engine plates being made in one piece, thus affording greater rigidity and strength as well as serving cleverly to conceal the inlet and outlet pipes from the main oil tank. A spring-up centre stand replaced the traditional rear wheel type, while revised, centre spring, front forks were fitted, having longer springs and side links, the latter incorporating large, adjustable, friction dampers, while a new, friction disc type steering damper arrangement was employed, the friction element being situated below the steering head. The brakes on the new models were improved having the benefit of larger diameter drums and stouter brake anchorages, while in keeping with the latest fashion, 'Brooklands Can' style silencers were fitted to the exhaust pipes, most having fish-tail end pieces. Other refinements included quick detachable rear wheels, improved, three point front lamp fixings, detachable rear carriers for some models, mechanical oil feeds to the primary chain drives, chromium plating for all bright parts and simple finger adjustments to all controls. Having realized that the bright, magenta coloured tank panels introduced during the previous year were proving unpopular, the Company reverted back to its traditional colour scheme, all models being finished in black with broad gold linings and transfers. Extras included electric lighting at £5.10s.0d. (£5.50) and chromium plating at £1.0s.0d. on models 'R5' and 'R12' only, while a chromium

1930 2.48 h.p. model 'R12'.
Photo: Author.

Close-up of drive and timing side model 'R12' engine.
Photo: Author.

or nickel plated, petrol tank finish was available on any model for an additional £1.0s.0d.

In the light of recent developments, the limited production 'R7' and 'R10' overhead camshaft models carried revised engine measurements. By adopting the specifications used by the successful Spring and Denly stable, the 'R7' received bore and stroke dimensions of 70 mm. x 90 mm. (346 c.c.) while the larger capacity 'R10' model 79 mm. x 101mm. (495 c.c.).

Meanwhile, as a result of the difficult trading conditions which had persisted for much of 1929, the Company's financial resources had been further affected. In an attempt to minimise any more losses, the A.J.S. board were forced to impose a 10% reduction in pay throughout the Company during the early part of 1930, as well as throwing more weight behind the light car project in order to keep Graiseley at full capacity.

On a much happier note, Millie Stevens married Tommy Spann at St.Peter's Collegiate Church, Wolverhampton in April 1930. The bride, who was given away by her father George Stevens, was attended by four adult bridesmaids and two children, while one of the two pages was none other than Master Murray Walker, son of Graham Walker and now the famous racing commentator. It was an extremely happy occasion with the popularity of the bride and her family in Wolverhampton evident by the large crowds who gathered in the church and the surrounding streets; many of the guests attending the reception held at the Victoria Hotel being well known racing motorcyclists.

On the racing scene, the talented Freddie Hicks was persuaded to join the A.J.S. camp for 1930, whilst also accepting full time employment in the experimental department at Graiseley, working on the research and development of new machines. Although the works 346 c.c. and 495 c.c. overhead camshaft racing engines featured a number of detailed improvements, they remained largely unchanged for the new season. Structurally however, a new sturdier straight line frame design having a large diameter top tube replaced the old familiar diamond pattern. In addition to the 346 c.c. and 495 c.c. machines there was a new and exciting 248 c.c. camshaft model, having a four speed, foot operated gearbox. It was the first time the Company had produced a lightweight racing machine and three were entered for the Isle of Man Lightweight T.T. Jimmy Guthrie riding one of these machines won the race at a record speed of 64.71 m.p.h. from the OK-Supremes of Paddy Johnson and C.S.Barrow. This incidentally was Jimmy Guthrie's first T.T. victory, there being five more to follow.

During 1930, A.J.S. enjoyed many successes on the Continent. In April, Leo Davenport won the 350 c.c. Hungarian T.T. at record speed, followed in August by the 350 c.c. Austrian Grand Prix and finally the Ulster Grand Prix in September. In June, it was Jimmy Guthrie's turn, winning the 350 c.c. German Grand Prix. While in July, Arthur Simcock claimed victory in the 350 c.c. Dutch T.T. and second place in the 350 c.c. Belgian Grand Prix a week later. Finally Freddie Hicks won the 350 c.c. French Grand Prix in September from fellow team mate Leo Davenport.

Further successes came in the 1930 Scottish Six Days' Trial held 5th to 10th May with 3.49 h.p. A.J.S. machines ridden by George Rowley, Clarrie Wise and Frank Turley gaining the best performance and manufacturers' team prize for solo machines up to 350 c.c. for the second year in succession; George Rowley also receiving a special award for best 350 c.c. solo performance. While in the Alan Trophy Trial, George Rowley riding a 2.48 h.p. machine won the 'Cumberland County Trophy' for the best solo performance of the day, as well as the 'Wrynose Cup' for the best performance by a 250 c.c. machine.

In August, the long awaited A.J.S. 'Nine' light car which had been announced as early as December 1929 was finally introduced. In an attempt to keep both works at full capacity during the trade depression, production of the car had been divided between Lower Walsall Street and Graiseley Hill, the former concentrating on producing body panels, while Graiseley became responsible for final assembly. The first cars to be produced were four-door, fabric bodied saloons and were priced at £230.0s.0d., although shortly after, two further models were added, a four-door, coachbuilt saloon at £240.0s.0d. and an open two seater with dickey priced at £210.0s.0d. Each model was fitted with a four cylinder, side valve, Coventry Climax engine having a capacity of 1018 c.c. (60 mm. x 90 mm. bore and stroke) and an RAC rating of 8.92 h.p., which put it in the £9.0s.0d. tax class at the time. A maximum power output of 24 b.h.p. was claimed at 3000 r.p.m. this being transmitted through a three speed gearbox. On the road the little A.J.S. more than measured up to expectations, finger tip steering combined with remarkable, low speed flexibility being among its most endearing features. Despite its comparatively high price, the car won much acclaim from the motoring press and as a result initial sales were encouraging.

Millie Stevens marries Tommy Spann at St. Peters Collegiate Church, Wolverhampton, April 1930. The Page seen on the right is none other than Murray Walker, (son of Graham Walker) the now famous racing commentator.
Photo: Susan Taylor.

In September, A.J.S. proudly announced advance details of its 1931 series 'S' motorcycle range. However, behind the bold advertisements, the Company was experiencing some of the worst effects of the continuing trade depression. Considering the strict financial restraints put on the business, the new models were extremely impressive; in fact there had never been a better time in which to purchase an A.J.S., the latest prices representing the best value ever.

Including the overhead camshaft models which were separately catalogued, the Company featured a ten model range, many of the machines incorporating important design changes over the previous series 'R' models. The most significant changes were to be found in the side valve models, which with the exception of one model, the 'S5', had been redesigned in line with car practice by fitting the valves into the cylinder casting rather than in the detachable head; the latest cylinder heads being produced in aluminium and held down on top of the cylinder by seven studs, a copper asbestos gasket being used to make the joint. With the exception of the camshaft racing models, a redesigned lubrication system was employed; a duplex 'Pilgrim' pump enclosed within the timing cover being driven from the crankshaft and fed from a separate tank, both top and bottom pump plungers being connected by a common internal lead. While the upper plunger delivered oil to the big end via the timing side of the crankshaft, the lower plunger returned excess oil back to the oil tank through a tell-tale, out flow pipe situated in the mouth of the filler neck. The oil supply was adjustable by means of a knurled thumb wheel located on the timing cover just above the pump. As in the previous model range, only one twin cylinder machine was listed, the 9.96 h.p. model 'S2' priced at £63.0s.0d. Although retaining the same basic specification as its predecessor, the 'S2' had been entirely redesigned, its engine fitted with the latest detachable, aluminium cylinder heads and housed in a new, semi-cradle type frame having duplex chain stays. The magneto had been repositioned behind the rear cylinder, while the earlier 'Brooklands Can' style silencer was replaced by a cylindrical expansion chamber transversely mounted in front of the crankcase and having a long exhaust tail pipe. In addition to following the latest side valve design, the De Luxe Side Valve model 'S4' had been increased in capacity to 399 c.c. (74 mm. x 93 mm. bore and stroke) and was priced at £44.10s.0d. (£44.50). In the popular 3.49 h.p. model range, two machines were listed; the Standard Lightweight model 'S5' priced at £40.0s.0d. and the Twin Port Overhead Valve model 'S6' priced at £53.0s.0d. Like its predecessor, the 'S5' was a 'no frills', low cost model retaining the same well proven, 349 c.c., side valve engine vertically mounted in the smaller 2.48 h.p. diamond frame, its standard specification weight totalling just 214½lbs. Three 4.98 h.p. models were listed; these being the Overhead Valve De Luxe Twin Port model 'S8' at £59.10s.0d. (£59.50) and the De Luxe Side Valve model 'S9' offered in a choice of light or heavyweight form. The lightweight model utilizing the same frame as the 'S4' weighed 293lbs. and was offered at £49.0s.0d., while the heavier version having the same frame as the 'S8' tipped the scales at 308lbs. and was priced at £52.10s.0d. (£52.50). Finally, the smallest machine in the range, the 2.48 h.p. Overhead Valve Twin Port model 'S12' weighing 219½lbs. in standard specification, was priced at £40.0s.0d.

Additional features and refinements to be found on the new 'S' series included a new, 'Cush Drive' face cam shock absorber fitted to the drive side engine mainshaft, while to facilitate rear wheel removal, hinged, rear mudguards were fitted to the 'S4', 'S6', 'S8' and 'S9' models; the 'man handling' of these machines also benefitting from the fitting of a new, low-lift centre stand. With the exception of the 'S5' and 'S12' models, redesigned, adjustable saddle mountings were fitted allowing forward and backward movement, while the operating cable of the front brakes passed down the front fork blade, adjustment being provided at the top of the forks. Similarly, the handlebar layout had been tidied up, black enamelled handlebars having integral levers and controls were employed, these being manufactured by the Sackville Company to A.J.S. design. Electric lighting and instruments were offered as additional equipment, options ranging from a simple, tank mounted speedometer to a comprehensive, tank mounted instrument panel housing speedometer, clock, ammeter and switches (not available on 'S5' and 'S12'). With the exception of the 'S2' twin cylinder machine, optional, four speed, gate change gearboxes were available at extra cost, while folding, pillion footrests were available for each model at an extra 12s.6d. (£0.65).

Although described as being replicas of the works' racing machines used during the 1930 season, the new 3.46 h.p. model 'S7' and 4.95 h.p. 'S10' camshaft models did not feature the latest, special straight line, frame design incorporating the large top tube, the makers choosing to continue using the existing diamond pattern type. Both models were separately catalogued and only produced in limited quantities. The 'S7' was priced at £80.0s.0d., while its larger brother the 'S10', £90.0s.0d. Chromium plated, petrol tanks with black enamel, 'D' shaped, side panels lined gold and A.J.S. transfers inset were supplied as standard on all models except the 'S5' and 'S12' which were finished in black with gold lining. However, chromium plated petrol tanks could be specified on these machines for an additional £1.0s.0d.

CHAPTER 6
1931

1931 was to prove an unhappy and tragic year for A.J.S.; the ripples of the 1929 Wall Street crash which had spread to engulf Britain and Europe had hit the car and motorcycle markets hard. The resulting slump in trade, coupled with the heavy investment necessary to get the car and commercial vehicle business off the ground, found the Company facing serious financial difficulties, capital being swallowed up at an alarming rate. The full extent of the problem became apparent following the Company's announcement that its accounts for the year ended 31st August 1930 had amounted to a loss of £89,201.0s.0d. News of the Company's performance was met with yet another fall in its share price, the market having witnessed a steady decline from 28s.0d. (£1.40) in May 1925 to a low of 5s.6d. (27½p).

With sales of the current 'S' series motorcycles proving much slower than expected, five new models were added to the existing range during January 1931; three of which were attractively priced, 'tax dodging' lightweights, pared down to take advantage of a concessionary £1.10s.0d. (£1.50) rate of Road Fund Tax for machines weighing less than 224 lbs. The first of these machines, the 'SA5' was a lighter version of the 'S5' side valve model weighing just 221lbs. complete with six volt 'Maglita' lighting set, tool box and horn. Price excluding lighting was £40.0s.0d. Next came the 'SB6 Big Port' model, a single port 3.49 h.p. overhead valve machine costing £45.0s.0d. which had been very skilfully engineered around the existing 2.48 h.p. design; the vertically mounted engine having a forward facing magneto and being mounted in the diamond pattern frame belonging to the twin port 'S12' model. The result was a remarkably lively machine weighing just 222lbs. and capable of returning a creditable

Millie Stevens seen behind the wheel of the first 'Richmond' saloon to leave the Graiseley Hill works.
Photo: Susan Taylor.

A.J.S. 'Admiral' reg. no. SC 7566 with Hayward coachwork, originally supplied to W.M. Herd of Edinburgh, but pictured here in Scottish Motor Traction ownership.
Photo: David L.G. Hunter.

petrol consumption of over 100 m.p.g. The third model, the 'SA12', a 2.48 h.p., twin port, overhead valve machine offered at £40.0s.0d., was similar in specification to the existing 'S12' except devoid of a rear carrier and incorporating a number of weight saving modifications. The fourth addition came in the form of the 'SB8 Big Port', an inclined, 4.98 h.p., overhead valve machine which followed the same basic lines as the 'S8' except a single port head replaced the twin port design. To reduce costs further, no rear carrier or tool case were included, the model being offered at £49.17s.6d. (£49.87½), representing a saving of almost £10.0s.0d. on the existing twin port model. Finally, to qualify for a lower band of insurance, the factory produced a smaller 3.49 h.p. version of the 'S4' model. Designated the 'SA4' it was offered at the lower price of £44.0s.0d.

Strange as it may appear, in the case of the 'SB6' and 'SB8' models, this was the first occasion that A.J.S. had officially used the 'Big Port' title.

After its successful introduction during the summer of 1930, sales of the A.J.S. light car began to fall by the early part of 1931. Although the main reason for the decline was blamed on the effects of the recession, it was obvious that when compared to other cars in its class, the 'Nine' was overpriced. To help stimulate sales, steps were taken in February to reduce the price by £11.0s.0d. As a further measure, a new, cheaper, fabric bodied, four door saloon named the 'Richmond' was introduced costing £197.0s.0d.

The introduction of the 'Richmond' saloon coincided with the Company's announcement of its third commercial chassis, the 'Admiral'. Closely resembling a heavier version of the popular, normal control 'Pilot', the 'Admiral' was aimed at providing a suitable basis for a high performance luxury coach capable of carrying twenty six to twenty eight passengers over long distances. Although it had been decided to install a purpose built, Henry Meadows, overhead valve engine, because of technical problems during its development, the unit was far from ready in time. As an interim measure, the Company settled for the 'L6', Coventry Climax, power unit as fitted to the 'Commodore'.

Although it had been rumoured for some time that a new, twin cylinder A.J.S. of unorthodox design was on the stocks, the Company caused a sensation when it announced details of its new 'S3' model in April. Being of entirely new design, the latest machine featured a 498 c.c., transverse, V-twin engine arrangement; its 65 mm. x 75 mm. bore and stroke side valve engine having its cylinders arranged at 50°, so permitting a generous air gap between. A single Amal carburettor fed both cylinders, while unusually, two separate, chain driven, outboard camshafts were employed, each chain being

1931 4.98 h.p. model 'S3' transverse twin.
Photo: Chris Cooper.

Front view of the model 'S3' showing the minimal protrusion of the cylinders. Wheel rims would have been enamelled black on original finish.
Photo: Bruce Main-Smith.

automatically tensioned by a Weller spring-loaded blade. No cam followers were used, the tappets having wide curved bases acting direct on the cams; the rear of the left camshaft serving to drive a coil ignition distributor. In keeping with the practice used on the other side valve models, detachable, aluminium cylinder heads were employed, each held down to the barrels by seven studs, the spark plug threads being located in a steel insert. Each side of the crankshaft was supported in ball bearings, while large, single row, caged roller big ends were used. Because the cylinder axis were in line and both big ends sat side by side on the crankpin, the small end bearings had to be offset. Domed, aluminium pistons were fitted having three narrow rings at the top and one at the base of the skirt.

Lubrication followed the same improved principle as the other models, an adjustable, double-acting Pilgrim pump mounted on the timing cover at the front of the engine being driven from the half time shaft; one side of the pump serving to indicate the correct functioning of the system through a tell tale return.

A hollow, primary drive shaft fitted with Hardy fabric couplings took the drive to an in-line, multiplate clutch and three speed gearbox having ratios of 5, 7.9 and 13.6:1. Interestingly,

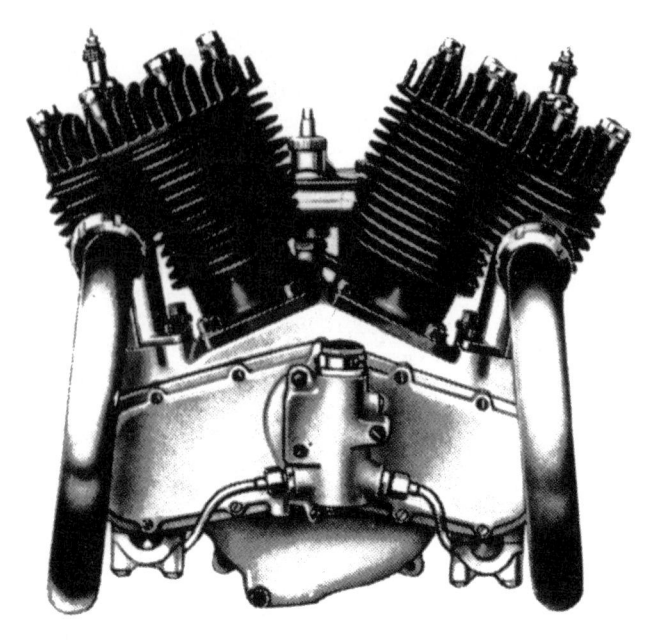

Front view of the 'S3' engine showing double - acting Pilgrim oil pump mounted on the timing cover.
Photo: Manufacturers catalogue.

Rear view of the 'S3' engine showing the neat positioning of distributor and dynamo.
Photo: Manufacturers catalogue.

shaft in its final drive, the gearbox incorporating a spiral-bevel, right angle drive to a totally enclosed rear chain.

The engine and gearbox were carried in a widely splayed, duplex cradle frame having a single top tube; the engine supported directly by the lower tubes, while the gearbox was mounted on a heavy steel platform forming an undershield between the tubes. Webb type girder forks were employed, being of A.J.S. manufacture. Wide, efficient mudguards covered 26" x 3.25" tyred wheels, while a three gallon fuel tank was topped by a fashionable, diamond shaped, instrument panel containing a Smith's speedometer and Lucas electrical gear.

Weighing in at 353lbs., the 'S3' was not intended as a fast sports machine, more a luxury tourer capable of cruising effortlessly at 45-50 m.p.h. Maximum speed was quoted as 65 m.p.h. with petrol consumption working out at about 60 m.p.g. Superbly finished in black and chrome, the machine carried a £65.0s.0d. price tag, standard equipment including electric light-

the clutch which was fitted to the front of the gearbox on production models, had originally been mounted on the back of the engine on the first experimental prototypes. During early tests it was discovered that the additional weight of the drive shaft using this arrangement prevented clean gear changes from being made. Because of the unusual position of the clutch, its operating mechanism comprised a jointed push rod carried inside the hollow drive shaft, this being operated by a ball thrust race arrangement surrounding the shaft. The same shaft also served to drive a Lucas dynamo mounted directly behind the crankcase, a flat, endless, rubber belt drive being taken from a pulley mounted on the shaft, close to the engine coupling. Surprisingly, the 'S3' did not feature a

Freddie Hicks No. 19, pushes his Senior T.T. A.J.S. to the weigh - in.
Photo: Les Henshaw.

The Senior A.J.S. machine belonging to Australian rider D. Brewster.
Note the Bowden carburettor, specially adapted A.J.S./Sturmey - Archer four speed gearbox and Brampton front forks and brake.
Photo: Les Henshaw.

George Rowley No. 13, pictured at the Senior T.T. weigh - in.
Photo: Les Henshaw.

ing, horn, tank mounted instrument panel, rear carrier and twin, leather fronted, tool panniers.

On the international racing scene, the season got off to a good start for A.J.S. with Freddie Hicks winning the 500 c.c. class of the Grand Prix of the Nations at Monza in April from Tommy Bullus (N.S.U.) and Jimmy Simpson (Norton). Given the dreadful weather conditions, in which the machines taking part were said to resemble speed boats as they screamed along the flooded track, Hicks's winning average of 76.92 m.p.h. for the forty lap (170 miles) race was described by the press as "simply magnificent". In the twelfth post war Isle of Man T.T. series in June, Freddie Hicks was the only official A.J.S. entrant for the Junior and Senior events, George Rowley's machines being privately entered, while those of Tommy Spann and George Himing were entered by their own companies. In a Junior event dominated by the Nortons of Tim Hunt and Jimmy Guthrie, George Rowley was the highest placed A.J.S. rider in ninth place, while George Himing was fourteenth; Freddie Hicks retiring with mechanical problems on lap three. Tragedy struck in the Senior race, when on lap five, Freddie Hicks fighting a lonely battle with the leading

This 1930 model 'R10' camshaft machine, seen here in 1964 with current V.M.C.C. Research Officer Phil Heath, is reputed to be the same machine on which Freddie Hicks met his untimely death while competing in the 1931 Senior T.T. race.
After being rebuilt by the works following Hicks's fatal crash, the machine was loaned to Amal for carburettor development. When A.J.S. collapsed in October 1931, it was retained by Amal as part settlement for debts. Eventually, after being used on trade plates for a time, it was registered as EON 642 in 1939. After passing through several hands, it eventually came into the possession of the late Dan McDiarmid, first secretary of the racing section of the V.M.C.C. who converted it to racing trim. Having been loaned to Phil Heath and Mick Broom it was raced with a fair measure of success throughout the 1960's.
Photo: Ivan Rhodes.

Nortons of Tim Hunt, Stanley Woods and Jimmy Guthrie, lost his life while lying some two minutes behind the leader. After approaching the left hander at Union Mills very fast and nearly colliding with a telegraph pole, he lost control and crashed into the doorway of a small shop, sustaining severe head injuries from which he later died while on the way to hospital. Sadly it was to be the last appearance of a Wolverhampton works A.J.S. on the island.

Back at Wolverhampton, all was not going well for the Company. Despite strenuous efforts to reduce costs and improve its trading performance, income continued to fall short of expenditure. Sadly with so many good businesses going to the wall at this time, banks began to panic and loans were called in. A.J.Stevens & Company (1914) Ltd. were not immune. Their bankers, the Midland Bank, seemingly unhappy about the Company's ability to repay a substantial business loan, (essential to finance the expansion of its commercial vehicle and car business) decided to foreclose. Although A.J.S. were able to repay the loan, most of its working capital was swallowed up in the process. After unsuccessful attempts to raise further capital, (few wanted to invest in a company which had failed to declare a dividend since 1926) the directors informed its creditors and shareholders, that a resolution for the voluntary liquidation of the Company would be moved at an Extraordinary General Meeting to be held at the Victoria Hotel, Wolverhampton on 2nd October 1931. As a prerequisite of going into a members' voluntary liquidation, the directors filed a declaration of solvency with the Registrar of Companies on 22nd September 1931, stating that in their opinion the Company would be able to pay off all its creditors in full within a twelve month period of winding up. It was

1931

An aerial photograph of the Lower Walsall Street works, taken in 1932 following the sale to the Ever Ready Company (Great Britain) Ltd.
Photo: Ever Ready Ltd.

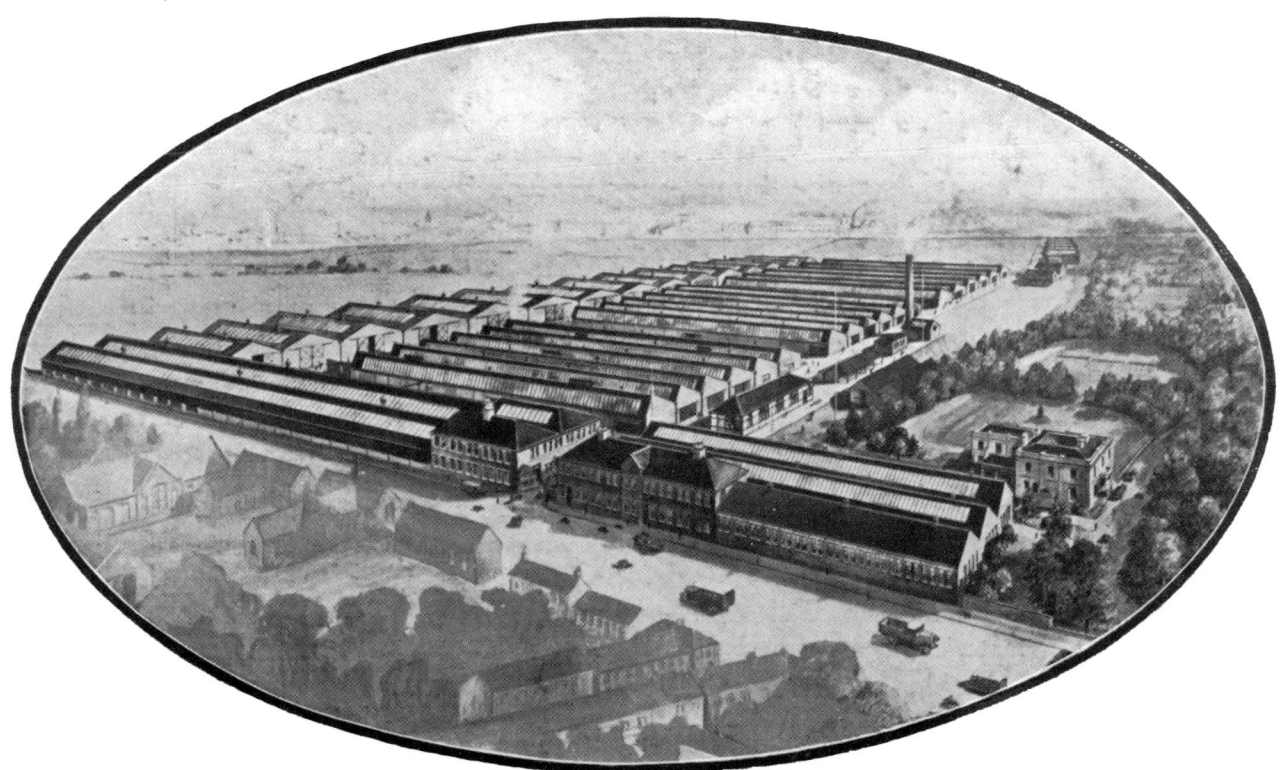

An artists impression of the Graiseley Hill works, sold as two lots in 1933 and 1934.
Photo: Manufacturers catalogue.

resolved on 2nd October that the Company be wound up voluntarily. John Todd Lewis of Agar, Bates, Neal & Company, 106 Edmund Street, Birmingham being appointed liquidator.

Following the subject of a bid, an offer of £20,000.0s.0d. was accepted from Matchless Motorcycles (Colliers) Ltd of Plumstead, London S.E.18 to purchase the name, manufacturing rights and goodwill of A.J.S. Motorcycles Ltd; a £2,200.0s.0d. deposit being received on 12th November 1931 and the balance of £17,800.0s.0d. on 17th December 1931. B.S.A. had also made a bid, although this was less than the offer made by Matchless. By a strange coincidence, not only did B.S.A. share the same bank as A.J.S., but one of its directors, Dudley Docker (father of Sir Bernard Docker), also had a seat on the Midland board, a position he had held since 1912. Shortly after the sale of the motorcycle business, Sir William Letts, Chairman of Willys-Overland Crossley of Heaton Chapel near Stockport, announced that the rights to the A.J.S. 'Nine' Light Car had passed to his company for the sum of £9,500.0s.0d.; a deposit of £1,000.0s.0d. being paid on 19th November 1931 and the balance of £8,500.0s.0d. on 4th January 1932. The sidecar business was acquired by Diamond Motors of St.James Square, Wolverhampton, the 'Graiseley' name, stock and goodwill being bought for £475.0s.0d. When no buyer could be found for the commercial vehicle business, the bulk stock was eventually sold for just £250.0s.0d. (scrap value) to Charles Aaron Weight for the Briton Motor Company Ltd.

The declaration of solvency made by the A.J.S. directors proved well founded, all the Company's creditors being paid in full by the end of September 1932; a first dividend of 12s.6d. (62½p) in the pound being paid on 16th June 1932, while a final dividend of 7s.6d, (37½p) in the pound was paid on 26th September 1932.

The freehold properties and land belonging to the Company were eventually sold for a total of £28,828.7s.6d. (£28,828.37½). The Lower Walsall Street premises were bought by The Ever Ready Company (Great Britain) Ltd. on 25th January 1932 for a sum of £12,750.0s.0d. In order to obtain the best price, the large Graiseley Hill property was sold in two lots, Star Aluminium Company Ltd purchasing the Marston Road end of the site toward the end of 1933, while the Graiseley Hill portion was sold to Wolverhampton Die Castings on 17th February 1934. Even then, the total only amounted to £14,328.7s.6d. (£14,328.37½), a ridiculously low figure given that the entire Graiseley site was roughly four times larger than the Lower Walsall Street works. To complete the sale of property belonging to the Company, derelict land in Commercial Road was eventually sold toward the end of 1934 for a sum of £1,750.0s.0d.

Following a surplus of £33,750.0s.0d. a cash return of 3s.4½d (16.87p) per share was paid to preference shareholders; 2s.0d. (10p) being paid on 27th November 1933 and 1s.4½d. (6.87p) on 3rd December 1935.

When A.J.S. finally closed its doors in 1931, its work force and Wolverhampton were devastated. The loyalty of its workers is best symbolised by a Mr.Butterworth, who having been offered a job with Matchless Motorcycles, went to see Joe Stevens Junior to ask if it would be disloyal to accept the offer. Needless to say 'Mr.Joe' told him to take it.

When looking back over the Company's remarkable history of success and achievement it is hard to believe that it all took place during a period lasting just twenty two years. Long before the first machines were to bear the famous gold initials however, the talented Stevens brothers were already proving to be visionary men, of great technical ability, destined to play an important role in the history of the developing British motorcycle industry. Following its birth in 1909, the A.J.S. marque would eventually rank alongside the greatest names in motorcycle competition; four T.T. victories in a row, including Howard Davies's unique 1921 Senior victory on a 350 c.c. A.J.S., plus an enviable tally of Grand Prix victories, world records and successful reliability trials.

Undoubtedly, A.J.S.'s phenomenal run of success was inextricably linked to the Stevens brothers extraordinary innovative talents plus an insatiable appetite to develop their ideas in what was the golden age of motorcycling.

A.J.S. of WOLVERHAMPTON

Part II

CHAPTER 7
Sidecars

Making their first appearance in the 1913 catalogue, the introduction of the A.J.S. passenger combination would later emerge as the Company's most renowned product, forming the mainstay of production until 1925.

The origins of the sidecar can be traced back to 1893, as the result of a competition run by a French newspaper to determine the most practical means of carrying a passenger on a pedal cycle. The winning entry comprised a simple tubular structure, supporting a third wheel alongside the rear wheel of the cycle, the passenger being seated midway between. However, for some unknown reason, the idea did not catch on and appears to have gone unnoticed.

Following the introduction of the De Dion-Bouton tricycle, a trailer made a brief appearance, the occupant being subjected to the dirt and fumes created by the leading vehicle. A big improvement came about in handling and comfort, when the designers repositioned the passenger in front of the powered vehicle, the main structure being extended forward to include two wheels at the front as well as the rear, with the passenger seated between in a simple wickerwork or coachbuilt open chair. Known as the quadricycle, it was far superior to the awkward trailer arrangement, but placed the passenger in a very vulnerable position.

Over the next few years, great interest was shown in this expanding market. As a result, many new designs and ideas were put forward; the most popular to emerge being the tricar, with two wheels and forecarriage at the front, one wheel at the rear and the engine centrally mounted. Some manufacturers featured detachable forecarriages enabling the owner to convert the machine to a solo motorcycle if they wished, while others offered forecarriages with universal fittings designed to alter almost any solo machine to a passenger carrying tricycle. 'The Stevens Motor Manufacturing Company', which had been set up in 1899 to manufacture proprietary engines, did rather well during this period, supplying their products to a wide sector of the expanding motor trade. For a time, the passenger tricycle and quadricycle enjoyed a relatively small but enthusiastic following. In real terms they were underpowered, cumbersome machines, generally unsuitable for the task for which they had been designed.

The breakthrough came in 1902, when the firm of Mills & Fulford, renowned for their trailers, had decided to attach one of their wicker cane trailers, minus one wheel, alongside a solo motorcycle. This time the idea did not go unnoticed, several other makers being quick to join the market with similar designs. Invariably the competition led to a great many different ideas being put forward, but the most important aspect was, and remained, that the sidecar could be quickly and easily fitted or removed as well as being cheaper to produce.

The Stevens concern continued to develop and produce engines, gearboxes and carburettors for the trade until November 1909, when the brothers chose to form a new partnership to manufacture complete motorcycles under the title of A.J. Stevens & Company Ltd. The first A.J.S. passenger machine suitable for sidecar work was exhibited at the 1910 Olympia Cycle Show in November. Designed by Harry Stevens, the two speed machine had a 3½ h.p. 50° V-twin engine based on an earlier design produced for the Wearwell Company; the model did not go into production. It was to be another year before A.J.S. announced its first production passenger machine. Listed as the model 'D', the two speed, chain driven machine was fitted with a 5 h.p., 50° V-twin side valve engine (631 c.c.) having 70 mm. x 82 mm. bore and stroke dimensions. The gearbox and clutch was robustly designed for passenger work and incorporated a simple kick start lever which enabled the rider to start the engine from the saddle. The machine, having a 4'6" wheelbase tipped the scales at 238 lbs. and was offered at sixty guineas (£63.00).

At this stage, no sidecar or chassis was offered by the Company for use with their model 'D' passenger machine, the customer being expected to purchase from a recognized manufacturer. Despite this, the new model was well received and sold quite well.

With the rapid expansion of the cycle and motorcycle industry at this time, a local man,

This photograph of a cluttered corner of the 1870 sq.ft Retreat Street factory in 1913, shows a row of 6 h.p. model 'D' passenger machines and some early Hayward sidecars.
Photo: Ray Jones.

Charles Hayward, had a year or so earlier decided to set up in business to produce sidecars and tubular chassis. He had first taken a small workshop in John Marston's Paul Street Works, to produce a small number of sidecar bodies and chassis to fit to Sunbeam motorcycles. News of the business soon came to the attention of the Stevens brothers and as a result arrangements were made to supply A.J.S. as well as Sunbeam with up to ten complete bodies per week. The first of these sidecars was featured in the 1913 catalogue and was described thus :- "The chassis is all that a sidecar chassis should be, while the body - to the design of which we have devoted special attention - is unique in that it is built entirely of steel with electrically welded joints and seams, a construction which represents the only way to secure the desirable combination of maximum lightness and immunity from warping, rattle and eventual disintegration under hard road usage. For touring purposes its equal does not exist, the degree of locker capacity and personal comfort provided being the last word in such matters, while the finish of the whole is fully up to the standards of A.J.S. quality - than which we feel no more need be said as a guarantee to those who know our work." To accompany the new Hayward open sidecar, the twin cylinder model 'D' had been redesigned with a larger 6 h.p. engine (696 c.c.) having 74 mm. x 81 mm. bore and stroke and a new, bottom bracket, three speed gearbox, providing gear ratios of 4.75, 7.5, and 12.25:1. The clutch had also been redesigned, now having five plates and giving twice the original friction surface. The frame, fitted with the latest Druid forks, had been lengthened to give a wheelbase of 4'9", while the weight had risen to 255 lbs. Although the latest model 'D' passenger machine carried a sixty nine guinea price tag (£72.45), no figure was listed for the sidecar and chassis, suggesting no firm prices had been established between Hayward and A.J.S. at the time of going to press.

The new improved 6 h.p. combination proved so popular, that the thriving Hayward sidecar business operating under the new title of C.W. Hayward, was forced to move to a larg-

The grim exterior of the C.W. Hayward Church Street sidecar premises of 1913, rented for the weekly sum of 2s.6d (12½p).
Photo: Angela Rogers.

er workshop situated in a coal yard in Church Street for a weekly rent of 2s.6d. (12½p).

For the 1914 season, A.J.S. again redesigned its model 'D' passenger combination. This time the engine was increased to 748 c.c. (74 mm. x 87 mm. bore and stroke), while an improved gearbox carried gear ratios of 4.75, 7.5 and 16:1. On the cycle side, the Company introduced their new quickly detachable and interchangeable wheels, offered as an extra for an additional £3.3s.0d. (£3.15). This feature was to prove so popular that the factory decided to offer a conversion for earlier A.J.S. passenger machines. To improve braking, a new, internal expanding, rear brake was fitted, although strangely the existing stirrup pattern continued to be used on the front wheel. The sidecar took on a more luxurious appearance, with full weather equipment being available at additional cost. The basic combination scaled 423lbs. and was offered at eighty four guineas (£88.20).

Following the outbreak of the First World War, the newly formed public company of A.J.Stevens & Co. (1914) Ltd., found itself working full out on War Office contracts. However, two completely new passenger combinations were introduced for 1915, a 6 h.p., three speed

A rear view of the 1914 6 h.p. model 'D' combination featuring quickly detachable and interchangeable wheels and full weather equipment.
Photo: Manufacturers catalogue.

model and a smaller, 4 h.p. version. The 6 h.p. machine remained listed as the model 'D' and retained the same engine dimensions as for the

Above: The elegant lines of the 1915-16 Hayward coachbuilt sidecar. *Photo: Manufacturers catalogue.*

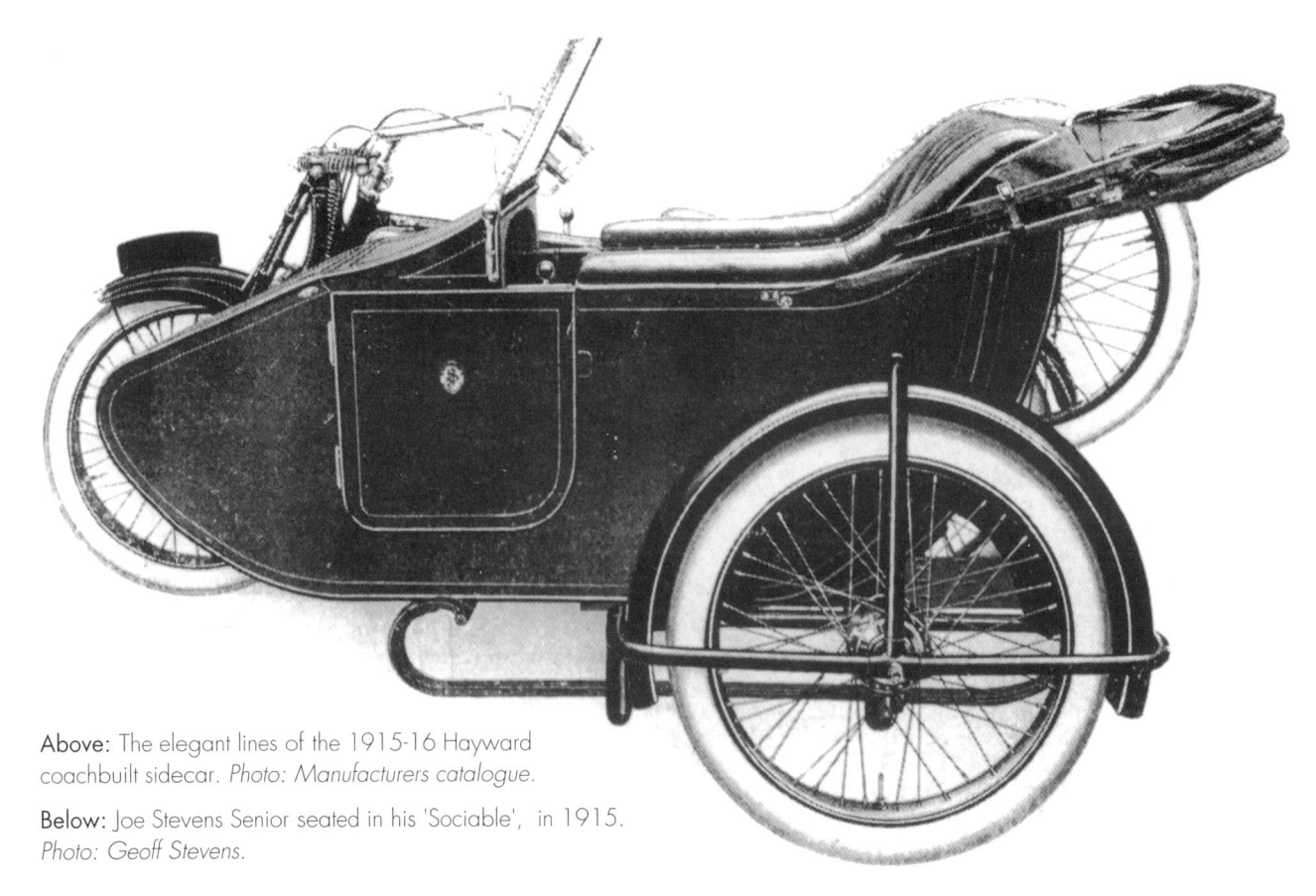

Below: Joe Stevens Senior seated in his 'Sociable', in 1915. *Photo: Geoff Stevens.*

Mr. & Mrs. Jack Clarke of the Wearwell Cycle Company enjoy a Sunday afternoon spin in their 6 h.p. A.J.S. 'Sociable'.
Photo: Geoff Stevens.

previous year, while the smaller 4 h.p. version was designated the model 'A' and fitted with a 550 c.c., 50° V-twin engine (65 mm. x 83 mm. bore and stroke). The coachbuilt sidecars fitted to each passenger machine were extremely well made and luxuriously upholstered in 'Levrine' leather, the seat and back rest being fully sprung. Each chassis was fitted with large, three leaf, 'Cee' type springs back and front with shackles interposed on the rear portion. In following a policy of continuous development, the detachable and interchangeable wheel design now extended to the sidecar also, a spare wheel carried high at the rear of the sidecar serving to cover all three wheels of the combination. As for the previous year a full set of weather equipment and extras were listed, with costs ranging from £2.0s.0d. for a folding hood to 6s.0d. (30p) for an Axminster mat. The model 'D' combination was listed at eighty eight guineas (£92.40) while the smaller model 'A' version eighty one guineas (£85.05).

During the same year a prototype machine christened the 'Sociable' was constructed. It was based on the current 6 h.p. model 'D' combination, but fitted with a side by side, double adult, Hayward sidecar of enormous proportions. The idea of this contraption was to protect the occupants from the elements, while the person seated nearer the motorcycle would steer by means of a tiller type control, from within the sidecar. It never really caught on (one wonders why!) and only a few were made.

In July 1915 Harry Stevens, out driving with his wife Annie in one of the 'Sociables', had received serious injuries, when they were involved in a collision with a car at cross roads near Tong, while driving towards Newport. The car travelling at an estimated 45 m.p.h. from the direction of Weston collided with the outfit, flinging poor Harry some fifteen yards up the road.

The twisted remains of Harry Stevens 'Sociable', following the road accident in 1915.
Photo: Joan Stevens.

Annie Stevens was lucky to receive only cuts and be badly shaken, as the sidecar was reduced to matchwood. Although Harry received serious injuries (from which he later recovered), he would have certainly been killed had he been riding a conventional motorcycle combination, as the motorcycle had taken the full impact.

Faced with an increasing shortage of labour and materials due to the effects of the war, the Company, now manufacturing from its new factory building at Graiseley Hill, reluctantly chose to cancel their popular 2¾ h.p., model 'B', solo machines and concentrate on the passenger machine market; the 1916 models 'D' and 'A' passenger combinations remaining much the same as in the previous year. A.J.S. sidecar bodies and chassis continued to be produced by C.W.Hayward under the terms of a special agreement. Due to a huge growth in the sidecar market, Charles Hayward had moved to much larger premises in Stewart Street, formerly those of The Star Cycle Co. and the Briton Motor Co. Ltd.

After the Ministry of Munitions issued an order on 3rd November 1916 prohibiting the manufacture of all motorcycles, except those required for war duty, A.J.S. were forced to cease further development of their civilian passenger range. However, despite the difficult circumstances, A.J.S. and C.W.Hayward did extremely well during the hostilities, supplying the Ministry of Munitions with large numbers of military motorcycles, sidecars and machine gun carriers.

The armistice in November 1918, saw a huge demand for new machines; the general shortage eventually leading to astronomical prices following the lifting of civilian market restrictions by the Ministry in January 1919. With their usual celerity, A.J.S. began work on a new, three speed, 6 h.p. outfit, embracing many of the features and refinements learnt from their experience of producing the military model. Listed as their 1919-1920 'De-Luxe' model 'D' combination, the most striking feature of the motorcycle was a new style saddle tank. Although the V-twin engine retained its previous 1916 dimensions, it was now constructed with detachable cylinder heads. The single seater Hayward sidecar was a superb piece of work, constructed of steel panelling and beautifully upholstered; seat and back being fitted with springs on a special underslung frame, the design of which enabled a spacious body to be used. Luxurious suspension, unrivalled in comfort, was ensured by three large 'Cee' springs fitted to the back and front of the chassis. Standard equipment included a hinged dash carrying the windscreen, side curtains, storm proof apron, folding hood and cover, integral luggage grid with a tool locker set beneath and a spare wheel mounted at the rear, the latter being quickly detachable and interchangeable with the wheels of the motorcycle. Prices fluctuated from £142.0s.0d. to £200.0s.0d. due to a brief period of inflation which followed its introduction in March 1919. The new 'De-Luxe' combination proved a real winner, resulting in an output of sixty five units per week.

As mentioned earlier, A.J.S. sidecars and chassis were manufactured by C.W. Hayward under terms of a special agreement struck with the Stevens brothers. Charles Hayward had now become a step-brother in the Stevens family, following his mother's marriage to Joe Stevens Senior. With the popularity of the sidecar combination at an all time high, the Hayward sidecar business had grown to such an extent, that by 1920 it was recognized as being the largest in the world, supplying most of the major motorcycle manufacturers. This important fact did not escape the attention of the A.J.S. board, who later in 1920, as part of their expansion programme, took over the business of C.W.Hayward as well as acquiring the freehold of the Stewart Street works. In view of the established trade which had been built up with many of the other motorcycle manufacturers, it was decided to allow the Company to trade under its old title, with Charles Hayward continuing as Managing Director.

The Stewart Street works consisted of two separate departments. A body building section having an area of 11,500 square feet, fully equipped with sawmill and joinery section, plus a chassis department measuring 25,700 square feet, complete with enamelling stores. The incorporation of C.W.Hayward was in itself an important move for the Company. Just as significant however was the overriding desire of the brothers to lay claim to all A.J.S. products.

For the 1921 season, the Company chose to concentrate solely on the passenger machine market. A larger 7 h.p. version of their popular model 'D' combination was introduced in November 1920. To provide a greater spread of power, the V-twin, side valve engine was increased to 799 c.c. capacity, the bore and stroke dimensions being 74 mm. x 93 mm. respectively, while on the cycle side, the old familiar stirrup front brake was finally replaced by an internally expanding type. Apart from minor alterations to the coachbuilt bodywork,

The A.J.S. 'Double - Seater' sidecar, introduced March 1922. It had an overal length of 6' 6" allowing passengers to sit tandem fashion.
Photo: Manufacturers catalogue.

the sidecar and chassis remained similar to the previous model.

Following their tremendous victories in the Isle of Man Junior and Senior T.T. events, the Company decided to 'cash in' on their double success, by introducing two new, 2¾ h.p., sporting models; the first machines intended for solo use since 1915. Later, in response to a growing number of requests, the Company introduced a smart, lightweight sidecar for the 1922 season. Primarily designed for use with the new, 2¾ h.p., model 'B' machines, the body measured 5'4" x 1'8½" wide and weighed 107lbs. complete with its chassis. Price, including a storm proof apron, was £25.0s.0d.

Due to the vast popularity in motorcycling at this time, the trade had never been busier, demand for passenger machines reaching an all time high. With the sidecar and chassis works at full stretch, Charles Hayward was appointed to the main A.J.S. board on 23rd November 1921. Owing to the cramped conditions at Stewart Street, the business moved to much larger premises in Lower Walsall Street towards the end of 1922 and during the next few years additional buildings were erected on the site bringing the total factory area to over 150,000 square feet.

Following its introduction in 1913, the A.J.S. passenger combination provided the backbone of the Company's business until 1925, when it began to lose ground due to the emergence of

Interior features of the 'Double - Seater' sidecar showing lift-up seat and hinged rear screen access for rear passenger.
Photo: Manufacturers catalogue.

the light car, headed by such notable competition as the Austin 'Seven'. However, until this time the popularity and development of the

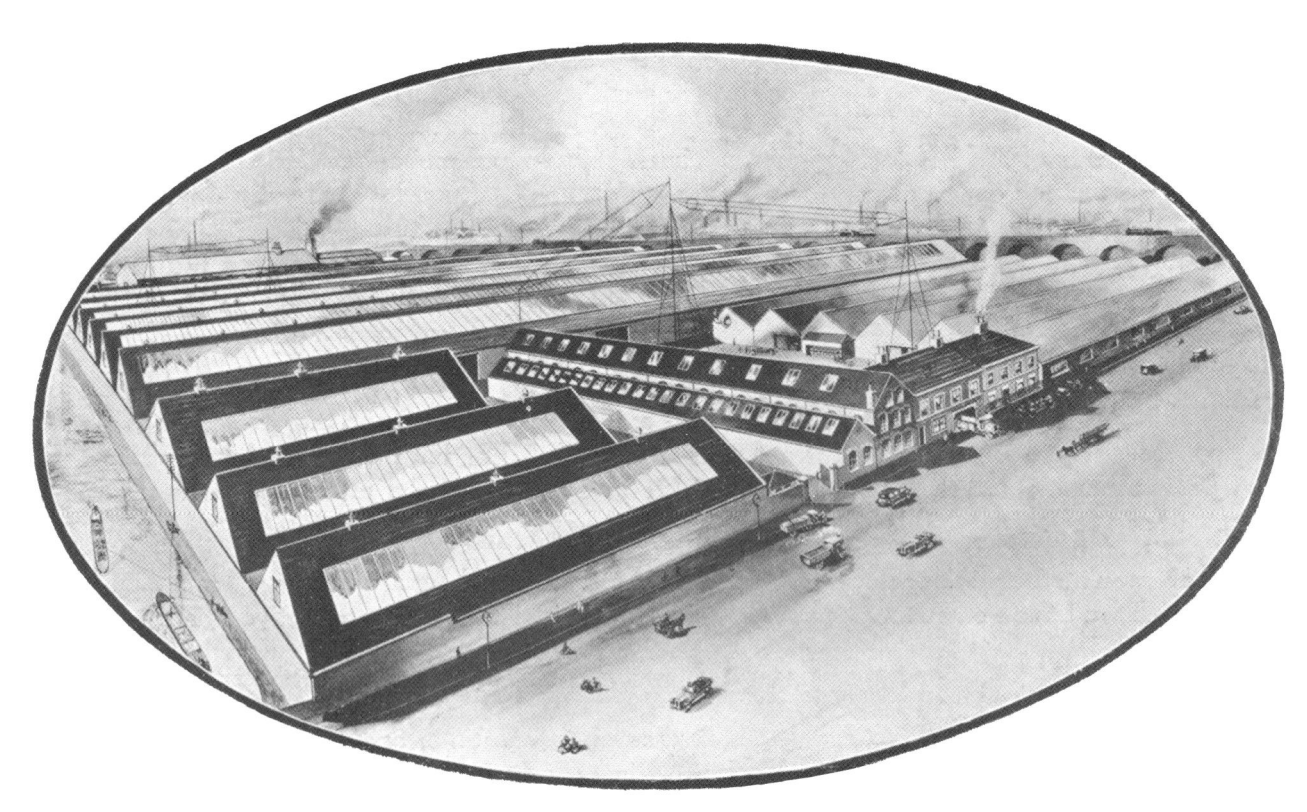

An artist's impression of the sidecar and chassis works at Lower Walsall Street 1925.
Photo: Manufacturers catalogue.

1925 7.99 h.p. model 'E1' De Luxe Passenger Combination.
Photo: Manufacturers catalogue.

Chassis shop, Lower Walsall Street works, 1926.
Photo: Geoff Stevens.

A.J.S. combination owed much to a remarkable run of competition success in the hands of the Company's competition manager Frank Giles. Frank, partnered by his wife Adelaide in the sidecar, represented a truly wonderful advertisement, being seemingly invincible whilst representing Britain in numerous international trials.

In order to bolster the sudden decline in the passenger sidecar market, C.W.Hayward extended its range of commercial sidecars. Primarily aimed at the 'one man band' type of business, this was an expanding market, with most door to door delivery or service work usually conducted by horse and dray; the cost of a van or car being well beyond the means of the average tradesman. In addition, fire fighting sidecar chassis were produced, comprising a Merryweather fire pump, with ropes and axes etc. Most orders for this type of equipment were for export, the appliance being ideally suited for fast travel over rough tracks to deal with the likes of bush fires. The production of lightweight, collapsible caravans was also considered, six prototypes being built, each having hinged, aluminium, side panels supported on a hardwood structure which could be folded down, so allowing the roof to be lowered. The base of the caravan was fitted with screw jacks, one at each corner and mounted on a pressed steel, channel chassis which was carried on two, spoked, motorcycle wheels. Incorporated in the base was a separate compartment for storing a complete range of cooking utensils, cups, saucers, plates and cutlery. This range of equipment was intended to be supplied as standard with each caravan and was carefully selected by Charles Hayward's sister Daisy, then in charge of the main sidecar, car body and general hardware stores within the factory. The caravan design was advanced for its time, but sadly never got beyond the prototype stage.

In 1927, the Company were successful in securing a long term contract to produce lightweight car bodies for the recently introduced Clyno 'Nine'. The contract entailed much use of fabric coachwork. Fabric covered bodies were enjoying a vogue at this time, led by the design of Weymann. As a result, this type of coachwork was utilized on the passenger and commercial sidecar body range for 1928.

Although A.J.S. motorcycle production techniques had become quite advanced, at their peak some six hundred machines were being produced at Graiseley each week, sidecar bodies were still hand built by teams of six people comprising of a section leader and five others, each paid on a piecework basis. Sidecar chas-

Upholstery Shop, Lower Walsall Street works, 1927.
Photo: Geoff Stevens.

Sidecar Erecting Shop, Lower Walsall Street works, 1927.
Photo: Geoff Stevens.

Sidecar Finishing Shop, Lower Walsall Street works, 1927.
Photo: Geoff Stevens.

sis however, were manufactured strictly on a day work basis, only the finest 'A' and 'B' quality, bright drawn, weldless steel tubing from Accles & Pollock being used, all finished parts receiving a high quality, black enamel, dipped coating. From about 1926 onwards, A.J.S. offered the Sunbeam patent, ball joint, chassis attachment as an extra on their chassis. Under terms of a special agreement between the two companies, A.J.S. manufactured their own ball joints, these being offered at an additional cost of 12s.6d. each (65p), the usual royalty charges being waived by Sunbeam. As several types of bodies were fitted to different types of chassis, it was found necessary to designate chassis and bodies separately, the section leader stamping each sidecar body so that a check could be made upon its progress through the works and also its eventual destination. Upon completion, each sidecar body would be thoroughly checked by an inspector who would then cross off each serial number on his list if the work was satisfactory. If not, then the work would be returned to the section responsible, who would be expected to rectify the fault in unpaid time. Finished sidecars and chassis would be taken by lorry either to the Graiseley works to be fitted to A.J.S. motorcycles, or delivered direct to rival motorcycle manufacturers such as Norton, Brough, Scott, Excelsior, Sunbeam, Ariel etc. The Swallow Coachbuilding Company of Blackpool (later to become famous as Jaguar Cars Ltd.) were one of Hayward's best customers. When Swallow moved to Coventry in 1928 both companies enjoyed a close business relationship. Various sprung wheel chassis underwent experiment, George Brough sending his own S.S.100 motorcycle to the works to test one particular design. This was driven over parts of the Victory Cup Trial course without difficulty, as a result a number were supplied to Brough.

Charles Hayward, by this time a relatively wealthy man, left A.J.S. in 1928 to pursue a successful career in London as a stockbroker and industrialist, forming a company to finance new inventions and processes. His position at Lower Walsall Street was taken over by Joe

Finished Sidecar Shop, Lower Walsall Street works, 1927.
Photo: Geoff Stevens.

Stevens Junior, who until this time had been chiefly responsible for production at Graiseley.

For 1929, A.J.S. completely redesigned its motorcycle range and listed no less than thirteen, different, sidecar body options in their series 'M' catalogue; these being eight passenger and five commercial types with prices ranging from £15.0s.0d. for a lightweight commercial model to £26.5s.0d. (£26.25) for an occasional two-seater including windscreen, sidescreens and storm proof apron.

Production of car bodies at Lower Walsall Street was suddenly halted early in 1929 following the appointment of a receiver to wind up the interests of The Clyno Engineering Co. (1922) Ltd. This action came at a very difficult time for A.J.S., for not only had the contract been a lucrative one, essential to help fund a new commercial vehicle venture, but it had also served to ensure full employment for a large number of people employed in the declining sidecar business. In a bold attempt to fill this void and at the same time provide additional production for Graiseley, it was decided the Company would produce its own light car, the A.J.S. 'Nine'.

Production of sidecars continued under the name of C.W.Hayward until September 1930, when A.J.S. chose to announce through various trade notices that "in responding to the pressing requests of numerous dealers, A.J.Stevens & Co.(1914) Ltd. will now supply sidecars to the trade for fitment to any make of motorcycle and that in future these sidecars will be known as the Graiseley". As it was common knowledge in the trade that C.W.Hayward and A.J.S. were one and the same, it is assumed that this new arrangement would allow the Company to relax its existing agreements.

As a result of the heavy investment necessary to get the commercial vehicle and car business off the ground, A.J.S. found itself in serious financial difficulties, eventually resulting in the Company's voluntary liquidation in October 1931. The Graiseley sidecar business however was not finished, the 'Graiseley' name and stock being bought for £475.0s.0d. from the liquidator by Diamond Motors of St.James Square, Wolverhampton. The main force behind

1927 7.99 h.p. model 'H1' De Luxe Passenger Combination.
Photo: Manufacturers catalogue.

Diamond's bid had been Alec Holder, chief designer of sidecar chassis at Lower Walsall Street at the time of the closure. Alec had joined C.W.Hayward in 1925 as a designer draughtsman and finding himself out of a job when the crash came had joined forces with Walter Ford of Diamond Motors and Harold Nock, another former employee of Haywards to purchase the sidecar business. In Alec Holder's case, the cost of the purchase meant postponing his forthcoming marriage for a further three years, the money used being the deposit saved for a house!

The new owners lost little time in setting up 'Graiseley' chassis production at St. James Square, leaving the task of producing 'Graiseley' sidecar bodies to the Specialist Coach Co.Ltd. based in Commercial Road, Wolverhampton, run by the one time general manager of C.W.Hayward, Sidney Jones. The new enterprise eventually became very successful, the new owners managing to persuade old customers to stick with the new set-up.

Although sidecar body production was short lived, the Specialist Coach Co. Ltd. closing its doors in 1935, chassis manufacture continued under Diamond Motors until 1939, when the company chose to concentrate its efforts on battery powered vehicles.

CHAPTER 8
Big Port

Few motorcycles can have attracted more worship than the legendary 349 c.c., overhead valve A.J.S. Its overwhelming run of racing successes during 1920, 1921 and 1922, including the phenomenal, record breaking, Isle of Man Senior T.T. win by Howard R. Davies, is unlikely ever to be equalled.

The first A.J.S. overhead valve engine was created by Harry Stevens as early as 1918, but it was to be a further five years before the factory listed an overhead valve machine in its catalogue. Indeed since making its sporting debut in 1920, the machine had remained very much a factory special. Its success in the Isle of Man T.T. series brought with it much criticism from those who chose to question its elegibility to take part. Quite right! After all, surely the very foundation of the Tourist Trophy series, had been built on the basis of being a proving ground for catalogued models available on the open market. To uphold their reputation, the Company set to work and in the autumn of 1922 announced the introduction of a new super sports machine the '2¾ h.p. Three Speed Overhead Valve T.T. Model', based on their T.T. winner. In 1924 this was listed simply as the 'B3' and from the following year A.J.S. adopted a prefix letter code system. Beginning with 'E', followed by 'G' for 1926, 'H' for 1927, 'K' for 1928', 'M' for 1929, 'R' for 1930, and 'S' for 1931. So how, why and when did the 'Big Port' name creep in? Over the years this question has created more than its fair share of argument. Let us put the matter straight once and for all! The 'Big Port' got its name from Joe Stevens Junior. Joe, the brother in overall charge of the Company's motorcycle production and racing activities at the time, had casually used the term to describe the outsize dimensions of the exhaust valve and pipe fitted to the 1922 works Junior T.T. machines; as simple as that. The nickname stuck and as a lasting measure of the charm attached to subsequent road models, it is still affectionately used by enthusiasts today.

1923. '2¾h.p. Three Speed Overhead Valve T.T. Model'.

The first production overhead valve model, was exhibited at the Olympia show held from 25th November to 2nd December 1922, on stand 67. Although flanked by the other popular side valve models, it soon became the main centre of attraction with visitors to the stand. Practically a true replica of the famous T.T. machine, it was listed in the Company's 1923 preliminary catalogue under its official title of the '2¾ h.p. Three Speed Overhead Valve T.T. Model'. But for the fitting of number plates and a silencer, practically no attempt had been made to alter the machine's sporting characteristics for ordinary road use. Close ratio gears, large diameter valves and competition timings were retained. Truly, 'a mount for the clubman', the 1923 T.T. model embodied all the features the sporting enthusiast could wish for:

The man who gave the 'Big Port' its name, Joe Stevens Junior. *Photo: Geoff Stevens.*

T.T. racing handlebars, the latest Druid forks, a potent engine, front and rear internal expanding brakes and an all up weight of just 204 lbs. There was one snag however, the price. At £87.0s.0d. very few could pretend to be a T.T. rider.

The single cylinder, overhead valve engine fitted to the new model, retained the now familiar bore and stroke dimensions of 74 mm. x 81 mm., giving a capacity of 349 c.c. A revised, vertically finned, cast iron, cylinder head replaced the earlier radial finned type fitted to the 1922 works racing machines. Internal port diameters for inlet and exhaust valves measured 1" and 1⅞" respectively, while longer valve guides were used to reduce premature wear. Single, conical shaped springs were fitted to each valve, retained by top collars secured by a round pin passing through the valve stem. The valves, each having a ⁵⁄₁₆" lift, were operated by hollow push rods, with a single, independent, return spring connecting the rocker gear. An important innovation was the use of an aluminium piston having four narrow rings set above a hollow gudgeon pin. The cylinder barrel had close pitch, symmetrical type finning running from top to bottom, and was held in place by a round section, steel strap, semi-circular in form, passing over the top of the cylinder head. The whole assembly was pulled down by screwed turnbuckles secured on either side of the crankcase. In the bottom half of the engine, the flywheels were carried in plain bronze bushes, whereas the big end assembly featured a twin row of uncaged, ⁵⁄₁₆" diameter rollers, supported in a steel outer race pressed into a light, nickel-chrome, forged, connecting rod.

Lubrication came in the form of a semi-automatic hand pump system, fed from a two pint oil reservoir contained within the main 1½ gallon flat fuel tank. On the drive side of the engine, the primary chain transmission incorporated a spring loaded, cam type, shock absorber fitted to the mainshaft and a hand controlled, cork inserted, multiple plate clutch. A three speed close ratio gearbox provided ratios of 5.52, 6.78 and 10.3:1. An Amac two lever carburettor was chosen, being well offset on the cylinder head to clear a steep, sloping, saddle down tube, while the ignition was provided by a Lucas magneto having a handlebar control for advance and retard.

Although of slender appearance, the frame was a beautiful piece of engineering, combining strength with lightness. In providing a wheelbase of 4'5½" and a saddle height of 28", it was perfectly proportioned in every way. For the benefit of the sporting rider wishing to enter speed events or hill climbs, the rear mudguard and carrier were quickly detachable, with easy access afforded to sprockets and clutch as only the top half of the chains were guarded. The specification included leather fronted pannier bags containing a full kit of tools and a 'kick-up' rear stand.

1924. Models 'B3' and 'B4'.

For 1924, the machine was listed in the Company's catalogue as the 'B3' and included a number of alterations. As a further option, a special sports model listed as the 'B4' was offered, stripped of its rear carrier and supplied with a high compression piston for sprint work. It is thought less than one hundred and fifty 'B4' models were produced.

The Druid pattern, side spring, front forks now included friction dampers by introducing new top links and matching steering head lug, the friction discs being located at the rear of the top link arms. The works later offered a conversion set at 14s.6d. (72½p) to update the earlier model. The footrest fitting was changed from a single rod passing straight through, to double rods one above the other passing through the engine plates requiring the hangers to be of different lengths to maintain the footrests at equal height. The magneto platform was modified to a two bolt fixing to effect improved chain adjustment, while the tyre inflator was repositioned from a vertical location beneath the nose of the petrol tank, to a horizontal position on the nearside rear, between a clip on the saddle stay at one end and a lug on the rear carrier at the other, an item not shown in the 1924 catalogue illustration.

In the engine, the single, conical shaped, valve springs used in 1923, were replaced by double (inner and outer), parallel springs for both valves. The spring top collar location on the valve stems, was changed from a pin to split collets. In an effort to silence the operation of the valve gear, the cam forms were modified. While the 1923 model had been devoid of a kick-starter, making it necessary to push start, the rear of the gearbox casting was extended to accept a kick-start quadrant and pedal. However, the mechanism was only included as a standard feature on the 'B3', costing a further £2.0s.0d. if required on the 'B4'. Prices were identical at £65.0s.0d.

1925. Models 'E6' and 'E7 Special Sports'.

For the next year the factory changed over to a prefix letter code system to denote the model year, with the result the 'Big Port' models were

1924 2¾ h.p. model 'B4'.
Photo: Author.

Close-up of drive and timing side of model 'B4' engine.
Photo: Author.

Freddie Hicks pictured on his 'Big Port' at Brooklands, May 1925, after winning the Three Laps Handicap Race for machines up to 500 c.c.
Photo: Dr. Joseph Bayley collection.

listed as the 'E6' and 'E7 Special Sports'. As with previous A.J.S. practice, each model carried a serial number stamped on the frame, engine and gearbox of each individual machine; now prefixed by the new code letter making it easier to identify the year of manufacture. Due to a programme of strict standardization, the frame dimensions became common to all 349 c.c. models making it possible to accommodate either side valve or overhead valve engines. It was necessary to amend the frame design because of a repositioned inlet tract, so the saddle tube took on a more vertical attitude in order to clear the carburettor. Its lower end was moved back from the front end of the main gearbox location bracket and positioned between the two adjustment slots. Twin head steadies were introduced from a location midway along the front down tube, to tapped holes in the cylinder head positioned on either side of the exhaust port. The combined petrol and oil tank was altered at the nose, being less rounded in shape and was now supported on two lugs brazed to the lower tank tube rail, being previously clipped to the top tube. This latter feature was incorrectly illustrated in the 1925 catalogue. The filler caps were moved from the offside to the nearside top of the tank, new, oval shaped, knee grips mounted into steel cups soldered to each side of the tank replaced the earlier, rectangular pattern type that were clipped over flat plates. All rear licence plates, which had previously been produced as a simple rectangular shape, were now made deeper and 'stylized' by having the sides tapered in toward the top.

In the engine department, the most striking feature was the introduction of tapered finning on the cylinder barrel, reducing in outline toward its base. A redesigned cylinder head was used, having a reduced exhaust port measuring 1⅝" diameter and a larger inlet port of 1¼" diameter. The inlet port was repositioned

George Rowley pictured at Graiseley on his 'Big Port' in 1926.
Photo: Beverley Shingler-Day.

opposite the exhaust, providing a more efficient straight through passage for escaping gases. The spark plug was repositioned from a point close to the inlet valve, to the front side of the semi-circular strap used for holding down the cylinder head.

Alongside the other alterations, the works decided to discontinue using the horizontal, return, rocker springs. New, one piece rockers produced in duralumin were fitted, but as so often happened at A.J.S., the factory would from time to time revert back to re-using the earlier, built up steel component.

A Binks two-jet carburettor replaced the earlier Amac two lever instrument, with an optional three-jet being available at an extra cost. On the lubrication side, a positive oil feed to the big end bearing was introduced via an oil gallery through the drive side mainshaft. For the first time the Company offered an option of mechanical lubrication in the form of an A.J.S.-Pilgrim pump mounted on the magneto drive case cover and driven from the exhaust camshaft, for an extra cost of £1.15s.0d. (£1.75). Standard silencing arrangements took the form of a front mounted, transverse, expansion chamber, situated beneath the magneto platform, identical to those used on the touring side valve models. As an option the factory offered a straight through 'sporting' exhaust system, which could be specially ordered. Although this system appeared to be identical to those used on the 1923 and 1924 models, the original, cast alloy, lozenge shaped silencer was replaced by a pressed steel counterpart finished in Britannia plate. In addition to dispensing with the standard, road going equipment as fitted to the 'E6', the 'E7 Special Sports' model featured main-

Leo Davenport poses for the camera on his works 'Big Port' in 1926.
Photo: Peter Allman.

shafts and timing gear shafts supported by roller and ball bearings respectively, whereas the 'E6' used plain bushes, rendering the crankcases incompatible. No provision was made for a kick-starter. Finally on the 'E7', 26" x 2¼" wheels and tyres replaced 650 mm. x 65 mm sizes. The 'E6' was listed at £60.0s.0d., whereas the price of the 'E7 Special Sports' was subject to final specification.

1926. Models 'G6', 'G7 Special Sports' and 'GR7'.

In 1926, there were three 'Big Port' models to choose from. A standard road-going machine listed as the 'G6', a special sports version the 'G7' and a special racing model under the title of 'GR7'. The principal difference between a standard 'G6' and the other two models, was the use of roller and ball bearings for mainshafts and timing gears, the standard machine retaining plain bushes. Further alterations were made to the engine, including a modified cylinder head and securing strap. The internal, exhaust port remained unchanged at 1⅝" diameter but now included a threaded, external stub to secure the exhaust pipe. The inlet port also remained unchanged from the previous year at 1¼" diameter. The semi-circular, holding down strap was replaced by a three piece bridge arrangement, with the crossbar bearing on a central location point cast into the top of the head. The factory again listed an A.J.S.-Pilgrim, mechanical pump, lubrication system as an extra at £1.0s.0d., being circular in shape without any sight feed facility.

On the fuel system side, a choice of optional tanks was available to replace the combined standard flat unit containing 1½ gallons of petrol and two pints of oil. The options being a slightly larger combined unit of 1¾ gallons of petrol and two pints of oil, or a petrol tank of 2 gallons capacity with a separate oil tank mounted on the saddle tube. The latter option included a foot pedal operation for the auxiliary oil pump, the pedal positioned beneath the offside footrest.

The earlier pattern gearchange was replaced by a completely new gear lever and gate assembly, designed and patented by Jack Stevens. In addition, two options were made available to the standard Brooks, leather covered, pan saddle: these being a Terry spring top saddle or a Brooks 'supple seat', having mattress springing covered by a leather top.

As could be expected for a machine designed for high speed competition work, the 'GR7' differed in many respects to the other two models. It was supplied with a specially finished cylinder head and two pistons. The piston fitted by the factory, was recommended for long distance events, while the other, having a much taller domed crown for higher compression, was more suited to short distance speed events, such as sprints or hill climbs, where the rider might use alcohol based fuels. Other special items included alloy clutch plates and chainwheel, alternative carburettor jets, T.T. handlebars and 26" x 2⅜" wired on tyres. A price of £53.0s.0d. was listed for the 'G6', whereas the 'G7' and 'GR7' prices were subject to final specification.

1927. Models 'H6' and 'H7'.

The Company produced two 'Big Port' machines for 1927. A road going sports model listed as the 'H6' and an uncatalogued racing machine known as the 'H7'.

Now a seemingly annual occurrence, the cylinder head received further modification. Externally the exhaust stub was finned and had a steeper angle of exit, leading into a sweeping pipe secured by a threaded retaining ring. The silencer was redesigned and took the form of a long tubular shape with conical ends leading into a plain tail pipe. Internally the cylinder head had both ports altered from the previous year. The exhaust being increased to 1⅞" diameter, while the inlet was reduced to 1" diameter. At the bottom end, the crankshaft was supported directly on roller bearings, while the timing gears were carried in plain bushes. The timing case was enlarged sufficiently to house and conceal the valve lifter mechanism, having an external operating arm only. For lubrication, a Pilgrim, sight feed, mechanical, oil pump was included in the standard specification, although a tank mounted, auxiliary hand pump was also provided.

The gearbox was uprated, using the same gear set as employed on the 4.98 h.p. models, with a choice of close or wide gear ratios, while a new end cover carried a revised clutch operating arm, being almost vertically disposed on its front face. The usual method of removing a screwed plug to check the gearbox oil level was replaced by a simple hinged lever situated at the rear of the main gearbox shell, making inspection much quicker. A twist grip control was included as standard for operating the Binks carburettor.

On the frame, the headstock was enlarged in diameter from 1½" to 1¾" and fitted with an improved top bearing race, permitting an increased handlebar stem diameter from ⅞" to 1". The fork links were altered to accommodate friction dampers fitted to the front ends of the lower links. Although incorrectly illustrated in the 1927 catalogue with a Brooks, leather, pan saddle, a Terry's spring top, pillar fitting saddle was standardized. The earlier flat-base wheel rims with beaded edge tyres were replaced by the later well-base units carrying 26" x 2¾" wired on tyres.

Mechanically the 'H7' racing model differed from its road going counterpart in the same way as the earlier 'GR7' model had in having a specially polished cylinder head, ball bearings for the timing gear shafts and no provision on the gearbox housing for a kickstarter. To reduce weight an aluminium alloy, rear wheel sprocket was fitted to a light steel brake drum and wheel hub and the tool bags were supported from the rear mudguard stays in the absence of a rear carrier. Dunlop cord, wired-on, 26" x 2⅜", rear studded and front ribbed tyres were fitted, covered by narrow, racing style mudguards. Fuel tank options were the same as offered on the 1926 models, however, twin T.T. style, pannier tanks were also available holding 3½ gallons, having a rectangular, metal, tool box mounted on top. One small, but unmistakable feature of the racing model was the larger finned exhaust pipe retaining ring. The 'H6' was listed in the catalogue at £53.0s.0d., but like the earlier racing models the price of the 'H7' was subject to final specification.

1928. Models 'K6' and 'KR6'.

In preparation for the 1928 season the Company announced its new model range in October 1927. Among the eleven model line up, there was one 'Big Port', the road going 'K6'. The usual practice of including a special over-

Big Port

1927 3.49 h.p. model 'H6'.
Photo: Author.

Close-up of drive and timing side of model 'H6' engine.
Photo: Author.

head valve sports or racing version had been dropped, in favour of a new, chain driven, overhead camshaft model listed as the 'K7'. In view of the serious problems which were encountered with the 'cammy' engines during the 1927 T.T. series (later traced to lubrication troubles), Joe Stevens Junior decided the team should revert back to racing push rod engined machines for 1928, while further development work could be undertaken on the camshaft engine. This bold decision eventually led to the introduction of the 'KR6' based on the latest, overhead valve, T.T. racing machine.

Considerable redesign work had gone into the 'K6' model. Radical changes to the top half of the engine meant the barrel and head were no longer secured by the strap arrangement of the past, this being replaced by a four stud fixing securing barrel to crankcase, while four bolts held the head to the barrel. Surprisingly, no tinkering of the ports had taken place, with sizes remaining the same as those adopted for the previous years' models. The earlier, roller bearing, bottom end was changed, with the new design reverting to plain bronze bushes set in a wider crankcase to support the crankshaft, while wider cam faces and two piece, oil tight tappets were introduced. The half-time pinion was machined with a flat back face to act as a register for the crankshaft end-float. A single head steady ran from the front down tube to the front centre of the cylinder head, level with the top of the exhaust port. Further strengthening of the gearbox was evident, the kickstart shaft being increased in diameter and splined at one end for the quadrant instead of the earlier, square type location. Although shaft lengths were different due to a wider gearbox shell, the heavier, 1927, gear pinions were retained, and a 'beefed-up' clutch spring common also to the 4.98 h.p. models was used.

On the cycle side, frame lugs were widened to accommodate the increased width of the new crankcase and gearbox castings. The side spring, Druid pattern, front forks were retained, but with wider fork blades of stronger construction, while tyre and wheel sizes were increased to 26" x 3" and a pressed steel, front brake drum replaced the earlier cast component. The combined fuel and oil tank retained its earlier appearance, but was now of welded construction rather than soldered tin plate and had an increased fuel capacity of 1¾ gallons. The clip-fixing system of attaching the saddle to a stem was replaced by a three point arrangement, in which a 'T' shaped extension of the lower tank rail extended rearwards. Tension springs were fastened to the ends of the 'T' bar, while the nose of the saddle was pivoted from a lug on the top frame tube. A new saddle frame being used in conjunction with this arrangement.

The eventual overhead valve ,'Special Sports' model, the 'KR6', reprieved following Joe's decision not to race the overhead camshaft models, was based upon the Isle of Man T.T. machines. Featuring dry-sump lubrication, the total loss Pilgrim pump of the standard 'K6' was replaced by a special feed and return pump mounted on the magneto drive case cover, with a direct feed to the cylinder base controlled via a needle valve on the driveside crankcase. The bottom end was fitted with roller and ball bearings to mainshafts and timing gear and the cylinder base had a thicker flange than the 'K6'. No provision was made for a kickstarter on the gearbox casing and the model featured separate fuel and oil tanks. The price of the 'K6' was listed at £50.0s.0d. whereas the price of the 'KR6', as usual, was subject to final specification.

1929. Models 'M6' and 'MR6 Special Sports'.
Although the term 'Big Port' would continue to form part of the enthusiasts' vocabulary to describe loosely all later 350 c.c., overhead valve models produced by the factory, 1928 was to mark what most dyed-in-the-wool A.J.S. enthusiasts would consider to be the last year of the real 'Big Port' models. It was also the final year of the flat tank styling; during the summer of 1928 designers at the works had taken the view that the 'Big Port' had begun to look old fashioned. They only had themselves to blame however, as earlier, like a handful of the bigger manufacturers, Triumph, Norton and Sunbeam, they had chosen to ignore popular demand for the latest 'top heavy saddle tank look' being produced by many of the other makers. On the other hand, there were many who felt fashion finally destroyed what was probably the most functional sports machine of its generation. When the advance 1929 model range was announced, it would appear as if everything that could be changed had been. The earlier, slim line look being replaced by models having a heavier, chunkier appearance. Fashion it would appear, dictating all. Gone was the unmistakable black and gold flat tank, replaced by a new saddle design emblazoned with magenta coloured, side transfer panels edged in black and gold and carrying revised lettering inset.

Two 'Big Port' models were available, the road going 'M6' and the 'MR6 Special Sports',

1928 3.49 h.p. model 'K6'.
Photo: Author.

Close-up of drive and timing side of model 'K6' engine.
Photo: Author.

the latter designed for competition work. In the case of the 'M6', a choice was offered of either a twin port cylinder head as standard, or a single port version at £2.10s.0d. (£2.50) less. In the interests of greater mechanical silence and overall external cleanliness, the new engines featured totally enclosed rocker gear, having grease gun lubrication and pushrods enclosed by steel tubes. Dry-sump lubrication became standard, with a Pilgrim recirculating oil pump cast-in as an integral part of the magneto drivecase cover, being fed from a separate 3¼ pint oil tank mounted on the rear mudguard immediately to the rear of the frame saddle tube, with an extended filler neck positioned on the offside of the machine.

Within the three speed gearbox, a larger diameter mainshaft of increased length was fitted to accommodate changes in the clutch. In order to retain an existing sleeve gear component, the increase of the mainshaft diameter made it necessary to delete the bronze bush within the sleeve, therefore allowing the shaft to run directly within the plain bore. The kickstart quadrant was repositioned between the clutch chainwheel and the gearbox sprocket instead of on the outside of the clutch face as hitherto. Another innovation was the adoption of a speedometer drive, positioned just below the clutch operating arm on the gearbox end cover, with a worm drive being taken from the gearbox layshaft.

The frame was redesigned with a sloping, top tube to accommodate the new style petrol tank, while the earlier, Druid pattern forks were replaced by Webb, centre spring type, incorporating friction dampers at the rear of the lower links. A steering damper was incorporated within the fork head stem, being slotted to accept two wedges that could be expanded inside, by means of a cone arrangement controlled by a handwheel positioned above the fork crown. A redesigned rear carrier was fitted, supporting leather fronted, tool panniers between symmetrical side stays, while a front stand was pivoted from the bottom of the front forks. The front brake included a water excluding flange, added to the backplate. A capacity of approximately 2½ gallons of fuel was contained in a welded saddle tank, which was fitted with new pattern, rubber knee grips which fitted over flat plates screwed to the tank sides. Provision was made in the top face for mounting a Smiths speedometer.

The 'MR6 Special Sports' was generally as the 'M6', but featured a specially tuned, single port, engine having ball bearing mainshafts, and a choice of two pistons, one to suit petrol - benzole, the other for alcohol fuels. Narrow style mudguards and rearset footrests were fitted and in order to reduce weight a specially designed, light, rear hub and brake drum assembly were set in a non-quick, detachable, rear wheel. There was no provision for rear carrier, front stand or kickstarter. The catalogue listed the 'M6' at £54.10s.0d. (£54.50.), whilst the 'MR6' was £62.0s.0d.

1930. Model 'R6'.
Despite mounting financial difficulties, the Company chose to completely redesign its model range for the 1930 season. Only one 'Big Port' machine was available, being the standard sporting 'R6'. The most striking feature of the model was the forward inclined position of the engine within the frame. Twin exhaust ports were retained and the cylinder head was modified to accept a flange fitting, Amal, needle jet carburettor. In the bottom half of the engine, the flywheel assembly was stiffened and carried in ball bearings, while a new, caged, double-row roller, big end bearing was fitted. The magneto was positioned to the rear of the cylinder on an adjustable, tilting, hinged platform, being chain driven from the inlet camshaft. The dry sump lubrication system remained practically unchanged in principle, except that the pipe work was cleaned up, the main tank to engine route consisting of steel tubes welded to the underside of the gearbox bracket; provision was made for an adjustable drip feed to the primary chain taken straight from the oil return pipe and regulated by a needle valve. The oil tank, now of rectangular shape was mounted from the frame saddle tube. A Sturmey-Archer three speed constant mesh gearbox and clutch replaced A.J.S. components, although the traditional, A.J.S. pattern, clutch withdrawal mechanism on the end cover was retained. The gearbox lever was located in a simple quadrant on the side of the petrol tank, with an indexing plunger located in the gearbox.

A completely redesigned, semi-cradle type frame was used, having a single top tube, duplicated chain stays, huge engine and gearbox cradle plates and lugs for saddle mountings. A spring-up centre stand replaced the traditional, rear wheel stand. Revised centre spring, front forks were used, being of sturdier construction and incorporating larger, friction dampers and a new, friction disc type, steering damper arrangement. Larger diameter brakes were employed, the front having longer anchor plates being fixed to both tubes of the fork blade. A

1931 3.49 h.p. model 'SB6 Big Port'.
Photo: Mark Baker.

detachable, welded, rear carrier was fitted having a four bolt fixing to the mudguard stays, while a single, leather fronted, tool box was carried between the offside saddle and chain stays. The front mudguard was now fully valanced and fitted with a small mud-flap at the lower end, while the rear carried a rectangular shaped number plate having a shoulder to the top edge for mounting and suitable provision for an electric lamp. When electric lighting was specified, a platform suitable for a six volt battery was positioned above the gearbox, immediately in front of the rear down tube. 'Brooklands Can' style silencers were fitted to the exhaust pipe with fish-tail ends.

The factory reverted back to an all black enamel paintwork, having gold lines to the petrol tank. All bright parts were chromium plated in lieu of nickel. The price of the 'R6' was £53.0s.0d.

1931. Models 'S6' and 'SB6'.

Due to the Company's worsening financial circumstances, the 1931 overhead valve models introduced in September 1930 remained largely unchanged. The official 3.49 h.p. overhead valve model for this season was the twin ported 'S6'. But a further model, a lightweight weighing under 224lbs to qualify for a concessionary £1.10s.0d. (£1.50.) rate of Road Fund Tax was later added to the range in January 1931. This model, catalogued as the 'SB6 Big Port' was in fact the first machine produced by its makers to adopt officially the 'Big Port' title.

Changes to the 'S6' included a petrol tank that was fully chromium plated, having black enamel, 'D' shaped, side panels lined gold with A.J.S. transfers inset. An optional, Lucas, tank mounted, raised instrument panel was available at 5s.0d. (25p) extra to house a speedometer, ammeter, clock and switches, while other popular options included a four speed gearbox at £1.10s.0d. (£1.50.), pillion footrests at 12s.6d. (65p.) and Lucas, six volt, 'Maglita' lighting set at £5.0s.0d. extra. To further facilitate the removal of the quickly detachable rear wheel, a hinged mudguard was fitted. New, 'clean', black enamelled handlebars produced by the Sackville Company to A.J.S. design were employed.

The lightweight 'tax dodging' single port 'SB6' had a vertical engine configuration based on the Company's 2.48 h.p. overhead valve design. The bottom half of the engine was fitted with a roller big end and ball bearing mounted mainshafts, whilst a forward facing magneto drive case was used. A Bowden carburettor having a twist grip control was a standard fitting.

A lightweight, Sturmey-Archer, three speed gearbox was fitted as standard, having the usual A.J.S. pattern, clutch withdrawal mechanism on its end cover. A four speed option was available, but if fitted, the overall weight of the machine then exceeded the 224lbs tax limitation. A saddle style petrol tank was used having a capacity of 1¾ gallons, whilst a separate, 3½ pint, oil tank was mounted on the frame saddle tube. To reduce weight and cost, no provision was made for a rear carrier or front mounted stand. Plain, unvalanced mudguards were fitted to front and rear, the latter had a spring clip to secure a simple, rear mounted stand. A 'Brooklands Can' style, exhaust silencer was used, but without fishtail, the tail pipe having a pinched end. Finally a return to an all black enamel finish was made, although the chrome and black finish to the petrol tank was available at an extra cost of £1.0s.0d. The price of the 'S6' was £53.0s.0d. while the 'SB6' was £45.0s.0d.

The 'Big Port' is best remembered as being one of the most popular and cherished of vintage motorcycles, but more significantly it is an important historical machine both in competition terms and because of its major role in British motorcycle development. Although 'Big Port' production at Wolverhampton was to span some nine years, it is generally accepted among A.J.S. enthusiasts that the model reached its peak around 1927.

CHAPTER 9
Wireless

The main driving force behind the decision of A.J.S. to enter the wireless market in 1923, was Harry Stevens. He was one of Britain's radio pioneers, responsible for many early designs. He had to persuade other members of the board, the time was right to introduce a programme of wireless manufacture at their Lower Walsall Street works.

Harry's interest in wireless could be traced back to its earliest beginnings. A keen amateur, he was fortunate to possess a receiving set prior to the outbreak of the 1914-18 war. On 1st August 1914, a few days before Britain declared war with Germany, the Post Master General issued an order to dismantle all experimental wireless apparatus. Harry was reluctant to comply. His defiance eventually led to a report to the police by his neighbours in Oaklands Road, who had suspected him of communicating with the enemy. Although innocent of any such crime, he was made to remove his equipment under the Defence of the Realm Act and was lucky to escape prosecution.

Until the many technical advances which took place during the First World War, the development of transmitting and receiving equipment had been a long and drawn out process. Wireless in those days had not been thought of in terms of broadcast entertainment, but merely as a form of 'station to station' communication.

As the war progressed, wireless was to become more widely accepted by the military as a vital addition to visual and line signalling among the troops. As a consequence, an urgent need arose for wireless technicians, instructors and operators to join the sevices. For the many thousands of men trained in its use during this period, it would provide them with their first experience of wireless, giving them a realization of the advantages to be gained from its use as a broadcasting medium. For many this initial contact would create a life-long fascination for the subject and would eventually lead them to form the foundation of the 'listening public'.

Following a relaxation in defence regulations, public broadcasting hesitantly became available in Britain. During the early part of 1920, the Marconi Company operated a transmitter at

Harry Stevens as photographed in 1920.
Photo: Geoff Stevens.

Chelmsford. This enabled the few owners like Harry Stevens, with the appropriate receiving equipment, to have their first opportunity of listening to music and voice transmission in Britain.

It was not long before other enthusiastic amateurs began to appreciate wireless for its home entertainment value. However, in the autumn of 1920 there was a temporary set back. Permission to broadcast from Chelmsford was withdrawn due to considerable interference with other stations, notably those broadcasting official communications. It was not until the winter of 1922 that the government felt sufficiently confident to allow the formation of the British Broadcasting Company to take place. The B.B.C. as it became known, comprised three hundred British manufacturers and dealers in wireless apparatus and accessories, headed by the so called 'Big Six'; Marconi, General Electric, British Thompson-Houston, Radio

Communication, Metropolitan Vickers Electric and Western Electric.

The B.B.C. first began broadcasting in London on 14th November 1922, from their single studio on the top floor of Marconi House in the Strand, two weeks after being granted permission for a two year period. The following day two further stations began broadcasting to listeners in Birmingham and Manchester. The funding of the B.B.C. was basically derived from a half share of a ten shilling (50p.) Broadcasting Licence which was introduced on 1st November 1922 for British manufactured receivers only, plus royalties levied on certain wireless equipment sold to the public. The use of imported parts was prohibited.

All commercially manufactured British valve receivers, valve amplifiers and crystal sets sold on the open market by a member firm of the B.B.C. first had to be 'specially' approved by the Post Master General. In order for the equipment to be approved, it was required to be tested to ensure that its construction would not cause interference to neighbouring receivers, this was the only equipment offered to the public. The G.P.O. issued a registration number, required to be displayed on each set, together with a circular B.B.C. stamp measuring approximately ¾" in diameter and bearing the peripheral wording 'TYPE APPROVED BY POST MASTER GENERAL'. This stamp of approval however, did not signify a guarantee of quality or design. Receivers ranged

B.B.C. Stamps.
Left: BBC/PMG stamp November 1st 1922 - September 1924.
Centre: BBC/EBM stamp September 1924 - 1927.
Right: B.B.C. 'Trademark' stamp September 1924 - 1927.
Photo: Jonathan Hill.

from crude and badly designed sets to expensive cabinets containing advanced equipment.

Toward the end of 1922 the B.B.C. transmitting within the medium-wave 'Broadcast Band', had four of its proposed eight main stations on the air. These were London (call sign 2LO) on 360 metres, Birmingham (51T) on 420 metres, Manchester (2ZY) on 384 metres and Newcastle (5NO) on 400 metres. Of the 36,000 people who had taken out ten shilling (50p) licences, most lived within the immediate areas of the four transmitters. They listened in to programmes of news and concert entertainment on head phones connected to simple crystal sets. These sets were by far the most popular, due mainly to cheapness, sheer simplicity in use, and compact size. A good crystal set would retail for around £2 to £3. However, they were limited in use, having a range of about fifteen miles. For those who could afford better, there was a choice of multi-valve, battery operated sets which were capable of receiving up to one hundred miles from the transmitter, costing upwards of £15.0s.0d.

For those wishing to build their own apparatus a ten shilling (50p) Experimenters Licence was available, instead of the Broadcast Licence. This arrangement quickly led to problems for the B.B.C. Considerable numbers of listeners had opted for the Experimenters Licence and consequently no B.B.C. share. They purchased cheaper, unstamped receivers sold in kit form, which were exempt from royalties. To avoid any further loss of revenue and curb the legal use of foreign equipment, the G.P.O. carefully redefined its existing licencing terms, by stipulating that experimenters would only be granted a licence, if they produced certain components themselves. Major parts required for the sets had to bear the B.B.C. approved stamp.

By October 1923, all eight of the proposed stations were on 'the air' and the number of Broadcast Licences issued had risen to almost 500,000 and increasing rapidly. In response to the demand for receivers the wireless industry began to show considerable signs of expansion, with many new manufacturers encouraged to enter the market.

The decision by A.J.S. to join the wireless industry had been made after recognizing the tremendous market potential, following the first B.B.C. broadcast from London in November 1922. However, it was not until the autumn of the following year that the first of the Company's wireless receivers appeared on the market.

Since acquiring the factory premises at Lower Walsall Street in 1922, measures had been taken to increase manufacturing capacity to produce car bodies as well as sidecars, by extending the existing floor space to 150,000 sq.ft. From the start of the wireless enterprise, separate departments were formed to deal with the interests of each business. All sidecar and coachbuilt body construction work was handled by C.W.Hayward, while the wireless business was dealt with under the grand title of 'A.J.S. Wireless and Scientific Instruments'. From the outset Harry Stevens had insisted that the Company should concentrate its efforts to pro-

Wireless staff at Lower Walsall Street 1924.
Charles Hayward who was in overall charge of the works can be seen with arms folded in the centre of the front row.
Photo: Pat Craddock.

duce suitable products for the quality end of the market. On receiving full support from his fellow directors, he had lost very little time in designing a high quality range of two, three and four valve receivers, all beautifully engineered and constructed in a choice of mahogany or oak cabinets. Initially these were constructed in the sidecar and car body areas of the factory, with the main assembly undertaken in a separate workshop area of approximately 4,000 sq.ft.

The price of the standard wireless ranged from £17.10s.0d. (£17.50.) for the two valve set, to £52.10s.0d. (£52.50) for the top of the range four valve 'Type F' pedestal model. In addition the Company offered a metal horn loudspeaker at £4.15s.0d. (£4.75.) plus two telescopic, tubular, aerial masts being 30ft and 50ft tall. The superb range of pedestal cabinets were designed to house a four valve receiver in the top, with the high and low tension batteries in the centre and loudspeaker in the base section. The metal horn of the loudspeaker was supplied in a hand painted, wood grained finish to match the chosen cabinet timber.

In order to promote their new business, A.J.S. decided to exhibit their products at the 1924 Wireless Exhibition held in London. Fifty six suppliers of wireless equipment supported this venture staged at the Royal Albert Hall, held from 27th September to 8th October, which attracted a paid attendance of 46,000. The A.J.S. products, displayed on stands 82 and 84 were very well received, resulting in the Company being able to appoint a number of important agents during the exhibition.

Harry's wireless designs soon established the business among the market leaders, with the products gaining an enviable reputation for quality and performance. A.J.S. quality however, did not come cheap. Prices quoted in cata-

1923 4 - valve 'Table De Luxe' model finished in oak.
Price £36.5s.0d. (£36.25).
Photo: Author.

1924 4 - valve 'Type F' sloping face model finished in walnut.
Price £27.5s.0d. (£27.25).
Photo: Author.

logues and advertisements did not usually include all the necessary equipment to be able to 'listen in'. For instance, in addition to the cost of the receiver, one would have to acquire a loudspeaker or headphones, aerial, high tension battery and several lead-acid accumulators. Add to this a quantity of spare valves, and it was not uncommon to find that a complete set in working order would cost at least twice as much as first expected. Even with cheaper brands on the market, to the average working man earning about £2 per week, the cost of owning a wireless set must have been prohibitive.

Prices became more realistic however, when member companies of the B.B.C. found themselves facing outside competition. This came from foreign and non member British manufacturers, following a decision in July 1924 to abolish the existing system of royalties, testing and registration of receivers. A few months later in September 1924, B.B.C. members were required to display a new stamp displaying the words, 'ENTIRELY BRITISH MANUFACTURE'. This was soon superceded by another stamp bearing only the B.B.C. emblem. Finally at the beginning of the following year, regulations governing the use of stamps were abolished altogether. A considerable number of B.B.C. member firms continued to display the stamp as it was thought this represented some prestige value and served to distinguish their products from those of foreign manufacture. By this time the wireles set had begun to creep into all levels of society. When a set was sufficiently powerful enough to work a horn speaker, it could provide regular home entertainment for all the family. During the summer of 1925 the number of licence holders had risen to one and a half million, a figure which probably in truth represented over ten million actual listeners to the B.B.C. programmes daily.

Following a dramatic increase in A.J.S. wireless sales, further manufacturing capacity was made available for cabinet production at Stewart Street. The Company also constructed a specially designed sound proof studio at Lower Walsall Street, containing the latest receiver equipment, which could be suitably demonstrated to prospective agents.

1924 4 - valve 'Type F' pedestal model finished in oak with built in horn speaker and battery compartment.
Price £52.10s.0d (£52.50).
Photo: Author.

Wireless

Wireless Sales Office, Lower Walsall Street 1925.
Photo: Pat Craddock.

Wireless cabinet and speaker production, Stewart Street 1925.
Photo: Jim Boulton.

1925 4-valve 'Type F6' table model finished in mahogany. Price £26.15s.0d. (£26.75).
Photo: Author.

On 10th September 1925, new, pestigious London offices and salesrooms were opened at 122-124 Charing Cross Road, the principal guest invited was Professor A.M.Low, a prominent figure in the wireless industry. All visitors to the showrooms were received by the Company Chairman, Edgar E.Lamb, who later read out a letter from the famous nineteenth century wireless pioneer Sir Oliver Lodge, expressing his appreciation of the results he had obtained from a four valve A.J.S. receiver. A few days later, the Company attended the second Wireless Exhibition held at the Royal Albert Hall from 12th to 23rd September, organised by the National Association of Radio Manufacturers and Traders. 'Radio' was a modern North American term for wireless which was beginning to spread across the Atlantic. A.J.S. were among one hundred and nine principal exhibitors, displaying an impressive range of two, three and four valve receivers. Ranging in price from £13.18s.6d. (£13.92½) for the simplest, two valve model to £75.0s.0d. for the top of the range 'S1' console model, complete with all accessories. Also included in their line up was a superb range of high quality cabinet and pedestal speakers costing from £4.15s.0d. (£4.75) to £22.10s.0d. (£22.50) as well as two horn loud speakers. For the constructor and enthusiast, A.J.S. components and accessories were offered, including for the first time A.J.S. headphones at £1.0s.0d. per set.

1926 was to mark the beginning of change in the wireless industry. There had been a gradual movement from the earlier designs with exposed valves and an array of complicated controls. Although the previous year had been a good one in terms of business for A.J.S., they had stuck to rather conventional designs and as a result sales had fallen. The market demand-

1925 2-valve 'Type Z' table model finished in mahogany. Price £13.18s.6d. (£13.92½).
Photo: Author.

Wireless

Metal Loud Speaker Shop, Stewart Street 1926.
Photo: Geoff Stevens.

A.J.S. Loud Speakers.(left) Large flared speaker finished in oak. Price £4.15s.0d (£4.75).
(right) 'Junior' metal loudspeaker type LSZ. Price £1.15s.0d (£1.75).
Photo: Author.

Wireless Cabinet Finishing Shop, Stewart Street 1926.
Note 'Symphony' circular frame aerials on top of the work benches.
Photo: Geoff Stevens.

ed that sets should have simple controls and fully enclosed workings. As a result shareholders were informed by the board that the Company had taken important steps to design a completely new range of 'radio sets' that would ensure a speedy market recovery.

New two, three, five and seven valve models marketed under the title of the 'Symphony Range', were unveiled in London at the first National Radio Exhibition held at New Hall Gallery, Olympia. The five and seven valve models were based on the 'Superhet' principle wherein the signal was converted to a fixed radio frequency, before amplification and detection. This gave increased power and ability to separate stations, in an already crowded waveband, simply at the twist of a knob.

The new models, were housed in high quality mahogany cabinets and were of modern design and appearance. Prices ranged from £17.10s.0d. (£17.50) for the 'Symphony Two' table model, to £67.10s.0d. (£67.50) for the top of the range 'Symphony Seven' bureau model. The Company went to great lengths to press home the point that prices included everything except the programme.

For a while the new models sold well and it appeared as if trading might get back to normal. The market however, had changed and radio sales became increasingly seasonal, forcing the Company to lay off part of its work force during slack periods. As a temporary measure, some of the employees were engaged on producing electrical products, such as the 'Cobra', a dual purpose heater, which could be used either to heat a room, or, when folded flat, it became a stove on which to boil a kettle of water. This instrument was named after the shape of its electrical element.

Towards the end of 1926, A.J.S. were forced to adopt mass production techniques in order to reduce manufacturing costs. Seasonal sales now made it necessary to take on extra workers during August to deal with peak production, only to lay them off in the spring when a downfall in the market would occur. As a result it became general practice in the industry to employ women rather than men, as they were considered more suitable for repetitive assem-

Wireless

Wireless Cabinet Shop, Stewart Street 1927.
'Symphony' two and three valve models can be seen in the course of construction.
Photo: Geoff Stevens.

Wireless Cabinet Shop, Stewart Street 1927, showing 'Symphony' loudspeaker and cabinet production.
Photo: Geoff Stevens.

Wireless Assembly Shop, Stewart Street 1927.
Photo: Geoff Stevens.

bly work, accepted lower wages and were easier to hire and fire.

The following year sales of A.J.S. battery operated sets took another set-back, as technical development was enabling 'all mains' sets to become more readily available. Mains operated sets became increasingly popular, as they enabled the cabinet design to become more compact and stylish, due to the absence of battery storage compartments, as well as doing away with the expense and inconvenience of recharging accumulators.

At this time battery operated, portable, wireless sets were increasing in popularity. Most rural homes had no electricity, nor did many town dwellers. An added advantage was the relative ease it could be carried outdoors. A.J.S., quick to spot this new market potential, had designed a five valve portable model to complement the existing 'Symphony' range. It measured 16" long x 13½" high x 8½" deep and was offered in the choice of an oak or mahogany case. It was designed with a single dial for control and tuning purposes. Another control was for volume, also a change over switch for long or short wave operation changing from the 200 - 550 metre to the 1000 - 2000 metre band. The case was designed to house the frame aerial, batteries and moving-iron speaker.

With early portable receivers, the term 'portable' could be rather misleading as almost anything with a leather carrying handle was listed in this category. Suitably a portable should be light and easily carried, but in 1927 most were bulky and heavy. The A.J.S. was no exception weighing in at 26½lbs when complete with batteries. The five valve portable was listed at £22.10s.0d. (£22.50) and, like the rest of the 'Symphony' range, was offered on easy payment terms.

During the summer of 1927, an important step was taken by the Company to enter the field of commercial vehicle production. To incorporate the new venture at Lower Walsall Street, it was decided to re-house the ailing wireless business at the Stewart Street works.

Although the Company went to great lengths to bring about a recovery in sales, the wireless industry remained unstable and A.J.S. finally gave up their struggle in the middle of 1928. Later in a statement, the directors had blamed the demise of the business on the problem of home produced equipment. However, this was unlikely as receivers had, in general, become far too complex in design for the average listener to construct. What was far more likely, was their failure to take advantage of new designs, such as incorporating multi-grid valves, which were introduced in 1927 and

1927 'Symphony Seven' bureau model finished in mahogany. Price £67.10s.0d. (£67.50).
Photo: Author.

Front and rear view of 1927 'Symphony Five' portable set finished in oak. Price £22.10s.0d. (£22.50).
Photo: Author.

which ensured a more stable, high gain amplification, without the setting up problems associated with earlier valve circuits.

The Stewart Street premises were eventually sold off and a new company 'The Symphony Gramophone & Radio Co. Ltd.', formed by its new owners. Soon, a modern range of radiograms and portable receivers were being produced, some of which contained obsolete A.J.S. components that had been included in the sale of the property.

A.J.S. were not the only motorcycle manufacturer to jump on the wireless bandwagon in the 1920's, as B.S.A. also became involved in the production of receivers. Indeed, B.S.A. had built some commercial vehicle chassis early in the decade, although their full name of 'Birmingham Small Arms' highlights that Company's origins. A.J.S., like B.S.A. will always be remembered primarily for their motorcyles.

Chapter 10
Overhead Camshaft

Despite the Big Port's remarkable record of sporting achievement, by 1926 the Company realized that its existing racing engine had reached its full potential and little improvement would be gained from further development. The design department was given the task of creating a new racing engine, an overhead camshaft design to replace the existing push rod layout.

As a result, two, entirely new, racing machines made their debut in the spring of 1927. Produced in 349 c.c. and 498 c.c. forms, each retained the same bore and stroke dimensions of their push rod ancestors. The design of the camshaft drive was a striking departure from the usual vertical shaft and bevels, the camshaft being centrally disposed across the cylinder head and driven by a chain enclosed in a long, cast alloy casing running up the outside of the cylinder barrel. To compensate for variations in chain tension brought about by heat expansion, an automatic, Weller patented tensioner was used. This comprised a long, slender leaf of sprung steel vertically mounted, anchored and pivoted from its lower end in the chain case and curved inwards like a bow to contact the slack side of the chain; a coil tension spring acting as a bow string between the point of anchorage and the free end of the steel leaf to take up any play. The cast iron cylinder head had deep vertical finning, carrying single inlet and exhaust valves fitted with coil springs and set at 90°, these being operated by exposed

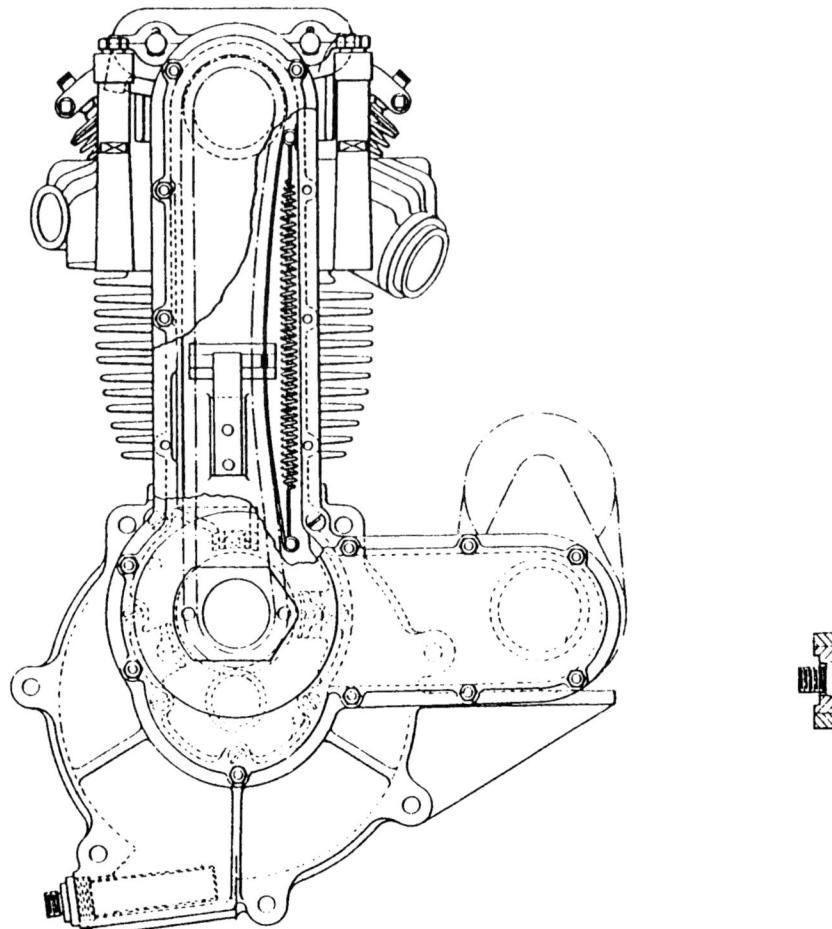

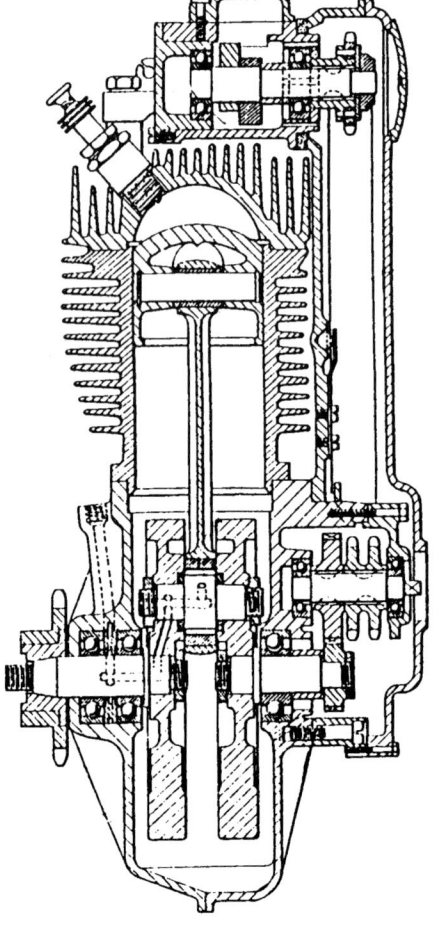

Two sectional views of the overhead camshaft engine showing chain driven camshaft and automatic 'Weller' tensioner. *Drawing: Author.*

Timekeeper Mr A.V. Ebblewhite prepares to start Charlie Hough in the 1927 Senior T.T. race. Charlie riding one of the new 4.98 h.p. camshaft machines went on to finish eleventh.
Photo: Doug Hough.

rockers fitted with end adjusters. Two ringed, aluminium pistons were fitted giving both engines a common compression ratio of 6.75:1. Dry sump lubrication was employed, a special, double Pilgrim oil pump being mounted on the side of the camshaft chaincase cover, delivering oil under pressure to the cam box and through the drive side crankshaft to a roller big end; the cylinder walls, piston and mainshaft bearings relying on splash feed.

Although a standard, close ratio, three speed gearbox was used for preliminary track testing, an advanced, four speed type was eventually fitted, operating through a car type, gate change mechanism using two selector forks, one controlling the engagement of first and second gears, the other, third and fourth gears. The ratios chosen for the 498 c.c. machine were 4.12, 4.98, 6.69 and 9.19:1; and for the 349 c.c. 4.61, 5.58, 7.49 and 10.29:1.

The factory chose to house the engine and gearbox in the same conventional diamond frame of the previous year, twin bolted, petrol tanks containing 3½ gallons of fuel being retained. Both brakes were foot operated, allowing the rider greater freedom to operate the remaining controls; the front brake measuring 6½" diameter, the rear 7¼". A.J.S., Druid type forks were used, fitted with an ingenious, Bowden steering damper, the tension of the friction pads being controlled by a handlebar mounted lever. A Lucas racing magneto provided the sparks, while a twist grip controlled, Binks carburettor supplied fuel to the engine.

During that year's Isle of Man T.T. races, the team suffered a serious set-back following a number of retirements due to lubrication failure; only four Junior machines from an entry of nine and five out of eight Senior machines completing the course. Jimmy Simpson however, managed to salvage some of the team's pride by finishing third in the Junior race despite losing a considerable amount of time removing a damaged primary chainguard, which had broken

*Drive side view of a 1928 3.49 h.p. O.H.C. model 'K7'.
Photo: Ivan Rhodes.*

away and become entangled in the chaindrive. Reliability returned a short time later with Jimmy Simpson taking the 350 c.c. international class by storm gaining victories in the Grand Prix d 'Europe, plus Belgian, Swiss and Austrian Grand Prix during July and August.

Although the earlier problems attributed to the lubrication system had been overcome, the overall performance of the 'cammy' engines was found to be lacking, so much so in fact, that after declaring himself a non-starter in both 350 c.c. and 500 c.c. classes of the Dutch T.T. held in June 1928, Jimmy Simpson never rode A.J.S. machines again: his entries being respectively taken over by Charlie Hough and Tommy Spann. Although 'cammy' A.J.S. machines successfully featured in a handful of international events during the year, the Company chose to revert back to the more established, three speed, push rod engines for much of 1928, enabling further development work to be undertaken. However, like Norton, A.J.S. in accordance with their traditional policy of offering the public what they raced, listed for the first time overhead camshaft models in their 1928 catalogue. Designated the 'K7' (349 c.c.) and 'K10' (498 c.c.), the new machines replaced the earlier 'H7' and 'H10', push rod, racing models. With the exception of three speed gearboxes replacing the special four speed unit, the new models were substantially the same as the T.T. machines, each featuring narrow, racing style mudguards, T.T. handlebars, tank mounted tool box and a steering damper. Apart from the fundamental difference in cubic capacity, both the 'K7' and 'K10' machines shared the same basic specifications, except that the 'K7' had a slightly shorter wheelbase, smaller capacity fuel tank, differ-

*Timing side close – up of model 'K7' engine.
Photo: Author.*

1929 346 c.c. long stroke (70mm. x 90mm.) four speed 'M7' racing replica of the machine ridden to victory by Leo Davenport in the 1929 350 c.c. Ulster Grand Prix.
Note: The machine was originally supplied with a Bowden carburettor and not the Amal instrument seen here.
Photo: Author.

ent gearbox ratios and lighter transmission chains. Considering the remarkably cheap, simple and straight forward principles behind the A.J.S. chain-driven design, it is not so surprising to discover that such advanced and exotic thoroughbreds as the 'K7' and 'K10' could be bought for the reasonably low price of £62.0s.0d. and £73.0s.0d. respectively.

The 349 c.c. and 498 c.c., 'cammy' racing machines were to reappear in 1929, each incorporating a number of important changes. On the engine side, modifications included strengthened rockers and a heavily ribbed crankcase; more important however, was the fitting of a modified camshaft. During exhaustive tests conducted at the works, it was discovered that the disappointing lack of engine performance lay in its valve timing. In truth, the original timings had been copied from the successful, push rod engines; the problem resulting from the increased efficiency of the overhead cam mechanism, allowing the valve to follow a much more precise path prescribed by the cam profiles, rather than the extended valve opening periods created by the action of valve float at high engine revolutions in the earlier, push rod layout. There was also a new, four speed gearbox and a redesigned frame having a straight top tube to accept a new, saddle type, fuel tank. Larger brakes were also featured, the front being 8" diameter, the rear 9".

With the camshaft engines more or less sorted out, the racing season got off to a fine start for A.J.S., Wal Handley coming a close second to Freddie Hicks on a Velocette in the Isle of Man Junior T.T.; Handley rather unlucky not to have won, with brake shoe damage slowing him on the last lap. At the German T.T. at Kolbergrennen in June, George Rowley won the 350 c.c. event; while Arthur Simcock was second behind Freddie Hicks on his Velocette in the 350 c.c. Dutch T.T. at Assen in July. George Rowley took second place to Wal Handley on a Motosacoche in the 350 c.c. German Grand Prix at Nurburgring at the end of July, then a few weeks later won the 350 c.c. Austrian Grand Prix in very wet conditions. In September, Leo Davenport went on to win the 350 c.c. Ulster Grand Prix, with team mate Rowley coming second and in October the same two riders were to finish in the same order at the end of the 350 c.c. European Grand Prix held at Amettla in Spain.

Back at home, the 1929 catalogue displayed the 'new look' A.J.S. machines, the Company finally succumbing to the latest fashions already adopted by most of the other manufacturers a year or so earlier. The most striking of these being the top heavy appearance of the new style, saddle tanks, sporting, much to the dislike of many A.J.S. enthusiasts, magenta coloured transfer panels. However, by far the most important feature of the new models was the change to dry sump lubrication. As in 1928, two camshaft models were listed, namely the 'M7' (349 c.c.) and 'M10' (498 c.c.) featuring much the same technical specification as for the previous year, except there was a choice of wide or close gear ratios available. The frames however, had been redesigned with a straight top tube to accommodate new saddle tanks; a 2½ gallon capacity being specified for the 'M7' model and 2¾ gallon for the 'M10', each recessed to accept a flush, top fitting speedometer driven from the end of the gearbox layshaft. The earlier, Druid pattern, front forks were replaced by Webb, centre spring type, having triangulated, tubular, fork blades with a single, barrel type, compression spring mounted between and lower links incorporating friction dampers. At a glance there was very little to distinguish between the two models, except the larger capacity machine had a 2" longer wheelbase at 4'7" and tipped the scales at 279 lbs compared to 260 lbs for the smaller machine. The 'M7' was offered at £62.0s.0d. and the 'M10' at £72.0s.0d.

That year A.J.S. turned its attention to track racing and record breaking. Having joined A.J.S. earlier in the year, the main thrust behind the Company's entry into this field lay with R.M.N. Spring and A.Denly, very experienced men,

Bert Denly (495 c.c. A.J.S.) pictured with Nigel Spring, (wearing trilby) at the B.M.C.R.C. 'Twenty-First 'Anniversary Meeting at Brooklands, 5th April 1930 following his win in the 500 c.c. One Lap Sprint at 90.88 m.p.h.
Photo: Dr. Joseph Bayley collection.

Bert Denly (495 c.c. A.J.S.) shakes hands with Nigel Spring after winning the 500 c.c. class at 97.26 m.p.h. in the 200 Miles Solo Races at Brooklands, 24th September 1930.
Photo: Dr. Joseph Bayley collection.

both of whom had established considerable reputations racing Norton machinery. Working as a team, Nigel Spring was responsible for A.J.S. interests at Brooklands and the preparation of special machines, while Bert Denly was responsible for riding them. In March 1929, Spring and Denly appeared at Brooklands with four, new, chromium plated, A.J.S., camshaft machines, having differing engine capacities of 346 c.c. (70 mm. x 90 mm. bore and stroke), 495 c.c. (79 mm. x 101 mm.), 598 c.c (79 mm. x 122 mm.) and 743 c.c. (84 mm. x 134 mm.). The team enjoyed a very successful season breaking no less than one hundred and seventeen records during the year on solo and sidecar machines. These included: the 200 mile, 1000 c.c. class sidecar race at Brooklands on 4th May, won by L.P.Driscoll riding Spring's 743 c.c. A.J.S. at a steady 77.15 m.p.h; also the 350 c.c. and 500 c.c. flying start kilometre records at 107.02 m.p.h. and 118.98 m.p.h. respectively at Arpajon in September; plus that most famous of all records, the Classic Hour and two hour record at Montlhéry a month earlier, Denly covering 104.51 and 202.52 miles respectively on the 495 c.c. machine.

Following his narrow victory over Wal Handley in the 1929 Isle of Man Junior T.T., Freddie Hicks accepted an offer to join A.J.S. Quite apart from being a brilliant rider, the Company recognized Hicks as being a talented engineer, capable of contributing just as much off the track in the development of new machines. As a result, the existing racing frame was redesigned for the 1930 season, the earlier, diamond shape giving way to a new, sturdier, straight line configuration, incorporating a large diameter, top tube and improved forks mounted on roller bearings. In addition to the 346 c.c. and 495 c.c. capacity models, the team received four, entirely new, 248 c.c. (62 mm. x 82 mm. bore and stroke) camshaft machines specially produced to compete in the Isle of Man Lightweight T.T. Although appearing as scaled down versions of their larger, stable companions, the smaller machines were fitted with entirely different cylinder heads and barrels. The former had revised, port angles, while a four speed, foot operated gearbox was fitted to make full use of the available power. As things turned out, the Lightweight race would provide the team's only success during the T.T. series that year, the Junior and Senior events proving a disappointment with the highest placed A.J.S. rider finishing eighth in the Junior event. Only three of the four machines entered for the Lightweight race actually took part, these being ridden by Leo Davenport, Jimmy Guthrie and South African J.G.Lind; Freddie Hicks declaring himself a non-starter due to wrist injuries sustained during the earlier Junior event. Jimmy Guthrie eventually went on to win the race at the record speed of 64.71 m.p.h., the only other A.J.S. to finish being that of J.G. Lind who crossed the line in fifth place. Jimmy Guthrie continued his winning form with a victory in the 350 c.c. class of the German Grand Prix, while Arthur Simcock won the 350 c.c. Dutch T.T. in July. Leo Davenport won the 350 c.c. Austrian Grand Prix in August as well as the 350 c.c. class of the Ulster Grand Prix in September; also during the same month, Freddie Hicks crossed the line first and Leo Davenport second in the 350 c.c. French Grand Prix. Further records fell to A.J.S., with Bert Denly not only raising the 500 c.c. hour record, but the Classic Hour too, to 108.60 miles at Montlhéry on 27th August.

A very special, overhead camshaft machine was produced by A.J.S. in 1930, a huge V-twin constructed for the express purpose of capturing that most prestigious of records, the world's flying kilometre, motorcycle, land speed record. The idea that the Company should make such an attempt belonged to Nigel Spring. He had previously been involved in an earlier record attempt at Arpajon and had little difficulty in persuading Jack Stevens that the existing record held by the Germans could easily be captured on a machine bearing A.J.S. initials. Despite the Company's difficult financial position, Jack's enthusiasm for the project was enough to convince the rest of the A.J.S. board that they should go for it. Jack, already in overall charge of the design and drawing office at Graiseley, took full responsibility for the project, entrusting much of the design work to one of his right hand men, Ike Hatch, while the ever faithful Bob Shakespeare was given the task of looking after the development work. Design work began in earnest during the summer of 1929, coinciding with the finishing touches being carried out to the new, 'R' model range to be announced in the autumn. The chosen design for the power unit eventually centred on a 50° V-twin configuration having a capacity of 990 c.c. (79 mm. x 101 mm. bore and stroke), which basically followed the lines of using a pair of the latest, 495 c.c., overhead camshaft singles sharing one common crankcase. For additional strength, the cylinders were machined from solid steel billets, particular attention being paid to the hardening of the bores by a special process ensuring the depth of hardness to a few thousandths of an inch. Aluminium was used for the construction of the cylinder heads, with cast iron valve seats inserted, the valve guides being bronze. One conspicuous change from the usual V-twin design, was the location of the inlet ports, being at the rear of both cylinder heads, thus allowing for greatly improved inlet tracts and cooling the exhaust valve in the rear cylinder. Huge, steel flywheels weighing 42 lbs. were housed in a generously webbed crankcase, supported in 1¼" diameter ball bearings, two races being employed on the drive side and one on the opposite. The connecting rods were of forked construction, additional strength and rigidity given by a cross member spanning the base of the forked rod. The big end assembly was designed with four rows of rollers enclosed in duralumin cages, the centre pair for the middle connecting rod and the outer pair for the forked rod, the crankpin measuring 1⁷⁄₁₆" diameter. The single, overhead camshaft, valve gear was identical to that employed on the single cylinder engines, both camshafts having separate chains enclosed in a one piece, three branch casting, one branch being used to enclose the chain-drive to an M.L. racing magneto. Both pistons and gudgeon pins were similar to those used in the 495 c.c. single cylinder engines, the former having three narrow rings, the bottom ring acting as a scraper. As was now normal practice, dry sump lubrication was employed, oil being carried in a separate, streamlined oil tank fitted into the right hand side of the rear stays.

Transmission was effected through a 7¼" diameter, four plate clutch, to a specially designed, three speed, Sturmey-Archer gearbox having ratios of 3.2, 4.3 and 7.8:1; primary drive being a ⅝" x ⅜" chain, while the rear was ¾" x ⁷⁄₁₆".

The engine and gearbox were housed in a huge, duplex, cradle frame of immense strength, the single top tube measuring no less than 2½" in diameter, while 1⅜" diameter twin cradle tubes swept down from a massive head lug to run beneath the engine and gearbox to the

Overhead Camshaft

The first photograph taken of the 990 c.c. big twin following its completion at Graiseley 1930.
Photo: Geoffrey St. John.

Captain Oliver M. Baldwin makes an appearance at Brooklands with the big A.J.S. in July 1930.
Photo: Geoffrey St. John.

rear spindle, providing a wheelbase of 60". Rigidity was further improved by an additional pair of frame tubes acting as chainstays, running from the rear down tubes to the rear fork ends. The front forks were the same type as used on the racing machines for the 1930 T.T. races and were fitted with an Andre steering damper. The dropped handlebars were made in two halves, each being supported below the top of the steering head by split lugs. The wheels were heavy, identical hubs being produced from solid steel forgings. For record attempts Dunlop 28" x 2.75" wired-on tyres were fitted, but for testing on the concrete at Brooklands 28" x 3.50" were used. To obtain the correct riding position a Lycett saddle was used, positioned low over the back wheel, while the footrests were set well back and fastened directly to the lower frame members. A beautiful, rakish teardrop, fuel tank straddled the giant top tube, being finished in chromium and black, lined in gold.

Once completed, the mighty twin produced almost 70 b.h.p. on the bench, running on an 11.5:1 compression ratio and fuelled by two, purpose constructed, Amal carburettors, fitted with 3" diameter float chambers. Using the 3.2 top gear ratio, it was calculated the maximum speed of the 426 lb. monster should be in the region of 150 m.p.h., fifteen miles per hour above the existing record held by Ernst Henne on a 743 c.c., supercharged B.M.W. at 134.75 m.p.h. It was rather hoped the task of capturing the record would go to Bert Denly, however this was not possible as the terms of his Shell oil contract clashed with the Castrol sponsorship of A.J.S. In the end it was decided that Captain Oliver M. Baldwin, an experienced record man and certainly no stranger to big twins, would ride the machine.

After fitting the machine out to his own special needs, Baldwin and the big A.J.S. appeared at Brooklands in July 1930, with the object of running the machine in and carrying out tests before travelling to Arpajon in August to make an attempt on the record. The attempt was to prove a huge disappointment for Jack Stevens and A.J.S., the big twin just managing to break the 130 m.p.h. barrier before a piston seizure in the rear cylinder brought the attempt to an end. Joe Wright riding a supercharged O.E.C. – J.A.P.,

Baldwin prepares for an attempt on the world flying kilometre motorcycle land speed record at Arpajon in August 1930. Note the elastic bands stretched over his socks and overalls to minimise wind resistance.
Photo: Geoffrey St. John.

Baldwin poses for the camera before making the unsucessful record attempt.
Photo: Dr. Joseph Bayley collection.

then took the record to 137.32 m.p.h. before Henne, who had been anxiously waiting on the sidelines, recaptured the record by increasing the speed to 137.66 m.p.h. Because of the Company's worsening financial position, further record attempts had to be postponed and the big twin reluctantly mothballed.

Despite the gloomy outlook, the Company still managed to produce a ten model line up for 1931. Two camshaft models were included, these being the 'S7' (346 c.c.) priced at £80.0s.0d. and the larger capacity 'S10' (495 c.c.) at £90.0s.0d. Alas there was to be no replica of Jimmy Guthrie's beautiful, 1930, Lightweight T.T., winning machine. Both camshaft models were depicted in a separate catalogue and only produced in limited quantities, each being specially built and tested by the racing department. Although the new models were reputed to be exact replicas of the works machines which had performed with such marked success in racing and record breaking during 1930, in reality neither shared the same straight line frame design, the factory continuing to use the familiar diamond pattern.

In October 1931, A.J.S. lost its financial struggle for survival. The manufacturing rights, stock and goodwill being acquired by the Collier brothers for Matchless Motorcycles Ltd. However, the big twin which had lain covered in the experimental department did not go unnoticed; in 1932 steps were taken by the new owners to continue where Jack Stevens had left off. In order to stand any chance of capturing Henne's latest 151.86 m.p.h. record, it was thought necessary to supercharge the existing engine. In due course, new, bronze cylinder heads were fitted and a Powerplus No.8. blower installed, mounted low down in front of the engine, the magneto being replaced by coil ignition. In May 1933, Matchless engaged the services of Joe Wright to make an attempt on the record at Southport Sands, Lancashire. Alas, the highest speed recorded this time was 136 m.p.h., the apparent lack of performance being the result of a bent valve stem. Later in September a further attempt took place in Hungary near Tat, Joe Wright pushing the blown twin to almost 145 m.p.h., very respectable but still well short of Henne's record. The Colliers decided to call it a day, the big twin eventually being sold to Charles Mortimer Senior a year later for £85.0s.0d. While under Mortimer's ownership, the frame was modified to rehouse the

Joe Wright poses for the press photographers on the supercharged twin at Southport Sands May 1933.
Photo: Geoffrey St. John.

The big A.J.S. pictured in Tasmania before returning to Britain.
Note the twin magnetos mounted in front of the crankcase, the hairpin valve springs and the blower support brackets mounted above the gearbox.
Photo: Geoffrery St. John.

Powerplus blower above the gearbox, the drive being taken from the drive side mainshaft, allowing twin magnetos to be mounted in front of the crankcase. The A.J.S. eventually found its way to Eric Fernihough who kept it as a reserve to his own, record breaking, Brough Superior machines. Following Ferinhough's tragic death in Hungary on 23rd April 1938 whilst trying to better his own record, the machine was sold overseas to Messr's E.T.H. and W.H. Jowett, A.J.S. agents based in Launceston, Tasmania. Although it changed hands a year later, it remained in Tasmania until 1981, when it was eventually sold and shipped back to Britain. By this time the machine was in a sorry state. But its new owner, Gloucester enthusiast and Vintage Motor Cycle Club member Geoffrey St.John, has painstakingly restored the big 'Ajay' to its former glory as when last owned by Charles Mortimer, except the twin magneto arrangement has now been replaced by a single M.L. unit.

After spending an interesting afternoon with Geoff St.John discussing the technical aspects of the machine, the Author was intrigued to learn that the record attempts could simply have failed, because the vent hole in the fuel tank may have been too small. In Geoff's opinion the system as it stood would not have been capable of providing enough fuel to meet the engine's requirements, the fuel being alcohol and the consumption about three miles per gallon. If correct this diagnosis would certainly explain the apparent hesitation and misfiring that was experienced by Oliver Baldwin and Joe Wright at high speeds.

By no means destined to become a lifeless museum exhibit, the big blown twin is fired up and used for demonstration runs whenever possible. After arriving back on her native soil half a century after passing out of A.J.S. ownership, the Company's most powerful motorcycle is thankfully preserved in good hands.

Geoffrey St. John's beautifully restored supercharged A.J.S. as photographed in 1983.
Photo: The Classic Motor Cycle.

A plumbers nightmare!
Timing side close - up of the supercharged O.H.C. Twin.
Photo: The Classic Motor Cycle.

Chapter 11
Commercial Vehicles

Toward the end of 1926 A.J.S. had, like so many of its contemporaries began to feel the effects of a general decline on its established markets.

The once buoyant and lucrative wireless trade had slumped, assisted by an abundance of cheap, imported receivers. The sidecar and car body business had suffered a substantial fall in orders and the Company's mainstay, its motorcycle business had become increasingly dependent on export trade to 'prop-up' a shrinking home market.

During the following year, the effects of the deepening recession had spread more widely and as a result the first of the Company's troubles surfaced, when it failed to declare a dividend to its shareholders.

In order to deal with the problem, it was felt the answer to full production lay in diversification. Following a general upsurge of interest in passenger vehicles, the Company decided to enter the commercial vehicle field. The strongest recommendation for a move in this direction had come from Charles Hayward, the director in charge of coachbuilding at Lower Walsall Street. This paralleled an earlier decision by their neighbours the Sunbeam Motor Co.Ltd. to adopt similar plans.

Once the ailing wireless business had been rehoused at Stewart Street, development work began in the autumn of 1927 to produce a coach chassis at Lower Walsall Street. The main task of getting the new venture off the ground was given to Edward Toghill (design) and Edward Jenner (sales), former employees of the Star Engineering Co.Ltd. Wolverhampton. These gentlemen had been responsible for much of the Star's success in the passenger vehicle market and had accepted offers from A.J.S. to join the Company as Chief Designer and Sales Manager respectively for commercial vehicles. After construction the prototype was driven around the Wolverhampton area to assess its handling and performance, before returning to the works to have make-shift Hayward bodywork fitted. It was then taken on a successful weekend trip to Blackpool, with members of the work staff as passengers.

In 1928 Charles Hayward who had played such a major role in encouraging A.J.S. to enter the commercial vehicle business, left the Company. He moved to London to form a new business involved in financing inventions and industrial processes. This company eventually became closely connected with the formation of the Firth Cleveland Group, of which he later became chairman. His position at A.J.S. in overall charge of Lower Walsall Street was immediately taken over by Joe Stevens Junior, who until this time had been in charge of production and racing activities back at the Graiseley Hill works.

Production of commercial vehicle chassis commenced at Lower Walsall Street about the same time as a long standing contract to produce car bodies for Clyno was halted. The termination of this contract had been brought about by Clyno unwisely getting involved in a price cutting war with Austin and Morris, culminating with the company offering their 'Century' model at £10.0s.0d. below that of the Morris 'Minor'. It was a decision that would later prove fatal, with Clyno going into receivership in February 1929.

The first A.J.S. chassis, designated the 'Pilot' was announced in February 1929 and was of conventional appearance and specification, designed along orthodox lines using bought-in components. A nautical theme was continued in naming all the A.J.S. commercial chassis types, although this may not have been the original intention with the 'Pilot', which appeared when air travel was hitting the headlines.

The chassis was primarily intended as a high speed, long distance coach, but was found to be equally at home when marketed as a service bus. The complete 'chassis' consisted of the axles, wheels, engine and all related parts. Except for the handful of Hayward designed examples, all bodywork was left to specialist businesses. Coach examples usually had twenty seats, with plenty of leg room and sumptuous luxury seats, their outward opening, hinge doors and small seating capacity made them unsuitable for service work, when they became unfashionable on front line work. A service bus was more basic, intended for the shorter dis-

"Pilot"

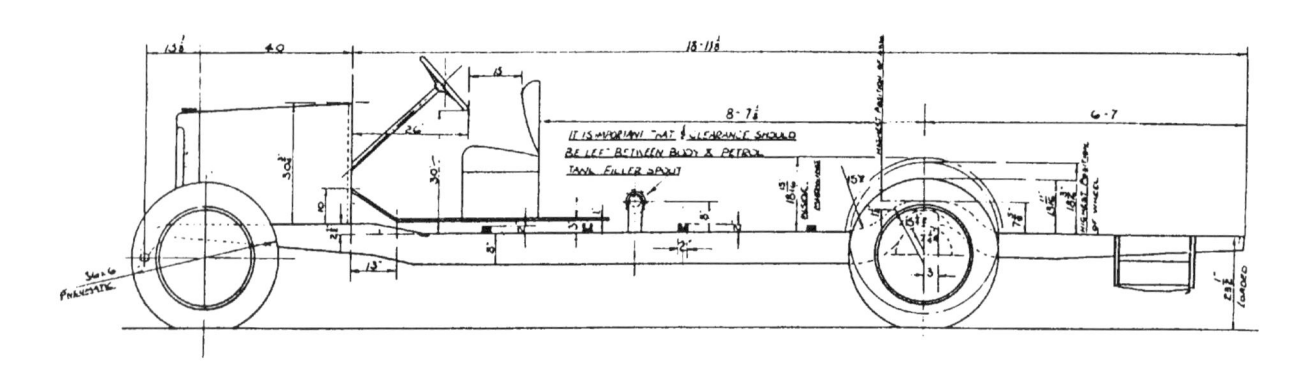

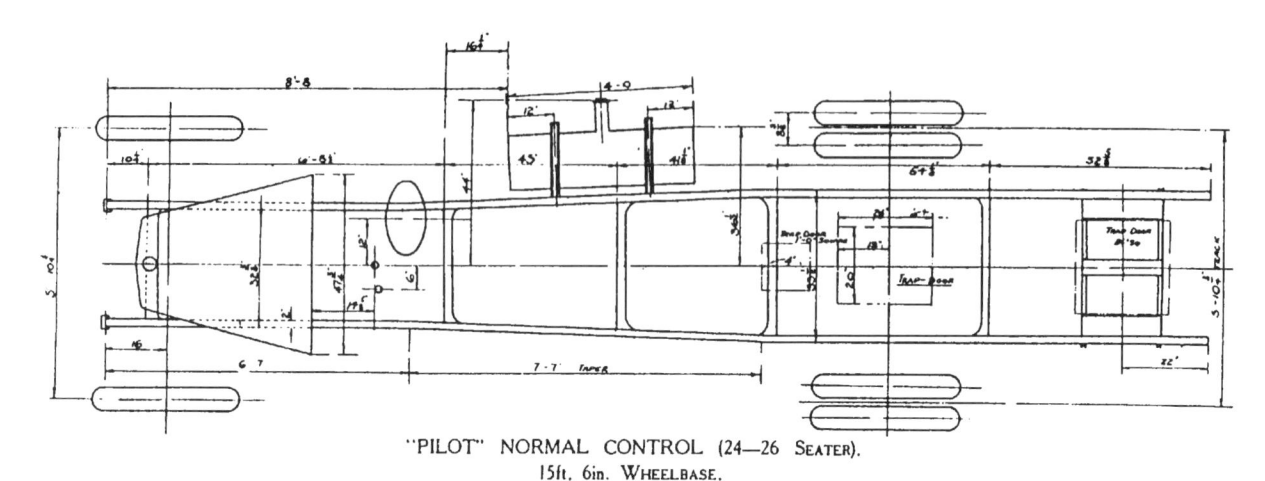

"PILOT" NORMAL CONTROL (24—26 SEATER).
15ft. 6in. WHEELBASE.

The normal control 'Pilot' chassis.
Drawing: Manufacturers catalogue.

Meadows type 6 ERC power unit fitted to the normal control 'Pilot'.
Photo: Manufacturers catalogue.

tance passenger. Twenty four seats could be fitted into such designs. When bodied, the main parts of the 'chassis' remaining visible were the wheels and radiator, the latter had to be prominent and easily recognizable, becoming the manufacturer's advertisement when out on the road.

The main frame was manufactured by John Thompson Motor Pressings Ltd. of Bilston, being of low level design. This gave a loaded height of approximately 1' 11½" between axles, consisting of 8", deep pressed, longitudinal channel sections approx 24' 0" in length and spaced 3'3½" apart at the rear, with a slight convergence towards the front. Five, well gusseted cross-members were riveted between the longitudinals to spread the load, forming a robust, rigid structure affording wheelbase and track dimensions of 15' 6" and 5' 10¾" respectively.

The 'Pilot' was designed as a normal control vehicle, giving the driver a position behind the engine. A further version was soon introduced with forward control, positioning the driver alongside the engine in a separate cab. This layout had the advantage of providing an increased distance of 3'3" behind the driver, allowing room for two further passenger seats.

160

Commercial Vehicles

Control mechanism and housing of the Dewandre servo braking system fitted to the 'Pilot'.
Photo: Manufacturers catalogue.

'Pilot' rear axle, showing underslung worm drive.
Photo: Manufacturers catalogue.

"Pilot"

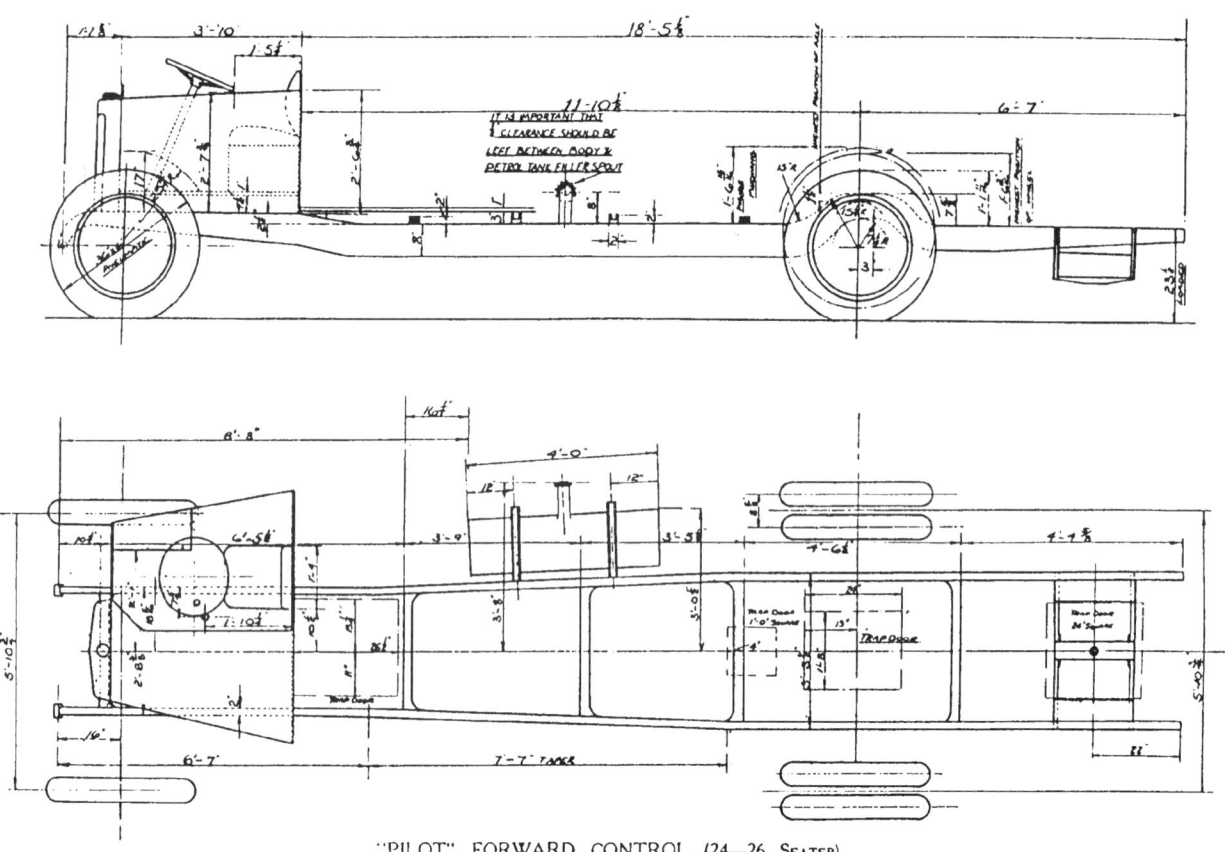

"PILOT" FORWARD CONTROL (24—26 Seater).
15ft. 6in. Wheelbase.

The forward control 'Pilot' chassis.
Drawing: Manufacturers catalogue.

Meadows type 6 ERC power unit showing forward control gear mechanism.
Photo: Manufacturers catalogue.

The engine chosen was a type 6ERC, built by Henry Meadows & Co. of Fallings Park, Wolverhampton. Being of unit construction design it had six cylinders, overhead valves and was fitted with a four speed gearbox. Bore and stroke dimensions were 82.5 mm. x 120.7 mm. providing a capacity of 3800 c.c. and an R.A.C. rating of 25 h.p. 54 b.h.p. was claimed @ 2000 r.p.m., while top speed was quoted as 55 m.p.h.

Initially, the 'Pilot' was priced at £685.0s.0d. for the normal control version and £705.0s.0d. for the forward control. It soon found a useful niche in the six cylinder market, with competition coming mainly from the Gilford 'CP6' (£595.0s.0d.), Thornycroft 'A6' (£725.0s.0d.) and Star 'Flyer' (£595.0s.0d.). None of these was offered with the choice of forward control like the 'Pilot'.

Following its introduction the 'Pilot' showed considerable promise and for a time sold reasonably well. It appealed to small independent operators in nearly all parts of Britain, but sadly not to the larger companies. It was found to perform extremely well, a number being employed on express coach services. Wolverhampton, being centrally situated, was ideal for reaching most parts of Britain, but as

Commercial Vehicles

DE 7121, forward control 'Pilot', supplied to D.H.Roberts & Son, Newport, Pembrokeshire.
Photo: Chris Taylor collection.

VD 230, forward control improved 'Pilot', originally supplied to G. Greenshields of Salsburgh but shown with second owner D.J. Morrison of Tenby.
Photo: Chris Taylor collection.

A.J.S. of WOLVERHAMPTON

SC 4807, normal control 'Pilot', originally supplied to W.M. Herd, Edinburgh but shown in Scottish Motor Traction ownership.
Photo: David L.G. Hunter.

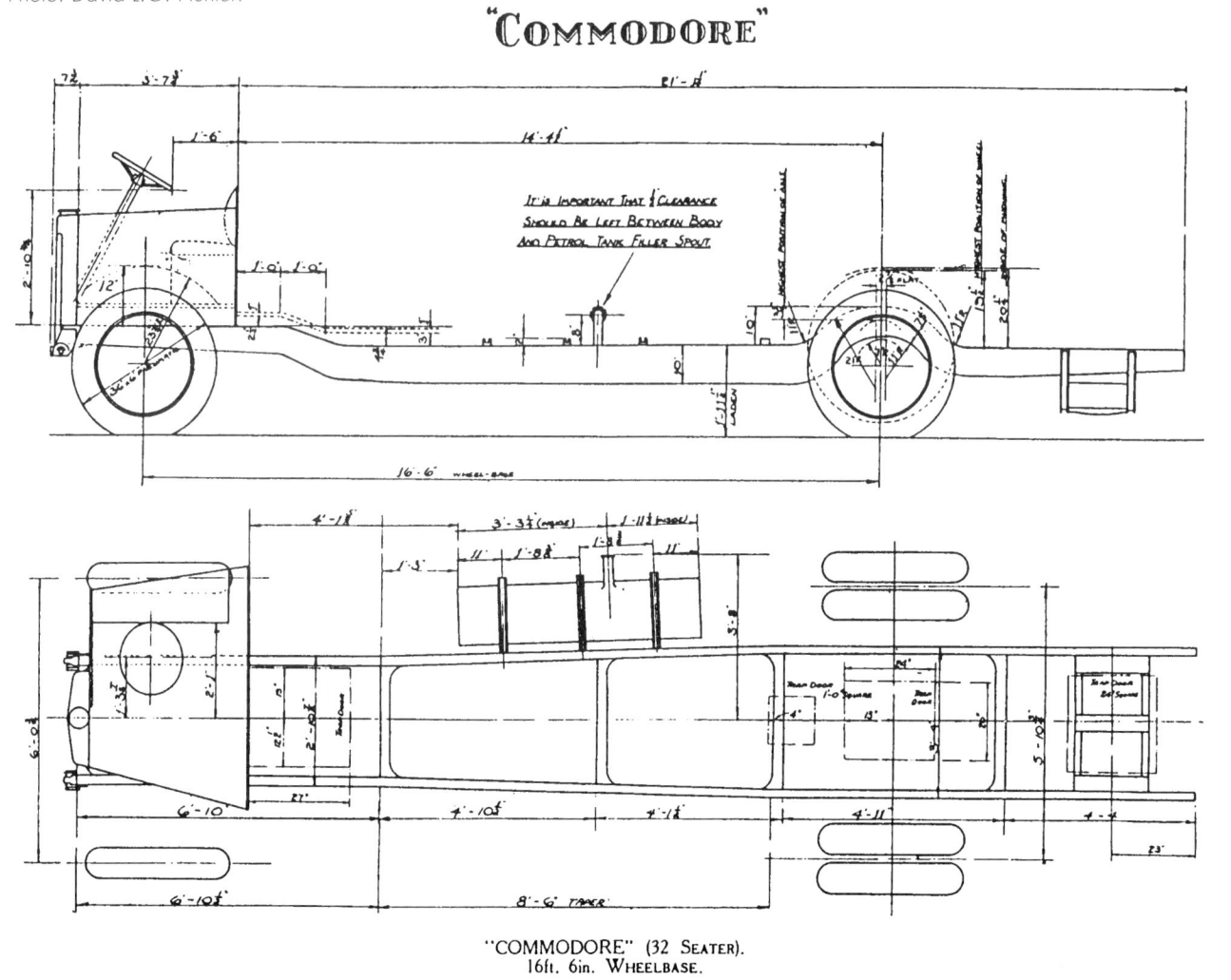

"COMMODORE"

"COMMODORE" (32 SEATER).
16ft. 6in. WHEELBASE.

The 'Commodore' chassis.
Drawing: Manufacturers catalogue.

in many businesses a London address was thought desirable. To this end a garage was opened in the capital at Victoria, S.W.1. Also around this time, D. & E. Petty of Hitchin, Hertfordshire were appointed agents and became responsible for many of the sales in the Home Counties. They also built bodywork, enabling them to offer a complete package to the independent busman in an increasingly competitive market. No attempt seems to have been made to make export sales, despite the large overseas market.

It was not long before the twenty to twenty six seat class with six cylinder engine attracted the larger manufacturers with access to more capital. A.J.S. found itself facing much stiffer competition from makes such as the Dennis 'Dart', REO 'Gold Crown' and Morris Commercial 'Viceroy'. Bedford were soon to flood the market with mass produced chassis, even Leyland were about to launch the 'Cub' from their Kingston on Thames factory. When the first of the 'Cubs' were entering service, the last A.J.S. passenger vehicle had already been built. During the 2½ year period the 'Pilot' was in production, some one hundred and forty in total were produced, initially using chassis numbers 101 to 226, then the sequence 1001 to 1014. These latter were 'improved Pilots', with modifications brought about as an effect of the 1930 Road Traffic Act. This act dictated spaces between seats and it was found that to qualify as a twenty six seater the forward control model would have to gain 3" in body space. This was achieved by moving the driver forward by that amount and fitting a less raked steering column. Existing vehicles were not affected.

The 'Pilot' sold well during the first eighteen months of production. It is interesting to note that the majority of small operators who bought them, opted for the simple, normal control layout, rather than the more advanced, forward control version often on the grounds of being able to carry out repairs and maintenance more easily. They could after all simply sling a rope over a beam in the garage and haul the engine out. Today's Health & Safety Inspectors would not be too amused at such practices! With the more complicated, forward control layout, the engine was not so easily removed; the radiator would first have to be taken off in order to withdraw the engine, involving much packing from beneath, greatly complicating matters.

In addition to the standard, passenger bodied vehicles, a few 'Pilot' chassis were supplied for light goods use. Horse boxes, furniture vans and light duty lorries were produced, being ideally suited to the low chassis height. The higher gearing made them swifter and much easier to handle than more conventional goods vehicles, as long as the overall weight was kept down.

The Company decided to follow up the success of the 'Pilot' with a new, full sized chassis capable of carrying a thirty two seat body. In October 1929, the 'Commodore' was introduced. A forward control design, based on similar lines to those of the forward control 'Pilot' and using experience gained in building and selling that model, the 'Pilot's' chassis height of 1' 11½" was used in the 'Commodore'.

To accommodate the greater load capacity, the longitudinal frame members were increased to a depth of 10" and spaced apart by six, deep riveted cross-members to distribute the load. Wheelbase and track dimensions were set at 16' 6" and 6'0¾" respectively. Like the 'Pilot', the 'Commodore' had grouped grease points; for access the bodybuilder needed to put trap doors in the floor. A Clayton Dewandre servo assisted braking system was used.

The choice of power came in the form of the Coventry Climax L6, of unit construction with six cylinders and 4 speed gearbox, having an R.A.C. rating of 36 h.p. The bore and stroke dimensions were 98.4 m.m. x 127 m.m. (5748 c.c.)with 75 b.h.p. being claimed @ 2000 r.p.m. This engine was of side valve layout, which could be regarded as a retrograde step, as most new developments involved the use of overhead valves, and in some cases, overhead camshaft. Indeed, Maudslay had been using an overhead camshaft since the turn of the century.

It soon became obvious the 'Commodore' was facing much competition in its class, but at £850.0s.0d. it was one of the lowest priced six

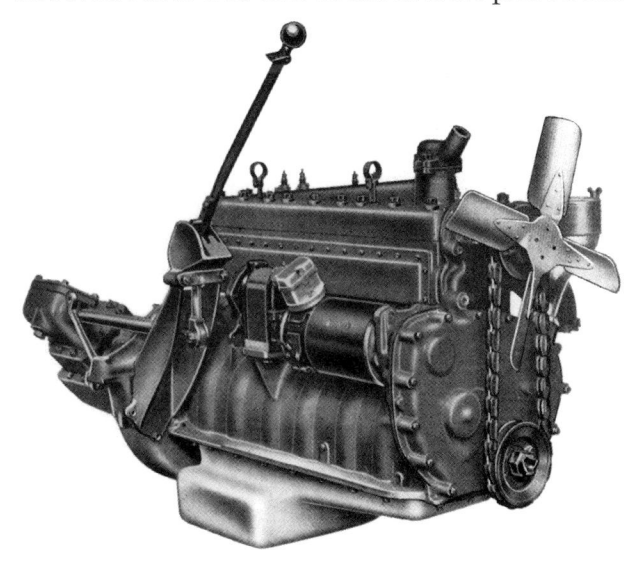

Coventry Climax L6 power unit fitted to the 'Commodore'.
Photo: Manufactures catalogue.

'Commodore' gearbox and servo motor.
Photo: Manufacturers catalogue.

cylinder chassis on the market. The main competition came in the form of the Gilford '1680T' at £895.0s.0d. (also fitted with a sidevalve engine), the Leyland 'Tiger' at £1,050.0s.0d. and the AEC 'Regal' at £1,050.0s.0d. not to mention the products of Albion, Bristol, Commer, Crossley, Daimler, Dennis, Guy, Maudslay and Thornycroft, all of British manufacture.

During the initial road testing, it was discovered the engine had a tendency to overheat. Subsequent hill climb tests carried out at Angel Bank near Ludlow, revealed the problem lay in the size of radiator being used. This was caused by choosing to use the same radiator as employed on the smaller engined 'Pilot'. In order to rectify the fault, the capacity of the original, honeycomb radiator was increased by extending the lower half and making it slightly wider. The result gave the 'Commodore' a modern and impressive appearance. Road tests were eventually completed following an exhaustive series of hill climbs on Porlock Hill in Somerset. The honeycomb pattern radiator was later replaced by a spiral wire gilled type.

The 'Commodore' soon gained a reputation for reliability and performance and, like the 'Pilot', became popular with the small operator. However, further sales in this market were severely hit when the 1930 Road Traffic Act, with its consequent regulation of bus and coach services, meant the slowing down of route expansion for the small independent busman. The sale of many of these small businesses to the large companies also helped to stifle sales.

Although A.J.S. tried hard to sell their vehicles to the large established companies, they met with no success. A solitary vehicle became the property of a municipal undertaking, many of which were busily replacing their trams. 'Commodore' chassis No.5026 (Reg.No.UK 9640) was first loaned to Wolverhampton Corporation, then purchased outright, plying the streets of its home town for the next seven years, as well as being used on the services to Bridgnorth, Cannock and Weston-under-Lizard.

Wolverhampton however, found itself in the embarrassing position of having two other chassis makers within its boundaries in the shape of

Commercial Vehicles

View of 'Commodore' rear axle, showing grouped lubrication.
Photo: Manufacturers catalogue.

EA 4464, a 'Commodore' with the earlier style radiator shell, supplied to G. Hill, West Bromwich.
Photo: Chris Taylor collection.

UK 9640, a 'Commodore' with Hayward coachwork and later, more modern radiator shell. An A.J.S. demonstrator supplied to Wolverhampton Corporation Transport Department.
Photo: John Mudge collection.

Sunbeam and Guy. The Corporation was following a conversion to trolley - buses and both these manufacturers could supply. It is interesting to relate that Sunbeam had entered the double - deck market, by introducing a six-wheeler, even so this company only built a handful of motor bus chassis; it did however become one of the leading trolley - bus manufacturers. In all, just over sixty A.J.S. 'Commodores' were completed over a two year period, with a few chassis being supplied as lorries. Chassis numbers 5000 to 5064 were issued.

In February 1931, A.J.S. announced the arrival of the 'Admiral', a third model to add to its range of passenger carrying chassis. The new chassis, aimed at providing a suitable foundation for a long distance, high performance, luxury coach, was designed only as a normal control machine, suitable for twenty six to twenty eight seat duty, being a little longer than the 'Pilot'.

The 'Admiral' looking every bit like a heavy weight version of a normal control 'Pilot', was in fact much more similar in detail design to the 'Commodore'. The main frame members were

SX 3254, a 'Commodore' originally supplied to W. Rendall & Company, Broxburn, but shown in Scottish Motor Traction ownership.
Photo: David L.G. Hunter.

SC 7566, an 'Admiral' supplied to W.M.Herd, Edinburgh.
Photo: David L.G.Hunter.

slimmed down to 8" deep and wheelbase and track measurements were set at 16'2" and 5' 10¾" respectively.

Following the uneasiness that had surrounded the 'Commodore's' side valve engine, the Company approached Henry Meadows & Co. to produce a new unit for the 'Admiral'. However, due to various technical delays in its development, this new engine was far from ready in time, leaving no alternative but to revert to the Coventry Climax L6 as an interim measure. In practice this power unit provided a 14.6 b.h.p. per ton power to gross weight ratio, resulting in a lively 5 to 55 m.p.h. top gear performance.

Priced at just £795.0s.0d., the 'Admiral' represented spendid value for money and seemed certain for a bright future, but alas, due to the effects of the recession, the Company's financial situation had deteriorated and as a result only eight 'Admirals' were produced, using chassis numbers 3001 to 3008. So quick was this model's demise, that no publicity material appears to have been produced.

During the 2½ years that A.J.S. produced its commercial vehicles, over 200 were sold. Quite a remarkable feat for a newcomer to the business, especially given the difficult trading conditions and competition that came from established builders during this time. In 1929, bus services were run basically on a free-for-all basis, although local licences were issued in cities and boroughs. The small busman wanted a swift machine, so as to race the large operator to the next stop and claim the passengers. By 1932, the 1930 Road Traffic Act had taken effect. Licences had to be issued, usually automatically to existing operators. Timetables and fares had to be registered and could not be altered without referral to the Traffic Commissioners. The large companies became associated with the railways and received injections of capital, enabling purchase of the small operator. In those 2½ years the bus world had changed, the markets had shrunk.

Sadly, there are no known A.J.S. commercial vehicles still in existence, nor is it likely that any will ever be found. The last known Wolverhampton built A.J.S. coach to operate for its original owner, belonged to Rose Bros of Chelmsford ('Commodore' chassis 5042) and was still sometimes used on their Chelmsford to London service until 1950. This may well have been the last such vehicle in passenger use.

It is likely that many of the A.J.S. commercial vehicles would have been scrapped, along with so many other makes, following the introduction of the seven year Certificate of Fitness, as part of the 1930 Road Traffic Act, governing the

DAB 341, Great Witley 'Commodore', A. Moore & Sons.
Photo: John Mudge collection.

safety and condition of passenger vehicles in service. However, it is possible a few may have survived in use as showmen's living quarters, travelling between fairgrounds and circuses until the late 1950's. It was not until 1959 that M.O.T. testing was introduced for private vehicles.

Faced with escalating losses, A.J.S. had in October 1931 elected to go into voluntary liquidation.

Other than a few 'Commodore' chassis, which were purchased from the liquidators by a couple of Pembrokeshire operators for £400.0s.0d. each, most of the remaining commercial vehicle stock, having a list price value of £40,000.0s.0d., was bought by Charles Aaron Weight for the Briton Motor Car Company Ltd. and stored in premises at Chillington Fields, Wolverhampton. During the next few years, some of the parts were sold to A.J.S. operators, keen to keep their vehicles on the road, until a couple of years before the outbreak of World War Two, when, to make room for a new business venture, the remaining parts were sold.

This should have been the end of A.J.S. as far as buses and coaches were concerned. But these parts, which included four complete chassis frames, were bought by Worcestershire bus operator, Arthur Moore & Sons of Great Witley. Mr. Moore and his staff assembled enough parts to produce a complete vehicle including coachwork built in his not over-equipped garage. The result took to the road in June 1939, registered DAB 341. This was the first 'modern' registered A.J.S. commercial vehicle; all Wolverhampton built specimens having a two letter registration. Then came the War, the scrap drive should have claimed what remained. But after a further seven years Mr Moore put EWP 476 on the road in May 1946, the chassis again made from his collection of

HWP 569, Great Witley 'Commodore', A. Moore & Sons.
Photo: John Mudge collection.

parts, this time carrying a mid-1930's Harrington body. In June 1948 GWP 20 was launched, again from spares, with coachwork built in Moore's garage. Not enough parts now remained to make a complete chassis, so EA 5181, 'Commodore' chassis No 5051 was cannibalized and married to what remained of the new parts, the result was furnished again with Moore's own coachwork. HWP 569 entered service in December 1949. A number of parts had to be specially made, the radiator was non-standard as were the front mudguards. A Leyland 8.6 oil engine was fitted, the only A.J.S. to be other than petrol powered. This excellent coach took to the road about the time the last, genuine, Wolverhampton built vehicles were being withdrawn from service. These 'Great Witley Specials', although being basically Moore's own creations, were licenced as A.J.S. and must be counted as such. Mr Moore gave them chassis numbers 1 to 4 in a separate series. HWP 569 remained in service until 1960, being seen in its last year at Skegness, Llandudno and Barry Island, indeed it was much sought by enthusiasts of the era. After withdrawal it remained at Great Witley falling into dereliction for another eight years, before being claimed by the scrap man. It can thus be said with certainty, HWP 569 was the last commercial vehicle to carry upon its radiator the evocative letters, A.J.S.

CHAPTER 12
A.J.S. Light Car

During the summer of 1927, A.J.S. were successful in securing a contract to produce car bodies for their neighbours, The Clyno Engineering Co. (1922) Ltd., through their subsidiary Company, Hayward Motor Bodies.

The contract had been drawn up following Clyno's occupation of a new four acre factory at Bushbury, during the spring of 1927, when they had decided to produce a small car, the Clyno 'Nine'. The new model, designed by A.G.Booth and costing just £160.0s.0d., was introduced during September 1927 and followed general Clyno practice in having a four cylinder, side valve engine, three speed gearbox and Cox-Atmos carburettor. Unlike their established models, the 'Nine' boasted a modern, single plate clutch rather than the usual, cone pattern type.

Production of the bodies was carried out at Lower Walsall Street, based on a batch system of fifty at a time. The chosen coachwork featured much use of fabric covered panels, supported on an ash timber framework.

The contract to produce bodies for the 'Nine' progressed well, until Clyno sought to take on the big battalions, Austin and Morris, by involving itself in a price cutting war. As a result, Clyno introduced a new, four seater, touring model, the 'Century', priced at a mere £112.10s.0d. (£112.50). This was a basic 'Nine' chassis, cloaked with a cheap, fabric, tourer body, which undercut the long awaited, overhead camshaft Morris 'Minor', introduced to compete with the Austin Seven by £12.10s.0d. (£12.50).

Clyno body production at Lower Walsall Street works, 1927.
Photo: Geoff Stevens.

A.J.S. Light Car

Body Panelling Shop, Lower Walsall Street, 1927, showing batch Clyno body production running alongside sidecar department.
Photo: Geoff Stevens.

Clyno bodies being trimmed in the Upholstery Shop at Lower Walsall Street, 1927.
Photo: Geoff Stevens.

Sadly the expected sales never materialized. The car became unpopular with the dealers and as a result only some three hundred were produced and sold. Cost cutting had simply gone too far and because of this, Clyno's reputation went the same way as their bank balance. The Century, dubbed the 'Cemetery' by its work force, proved too much and in February 1929 a receiver was appointed and a decision taken to wind the company up.

The demise of Clyno came at a very difficult time for A.J.S., coinciding with the introduction of their first commercial vehicle chassis, the 'Pilot'. In an attempt to recuperate their losses and provide additional production at Graiseley, it was decided to produce their own light car. Overall responsibility rested firmly on the shoulders of Arthur G.Booth, the designer of the original Clyno 'Nine', who had joined A.J.S. following the closure of Clyno. The result, the A.J.S. 'Nine', first announced in December 1929, was eventually introduced following exhaustive factory testing in August 1930, as a four-door, fabric saloon priced at £230.0s.0d. Shortly after, two further models were added, a four-door, coachbuilt saloon at £240.0s.0d., plus an attractive, coachbuilt, open two seater with dickey, at £210.0s.0d.

Production was divided between Lower Walsall Street and Graiseley Hill, the former concentrating on the bodywork, whereas Graiseley became responsible for final assembly. Although completely restyled, the new car followed the same general design layout as that of its predecessor. The main chassis frame, produced by John Thompson Motor Pressings of Bilston, provided wheelbase and track dimensions of 7' 7" and 3' 9" respectively and was designed on sturdy lines having deep pressed side-members, suitably braced by four, stout cross-members. Semi-elliptic springs having 'Silentbloc' bushes for the shackles were used front and rear. Both sets of springs lay practically flat, those at the front being controlled by Hartford dampers, whilst Smith units fitted transversely were used at the rear. The rear springs were underslung beneath the semi-floating, spiral-bevel type, back axle.

The car was fitted with a four cylinder, side valve, Coventry Climax engine, having a capacity of 1018 c.c. (60 mm. x 90 mm. bore and stroke) and an RAC rating of 8.92 h.p., which put it in the £9.0s.0d. tax class at the time. The crankshaft, produced as a forging in S26 high tensile steel, was dynamically balanced and ran on three main bearings, which had high pressure, cast, white metal linings in gunmetal shells. Both inlet and exhaust valves were produced in heat treated, 'Silico', chrome steel alloy. Following modern practice, a full-pressure lubrication system was employed; a gear pump driven from the centre of the camshaft, supplying the main and connecting rod bearings with lubricant at an approximate pressure of 25lb per square inch. A cast iron, detachable, cylinder head providing a 5.75:1 c,ompression ratio was fitted, having specially designed combustion chambers, based on the principles of the 'Whatmough' system for streamlining gas flow. This plus a twelve volt, Lucas, coil ignition system, ensured very smooth running and as A.J.S.

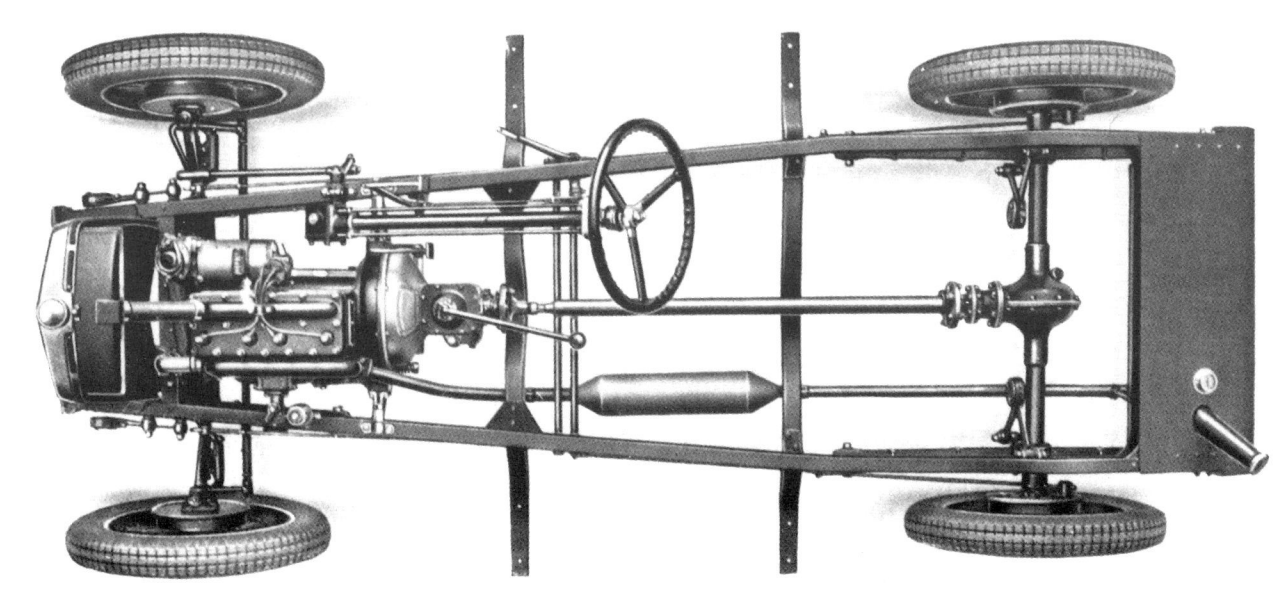

A.J.S. 'Nine' chassis layout.
Photo: Manufacturers catalogue.

Front and rear view of the 1930 A.J.S. 'Nine', four door, coachbuilt saloon.
Photos: Author.

Coventry Climax, side valve, power unit.
Photo: Author.

claimed, the ability for the car to be driven at speeds as low as 5 m.p.h. in top gear.

A maximum power output of 24 b.h.p. at 3,000 r.p.m. was claimed, being transmitted through a single, dry plate clutch carried in a flange mounted, steel flywheel, to a three speed gearbox in unit with the engine, having ratios of 19.0, 10.2 and 5.5:1. Transmission from the gearbox to the back axle was by a Hardy Spicer propellor shaft having enclosed, metal couplings. Fuel to the engine was supplied by a horizontal type, Solex carburettor fed by an Autovac, drawing from an eight gallon fuel tank located between the dumbirons at the rear of the chassis.

Bolted type, detachable, wire wheels were shod with 27" x 4.4" Avon tyres, with a spare being supported high above a sturdy, folding luggage carrier mounted at the rear of the vehicle.

Expanding shoe brakes of 9" diameter were fitted to all four wheels, operated by tie rods and levers. To comply with legal regulations at the time, the front and rear brakes were designed to operate independently. A handbrake lever situated on the right of the driver operated the rear, whilst the front were applied by foot pedal. The system however, incorporated a trip link which transmitted movement from the cross-shaft of the front brakes, to a similar cross-shaft for the rear, allowing all four brakes to be applied simultaneously when the foot pedal was depressed.

Following its introduction in August 1930, the A.J.S. 'Nine' was well received by the motoring press, and despite a comparatively high price, sold extremely well. Sales were further enhanced when it was displayed at Olympia the following October. Four examples were exhibited, a fabric saloon finished in black with a sliding roof, priced at £237.10s.0d. (£237.50), a coachbuilt saloon having aluminium panels and finished in royal blue at £240.0s.0d., an open two seater with dickey at £210.0s.0d. and a chassis devoid of bodywork. Among the features which attracted much attention, were the quality of the seats upholstered in furniture hide and the overall spaciousness of the body interiors. The instruments grouped in a centrally placed, pressed steel, oval, facia panel, grained to represent walnut, consisted of speedometer, clock, oil gauge, ammeter, lighting and ignition switch and red,

1930 A.J.S. 'Nine', coachbuilt, open two seater.
Photo: Author.

Rear view of open two seater.
Photo: Author.

Front and rear axle assemblies.
Photo: Manufacturers catalogue.

ignition warning light. In addition, there was a switch to control the lighting of the instrument panel, which also served to illuminate the floor of the driving compartment. The starter motor switch was foot operated and placed well above the clutch pedal, thus avoiding accidental use. Adjustable bucket seats with tilting backs were set in the front, while the wide rear seat had arm rests and footwells set in the floor on each side of the propeller shaft tunnel, to provide additional leg room and comfort for passengers during long journeys. To complete the body specification, flush fitting doors of ample width were included, having vertically opening glass windows. The windscreen, constructed from safety glass, was fitted with a vacuum operated wiper, while the rear window came complete with a blind, controlled by a cord terminating within easy reach of the driver's hand. The Company offered two factory fitted extras; chromium plated bumpers at £5.5s.0d. (£5.25) and a sliding roof for the saloon model at £7.10s.0d. (£7.50).

On the road the little A.J.S. more than measured up to expectations. Finger light steering inherited from the Clyno, combined with remarkable, low speed flexibility made it a delight to drive. Under favourable conditions, the 'Nine' could be driven at a mile-a-minute gait, while a maximum speed of 40 m.p.h. in second gear ensured brisk hill climbing ability. With powerful brakes, capable of stopping the car in 38 feet from 30 m.p.h. and a fuel consumption averaging around 36 m.p.g., the car won much acclaim from the motoring press. However, as far as the public were concerned, the 'Nine' stood out for quite another reason: its price! Compared to many other makes in its class, the A.J.S. was simply too expensive. As a result, in February 1931, the Company reduced prices by £11.0s.0d. on all models and introduced a new, four door, utility, fabric bodied saloon, christened the 'Richmond' at £197.0s.0d. Although identical in overall appearance to the more expensive, de-luxe, saloon models, close examination revealed a number of cost saving specifications had been included. Leather cloth now replaced hide and the vertically opening, side windows had been

(Above) Interior of 1930 coachbuilt saloon.
Photo: Author.
(Below) Millie Stevens seen standing beside the first 'Richmond' saloon to leave Graiseley.
Photo: Susan Taylor.

changed to simple, horizontal sliding units.

In a bid to reduce overall production costs, it was decided there was sufficient spare capacity and skills at Graiseley to produce their own engines. When word reached Coventry Climax, they were none too pleased. As a result the final batch of engines supplied were of such poor quality, it was necessary for them to be stripped down and rebuilt. The resulting A.J.S. engine turned out to be a carbon copy of the Coventry Climax, with nothing to distinguish between them.

Unfortunately, all was not well with the Company and just like the commercial vehicle venture, the A.J.S. 'Nine' did not improve the Company's fortunes. By the time of the shock announcement in October 1931, that the Company was in voluntary liquidation, some three thousand cars had been made at Graiseley; quite a remarkable achievement given the short life span of the car's production.

The rights of the 'Nine' eventually passed to Willys-Overland Crossley Limited of Heaton Chapel, Stockport in January 1932, for a sum of £9,500.0s.0d. Re-launched in March 1932 as 'The New A.J.S. Nine', the car differed from Wolverhampton produced machines in two main aspects. Firstly, only one body type was produced, being a re-styled, coachbuilt, four door saloon, offered in a choice of three quarter or half panelled forms and a fabric covered top. Secondly, the original, three speed gearbox had been replaced by a 'silent third', four speed unit. Priced at £229.0s.0d. it was soon realized by the Company, that the new model was in direct competitiion with their own Crossley 'Ten'. As a result the 'Nine' was reduced to £189.0s.0d. Despite this drastic price reduction, the expected sales never materialized with only about three hundred cars leaving the Stockport company before they too went into liquidation.

It is not surprising, given the relatively small number of A.J.S. cars produced at Wolverhampton, to discover how few examples survive today. However, the odd 'Nine' may still be seen at vintage car displays, where it usually attracts much attention from the viewing public, most of whom are unaware A.J.S. ever produced cars.

CHAPTER 13
Stevens

Although the Stevens brothers lost much of their own personal wealth during the collapse of A.J.S. they were fortunate to retain the private ownership of the Retreat Street works, used by their father as additional workshop space for the Stevens Screw Company Ltd.

In spite of their set-back they still had tremendous pride and faith in themselves as engineers and in the industry to which they had devoted themselves practically since boyhood. In May 1932 they formed a new company, Stevens Brothers (Wolverhampton) Ltd. Using a hand picked team and a number of unpaid volunteers, they set to work from early morning until ten o'clock at night to produce the 'Stevens Light Commercial Vehicle', a three wheeled van, powered by a single cylinder, water cooled, side valve engine of their own design and manufacture. During the early stages, the brothers were delighted to discover that help was at hand from many loyal business associates from the past. Harry Weston (later to become the Lord Mayor of Coventry) of Modern Machine Tools, Coventry, supplied two useful machines, telling the brothers: "Take the machines now and pay for them when you can". A deed which made George Stevens exclaim, "There really is a Father Christmas!"

This three wheel van was the brain-child of Harry Stevens. Although similar in appearance to the Raleigh three wheel van, Harry's original concept of the Stevens vehicle is thought to have originated from earlier times whilst at A.J.S. Ernie Hicks, a veteran of the Graiseley experimental shop, who had worked long and hard, had the privilege of driving the prototype from the factory doorway in Penn Street, to turn circles and figure eights in the road.

The chassis, designed to carry a maximum pay-load of 5 cwt. (560lbs) was fitted with a body shell having a capacity of 91 cu.ft., internal length, width and height being 5' 6", 4' 5" and 3' 9" respectively, while the rear doors provided an access of 3' 8". A single, front wheel was carried in centre spring type, heavyweight, motor cycle forks, incorporating friction dampers at the front of the lower links. A car type steering wheel was fitted, coupled to the fork stem by two separate roller chains passing around sprockets of differing size to form a simple method of reduction. The prototype however, had been designed with a single chain, and although of ample strength for the job in hand, it was later changed to satisfy safety doubts raised by prospective customers. A stop was later fitted to the steering lock after a number of the early vehicles had suffered broken front fork legs, the drivers having carelessly driven away with the front wheel locked over at right angles. Early models were driven by a duplex chain via a three speed, Burman gearbox fitted with reverse, to a semi-floating rear axle incorporating a differential. To provide adjustment for the chain, the axle was attached at each end by slotted brackets pivotally carried on each side frame of the chassis. These could be locked in position after adjustment by a bolt passing throught the slot, clamping the brackets to the sides of the chassis frame. Adjustment was carried out by means of a screwed rod extending through a fixed, cross frame member to a location on the axle casing. While the two rear wheels were not sprung in relation to the chassis, pressed steel frame members supporting the body were pivoted from the front end of the chassis, the rear end of the body being supported on leaf springs, extending rearwards from the main chassis frame.

A specially designed, 'Stevens', single cylinder, water cooled, 588 c.c., side valve engine was fitted, having bore and stroke dimensions of 84 mm. x 106 mm. respectively. The engine featured dry sump lubrication, oil being supplied from a 4¾ pint oil tank mounted on the offside of the driver's compartment below the dashboard. A Bowden carburettor was chosen, gravity fed from a long, rectangular, four gallon petrol tank cross mounted internally beneath the windscreen, while a seven pint radiator was mounted immediately behind the front forks.

Inside the driver's compartment, the steering wheel and controls were centrally positioned. Early vehicles were fitted with a full width bench seat, but this was eventually replaced by a large, motorcycle saddle, the driver being required to adopt a straddled position, with his

Light-fast-cheap — and profitable

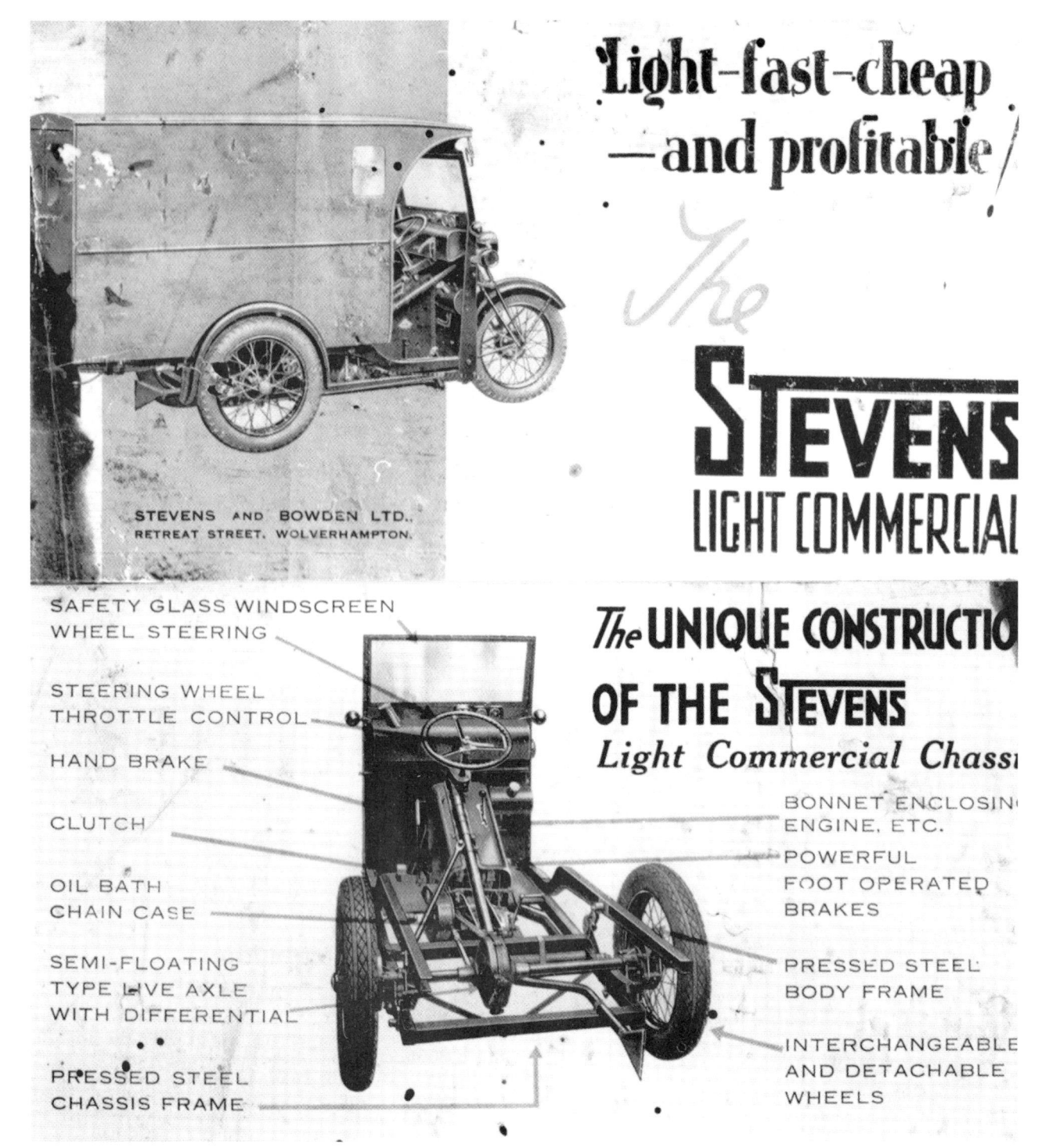

The STEVENS LIGHT COMMERCIAL

The **UNIQUE CONSTRUCTION OF THE STEVENS** *Light Commercial Chassis*

STEVENS AND BOWDEN LTD., RETREAT STREET, WOLVERHAMPTON.

- SAFETY GLASS WINDSCREEN
- WHEEL STEERING
- STEERING WHEEL THROTTLE CONTROL
- HAND BRAKE
- CLUTCH
- OIL BATH CHAIN CASE
- SEMI-FLOATING TYPE LIVE AXLE WITH DIFFERENTIAL
- PRESSED STEEL CHASSIS FRAME
- BONNET ENCLOSING ENGINE, ETC.
- POWERFUL FOOT OPERATED BRAKES
- PRESSED STEEL BODY FRAME
- INTERCHANGEABLE AND DETACHABLE WHEELS

Advertising literature for Stevens Light Commercial Vehicle.
Photo: Manufacturers catalogue.

feet planted on either side of the engine and gearbox. Starting was performed by a foot operated, kickstart lever, while a hand throttle lever was positioned from the centre of the steering wheel. The road wheels, shod with 27" x 4.00" tyres, were of quick detachable and interchangeable design, having internally expanding brakes; the two rear units being controlled by a foot pedal, whilst the single front brake was operated by a hand ratchet lever. Lighting and ignition was taken care of by a Lucas 'Magdyno' unit. On a good day, top speed would be of the order of 45 m.p.h. Total weight of the van was 7¾ cwt (868lbs.) and it was priced at £83.0s.0d. complete.

The early model was devoid of front doors, produced as a simple, cheap to run utility vehicle, ideally suited for short deliveries. When doors were later added, the vans became increasingly popular with the small tradesman.

1936 Stevens Light Commercial Van CHW 562 displaying identical livery and sign writing as used by the Company. Photo: Author.

The early production models suffered from one particular weakness, the chaindrive. This would break quite regularly, especially if the maximum pay-load was exceeded. One driver, then a teenager driving a Stevens van on a bread round in a rural district of Staffordshire during the early 1930's, recalled how when the chain broke on his van he would have to go back up the road to recover it. After getting out the rivet press from the tool box and pressing out the broken link, he would slacken the slotted chain tensioners on the rear axle, rejoin the chain with a spare link, then re-tension the chain before continuing his deliveries. He became so used to doing this, that he developed a special knack for carrying out the repair after dark which entailed holding one of the flat torches of the day in his mouth, leaving both hands free to rejoin the chain. He also used to remove the front doors during the summer months to make entry and exit much quicker, but in the winter it was 'too bloody cold'! He could also recount an episode when the front fork broke and a remote, country garage got him out of trouble by lashing a piece of 2" x 2" timber to it, allowing him to complete his deliveries. The relatively simple job of local van driving before the war, certainly had its interesting moments.

When production commenced in May 1932, the van chassis were produced in batches of six at a time. The bodies were bought in and all machining and assembly work had to be carried out in one small workshop. One of the first vans to be sold went to Tommy Silvers, an ex A.J.S. employee, who had been one of their top salesmen. So loyal was Tommy to the Stevens brothers that he asked for his vehicle to be painted in Wedgewood blue and offered to have their name and Company address sign written on each side, to give them free local advertising.

Toward the end of 1932, the Company entered into a working arrangement with Bowden (Engineers) Ltd. of London, whereby production of the van took place simultaneously in both Wolverhampton and London. This arrangement worked reasonably well for a time, but as sales increased an urgent need arose for additional manufacturing space to be made available at Wolverhampton, if the Company was to keep pace with demand. Unexpectedly, the answer came when the premises of S.Lloyd & Sons, a firm of storage and furniture removers situated opposite the Stevens workshop, became vacant. These were acquired by an old friend and close business associate Walter Hackett of Accles & Pollock, Oldbury. As an act of friendship, the premises were rented to the brothers for a small sum.

After the new business had become reasonably well established, two of the five brothers, Joe and Jack decided to accept offers of employment at Wolverhampton Auto-Machinists Ltd.,

CHW 562 as found derelict in a field near Ascot.
Photo: Alec Stevens.

a small company specializing in engine re-boring and overhauls; their decision to do so coming only after careful consideration and the realization that the new business would have difficulty in financially supporting five directors. This eventually left Harry, George and 'Billie' to continue running the business.

After a short spell of producing engines for E.C.Humphries of the O.K. Supreme Company, also A.J.W., using the name 'Ajax', they were sufficiently confident in March 1934 to re-enter the motorcycle market, choosing to do so with an attractive, up to date, 250 c.c., overhead valve single, designed by Harry Stevens. The new machine was compact and sturdily built, having wheelbase and saddle height dimensions of 54" and 27½" respectively and a fully equipped weight of 285lbs. Two models were listed; the 'D.S.1.' having a single, 2" diameter, downswept, chromium plated, exhaust pipe fitted with a cylindrical silencer and small fish-tail and the 'U.S.2' model, an upswept exhaust version. Apart from this cosmetic difference, both models shared the same overall specification. Alas the 'A.J.S.' name was no longer the property of the brothers. These second generation machines were sold under the 'Stevens' name.

A welded, duplex, cradle frame was used, fitted with Druid forks incorporating a hand adjustable shock absorber, steering damper and adjustable spindles. The cycle parts were both neat and refined. Deep section mudguards having ribbed edges were used, the rear guard having a quick, detachable section to facilitate wheel removal. The top strand of the rear chain was covered by an unusual, spring tensioned, chain guard, the rear end being rigidly secured to the brake anchor plate, whilst the sprung end allowed freedom of movement to slide back and forth when adjusting the chain. The machine was fitted with 19" diameter wheels shod with 26" x 3.25" tyres, the front having a 6" diameter

Interior of CHW 562 with engine cover and dash mounted fuel tank removed.
Note twin chain steering arrangement and Bowden carburettor.
Photo: Alec Stevens.

brake, while the rear had a 7" diameter unit; both drums being of special cast alloy bolted to ball bearing hubs and generously ribbed for greater rigidity and improved cooling.

A 3 gallon fuel tank having a right hand filler cap was used, supported on three, rubber, cushion mountings and equipped with a simple, top mounted, instrument panel containing an ammeter and lighting switch mounted longitudinally; large rubber knee grips and chromium plated name panels having rubber beadings were attached to the tank sides. Stands were fitted to both wheels, the rear being of the spring-up variety, whilst a leather tool box housed a comprehensive tool kit. In the interests of rider comfort, the machine was fitted with an adjustable, Dunlop, moulded rubber saddle, whilst the handlebar controls could be altered to suit individual tastes.

The vertically mounted engine, bearing all the old familiar hallmarks of a Stevens product, featured dry sump lubrication and was similar to late A.J.S. designs, having a chain driven, Lucas 'Magdyno' mounted directly behind the cylinder, and an oil pump built into the front of the chaincase casting, oil being stored in a 3½ pint, oil tank mounted in front of the crankcase. The engine had bore and stroke dimensions of 63 mm. x 80 mm. respectively, giving a capacity of 249 c.c. In the bottom half, a steel flywheel assembly was supported on three, heavy duty, ball races, one being on the timing side and two on the drive side, whilst a steel connecting rod carried a double row, roller big end. Two separate camshafts were employed, each being directly driven from the mainshafts, while light duralamin rockers operated from cupped push rods were mounted on stationary spindles supported on steel side plates, similar to the earlier 'Big Port' engines. Although cleverly concealed behind cover plates, the grease lubricated rockers were in fact exposed. The single ported cylinder head was finished with a polished, spherical combustion chamber and

Map showing location of Stevens Brothers (Wolverhampton) Ltd. and Stevens Screw Co.Ltd. in 1933.
Map: Jim Stevens.

featured a sharply inclined induction port, the valves being controlled by duplex, aero springs. A three ring, alloy piston having a fully floating, gudgeon pin was used, giving a compression ratio of 7.25:1.

The engine was coupled to a four speed, Burman gearbox with multiple plate clutch, being offered with a choice of foot or hand controls, and providing ratios of 6.06, 7.76, 9.93 and 16.58:1. The primary chain transmission incorporated a shock absorber mounted on the engine shaft and was housed in a fully enclosed, two piece, oil-bath case, the vertical joint between the two halves being gripped and sealed by an outer metal beading containing a special, rubber type seal.

Lucas 'Magdyno' ignition and six volt lighting set were included in the standard equipment, an 8" diameter headlamp and small, cylindrical, rear light being fitted as well as a push button, high-frequency horn.

Other than gold lining, the machines were finished in black enamel, all bright parts being chromium plated. Wheel rims were chromium plated with black centres lined gold, while mudguards were black with ribs pinstriped gold, the rear carrying a Stevens transfer, while the front had a chevron pattern transfer with the Stevens name inset. On the early machines however, there was a choice of petrol tank finish, this being either a chromium plated finish with black panels lined gold, or black enamel with continuous gold lines running from front to back, encompassing the rubber knee pads.

The new, 250 c.c. Stevens, heralded a welcome return of the brothers to the motorcycle industry. Blessed with exceptional handling and brakes, it was a joy to ride and was soon to prove popular. Due to a limitation of space and finances, a large proportion of the components were bought in, assembly being restricted to a batch of twelve machines at one time. Meanwhile production of the three wheel, commercial vehicle had been transferred across the road to the newly acquired premises. Both the 'D.S.1' and 'U.S.2' models were offered with a choice of Bowden or Amal carburettor and were priced at £51.0s.0d. complete.

Although remaining largely unchanged, a number of detailed improvements to the 250 c.c. models were announced in September for the 1935 season. These included flexible, handlebar mountings to insulate road shocks and collapsible footrest mountings to avoid breakage in the event of impact. A larger, combined stop and tail light was specified, switch operated from an extension on the rear brake pedal arm, while the earlier, leather toolbox was replaced by a steel counterpart, carrying an identical, chevron pattern transfer as displayed on the front mudguard. On the mechanical side, lubrication was extended to the inlet valve guide and the rear chain, whilst a speedometer was available as an optional extra, being driven from the front hub. Small alterations to the finish took place, the petrol tank being standardized in black (chrome being offered at extra cost) having two, separate, gold lined sections on each side, the largest carrying a gold name transfer inset.

Soon after these improvements had been announced, the Company introduced a 350 c.c. model. Close examination soon revealed however, that the larger capacity model was almost identical to its smaller brother, except the bore and stroke dimensions of the engine had been enlarged to 74 mm. and 81 mm. respectively and that the compression ratio had been reduced to 7:1, whilst gear ratios were altered to 5.5, 7, 9 and 15:1. The new machine was offered in two distinct forms, the model 'H.L.3' having a high level exhaust system, and the 'L.L.4' being a low level version. Both models were listed at £52.0s.0d. complete, just £1.0s.0d. more than the 250 c.c. machine.

A subsequent road test conducted by the 'Motor Cycle' in January 1935 commented on

1935 Stevens '350'.
Photo: Author.

Close-up view showing the compact lines of the Stevens 350c.c. engine. Note the down-draught carburettor.
Photo: Author.

its refined nature, while reporting its road holding as being the same as a T.T. thoroughbred combined with nigh on perfect brakes, the Company's slogan 'The Most Refined Sports Machine In The World' being justified.

In April 1935, the Company completed its range with the addition of a 500 c.c. single. Generally the overall specification was similar to the smaller models, except the frame was larger (55" wheelbase), heavier and incorporated lugs for attaching a sidecar. Two types were available, the 'H.P.6' (high pipe exhaust) and 'L.P.5' (low pipe exhaust). A larger, 3¼ gallon petrol tank was used having a left hand filler, while engine oil was carried in a separate, 3 pint tank mounted beneath the saddle on the offside. The front brake was increased to 7" diameter to match the rear and a new, sprung loaded chainguard was fitted incorporating separate covers for top and bottom chain strands. The engine had bore and stroke dimensions of 79 mm. x 101 mm. respectively, giving a capacity of 495 c.c. Unlike the smaller models, the engine was fitted with double hairpin springs, and had a lower compression ratio of 6.5:1. A Burman, four speed gearbox with foot control was fitted as standard, the gear ratios being 4.4, 5.55, 7.43 and 11.75:1. A hand operated control was available however, if preferred. The weight of the machine, fully equipped, scaled 316 lbs.

while a maximum speed of 85 m.p.h. was claimed. The price complete with Lucas electric lighting was £63.0s.0d. A competition version in trials trim was available for £6.0s.0d. extra. This also applied to the 250 c.c. and 350 c.c. models.

Soon after the 500 c.c. models had been added to the range, George Stevens, who was in overall charge of sales, took steps to expand the Company's export market. On one occasion George, together with solicitor Frank Cooper, entertained two Japanese visitors to a business lunch with the purpose of selling Stevens motorcycles to Japan. One of the Japanese introduced himself as an interpreter, saying that the other, who was in authority, could not speak English but only he could make decisions. At the luncheon meeting, the interpreter excused himelf and left the table, leaving his chief with George and Frank. George said: "This is how we will play it", Frank gave him a mighty kick beneath the table and changed the topic. Afterwards Frank explained to the indignant George: "You bloody fool, that man could understand and speak English as well as you can, it was just a trick to find out what our plans were". Fortunately in the end everything went according to plan, and George was successful in completing the deal.

While the motorcycle business had been steadily getting off the ground, careful redesign work had been undertaken to overcome the three wheeled, commercial vehicle's main weakness, its chaindrive. In October 1935, the Company announced important changes to its transmission system. In place of the fragile chain, a shaft drive was used, the mainshaft of the sturdy, three speed gearbox now being arranged fore and aft instead of across the chassis. At the rear, the chassis was now completely sprung. Two, half elliptic springs were interposed between the axle and the main chassis frame. The improved design enabled a pay load of up to 8 cwt. (896 lbs.) to be carried, representing a remarkable improvement over the previous model. The new chassis was offered with a choice of van or open truck body, both models being priced at eighty nine guineas (£93.9s.0d.).

Changes to the motorcycle range announced in the autumn of 1935 were largely cosmetic. Generally, all petrol tanks were lined in blue and gold, blue being the predominant colour, while the black wheel centres of the chromium plated rims were edged in blue. All models received new, heavily valanced, front mudguards, each having a lower mud apron, while the tubular fish-tail exhausts on the 350 c.c. and

Ace rider Tommy Deadman astride his successful Stevens motorcycle in 1935.
Photo: Lilian Deadman.

500 c.c. models were replaced by megaphone style silencers.

Toward the end of 1936, the Company chose to discontinue its production of the three wheeled, commercial vehicles after some five hundred had been built and concentrate its efforts solely on motorcycle manufacture. Despite the earlier improvements to the transmission and load carrying capacity, sales of the commercial vehicles had declined, prospective buyers it would seem, preferring to spend their hard earned cash on vehicles affording more comfort and four wheels.

The Stevens motorcycles however, were proving extremely popular, with the factory producing some two hundred machines per year. As with the earlier A.J.S. marketing strategy, the Company had boosted their sales by successfully entering their machines in competition, the 500 c.c. version proving extremely successful in the hands of their chief tester and works competition rider, Tommy Deadman.

Only a few changes were made to the 1937 range, these being limited to the fitting of a larger, 3¼ gallon, petrol tank having a left hand filler cap and a megaphone style silencer to the 250 c.c. models. The following year, the brothers were approached by George Brough of

The Directors of The Stevens Screw Company Ltd., 1948.
Standing from left: Daisy Jones (daughter of Lucy Stevens), William Stevens ('Billie'), William Simpson (married to Ethel Stevens) and Gladys Barrett (Daisy Jones sister).
Seated from left: Lily Woods (née Stevens) and Daisy Weir (née Stevens).
Photo: Jim Stevens.

Nottingham, then making what was considered to be the 'Rolls Royce' of motorcycles, the famous 'Brough Superior'. George wanted them to build an engine for a new machine that was to be exhibited at the 1938 Motor Cycle Exhibition at Earls Court. According to George, it would be a bike to end all bikes. It was called the 'Dream', or the 'Golden Dream' as it later became known, with its gold finish. It had a 1000 c.c., four cylinder, horizontally opposed engine with crankshafts geared together, set across the frame and a four speed gearbox with shaft drive. Apparently none of the Stevens was particularly happy about the design, but kept quiet about it. Although they managed to complete the work on time, sadly the project remained just a pipe dream. Only one 'Golden Dream' was ever built, fortunately this is now on display at the National Motorcycle Museum in Birmingham. Production of Stevens motorcycles came to an end in the Summer of 1938, by which time about one thousand had left the factory. With comparatively limited production, the 'Stevens' marque became a rare bird.

With the threat of war looming, it was decided to concentrate on general engineering, as it was obvious that contracts for motor cycles from the War Department would be given to the larger manufacturers. Throughout the period leading up to the outbreak of war, Britain was rearming, preparing to stand against the might of the German army. The Company was directed to defence work, mainly producing aircraft components for the Ministry of Aircraft Production; one of many small engineering firms that helped Britain to victory through those dark years.

There were however, two motorcycles still left to be made. Close cousins Alec and Jim Stevens, both sixteen years of age at the time, quite naturally wanted motorcycles to ride. Their fathers, Joe Stevens Junior and 'Billie', reckoned there would be enough bits and pieces left over at the works to complete two machines. These were the last Stevens motorcycles ever made.

After the war, the Stevens did not return to motor cycle manufacture. Britain needed rebuilding and there was plenty of general engineering work on offer. Old age and illness gradually took their toll, until only Jack Stevens was left. Appropriately it was his initials, A.J.S. that will always remain as the family's memorial. He died in 1956.

The last remaining Stevens link with engineering in Wolverhampton, was finally broken when the Stevens Screw Company Ltd., founded in 1906 by Joe Stevens Senior, closed its Retreat Street factory in December 1992. For the first time in almost a century, there was not a Stevens family engineering business in Wolverhampton.

A.J.S. *of* WOLVERHAMPTON

Appendices

Appendix 1

A.J.S. Transfer Details

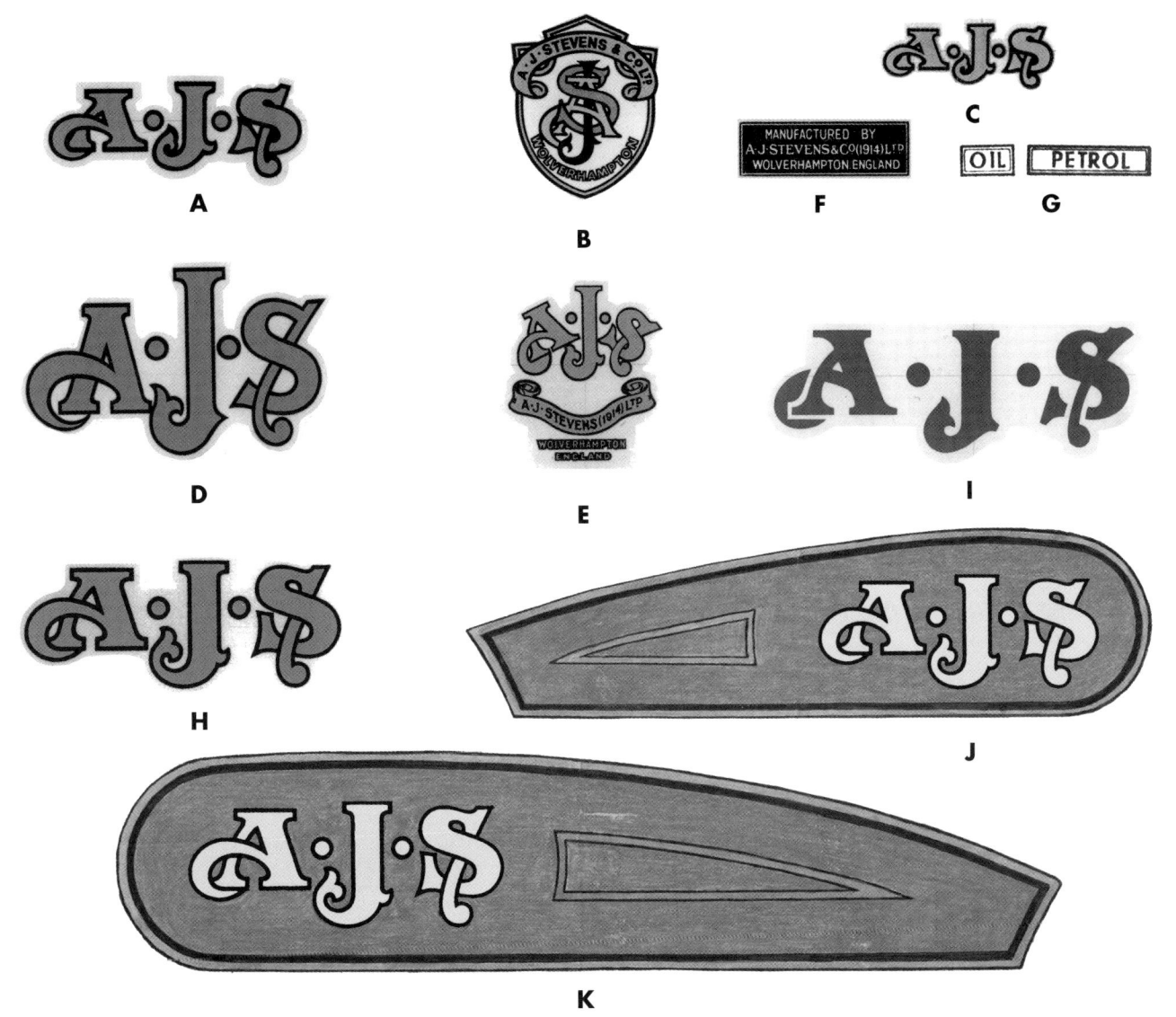

Type	Size (mm)	Year	Location	Finish
A	75 x 28	1912 - 28	Petrol tank & sidecar door.	Gold with black outline.
B	54 x 45	1914 - 27	Headstock, clutch cover & sidecar door.	Blue, black and red initials on cream ground. Gold outer shield with black outline.
C	48 x 17	1922 - 29	Rear mudguard.	Gold with black outline.
		1928 - 29	Clutch cover.	
D	89 x 54	1928 - 31	Sidecar door & body.	Gold with black outline.
		1930 - 31	Rear mudguards 9 h.p. car.	
E	51 x 46	1927 - 31	Headstock.	Gold with black outline.
F	51 x 17	1921 - 28	Top tube & sidecar chassis.	Gold lettering & lines on black ground.
G	10 x 6 & 25 x 6	1914 - 28	Petrol tank.	Gold.
H	87 x 35	1924 - 31	Sidecar door & body.	Gold with black outline.
		1930 - 31	Petrol tank.	
I	102 x 35	1924 - 26	Wireless horn speakers.	Gold.
J	210 x 56	1929	Petrol tank (250 c.c. & 350 c.c.)	Gold initials & lines with black outline on magenta ground.
K	261 x 58	1929	Petrol tank (500 c.c. & 996 c.c.)	Gold initials & lines with black outline on magenta ground.

Prior to 1912 A.J.S. initials were painted gold on black panels lined green. All original transfers were produced by Harold E. Peace & Co. Birmingham. Transfers A - I kindly supplied by the Vintage Motor Cycle Club Transfer Service

/ Appendix 2

Patents held by A.J.S. & Stevens Bros. (Wolverhampton) Ltd.

Application Number	Application Date	Applicants	Details
11886/1912	20.5.12	A.J.S. & J. Wood	Claw clutches for gearbox
26015/1912	13.11.12	A.J.S. & H. Stevens	Petrol level indicator
17464/1913		Abandoned	
24173/1914	25.10.13	A.J.S. & G. Stevens	Gear change lever
108,077	14.10.16	A.J.S. & H. Stevens	Transmission shock absorber
133,858	8.1.19	A.J.S. & H. Stevens	M/C rear stand with lever
139,331	31.3.19	A.J.S. & A.J. Stevens	M/C foot board
144,894	11.7.19	A.J.S. & H. Stevens	Frame work of 3 wheeled motor vehicle
152,131	11.7.19	A.J.S. & H. Stevens	Ignition system
168,795	30.1.20	A.J.S. & A.J. Stevens	Leaf spring
169,906	30.9.20	A.J.S. & H. Stevens	Wedge type head gasket
174,501	29.11.20	A.J.S. & G. Stevens	Grommet for tube passing through sheet
175,079	16.11.20	C.W. Haywood & A.J.S.	Draught and rain excluder for sidecar
175,120	29.11.20	A.J.S. & H. Stevens	Gearbox mounting frame
175,407	16.11.20	C.W. Haywood & A.J.S.	Sidecar seats
175,446	29.11.20	A.J.S. & H. Stevens	Detachable front wheel
175,722	16.11.20	C.W. Haywood & A.J.S.	Sidecar side screen
200,239	19.4.22	C.A. Ely & A.J. Stevens	Lubricant controller for racing engine
209,986	10.3.23	A.J.S. & H. Stevens	Variable capacitor
225,358	9.11.23	A.J.S. & C.W. Haywood	Sidecar mudguard
227,210	15.10.23	A.J.S. & J. Stevens	Shock absorber for front forks
227,222	20.10.23	A.J.S. & C.W. Haywood	Wireless cabinets
228,836	16.11.23	A.J.S. & C.W. Haywood	Beading to cover joints between metal sheets
230,950	16.1.24	A.J.S. & C.W. Haywood	Sidecar construction
231,973	29.1.24	A.J.S. & A.J. Stevens	Dry sump lubrication, scavenge from below crankcase
238,280	10.5.24	A.J.S. & A.J. Stevens	Petrol tank knee pads
243,146	3.11.24	A.J.S. & H. Stevens	Wireless capacitor
244,555	21.10.24	A.J.S. & C.W. Haywood	Sidecar construction
245,549	3.11.24	A.J.S. & H. Stevens	Coil holder
246,233	3.11.24	A.J.S. & H. Stevens	Electrical resistor
246,234	3.11.24	A.J.S. & H. Stevens	Electrical switch for wireless
246,235	3.11.24	A.J.S. & H. Stevens	Electrical connector
251,062	13.3.25	A.J.S. & C.W. Haywood	M/C cover
262,981	30.1.26	A.J.S. & A.J. Stevens	Gear lever assembly
263,978	6.11.25	A.J.S. & H. Stevens	Rear wheel alignment gauge
267,693	24.2.26	A.J.S. & C.W. Haywood	Sidecar suspension
268,570	19.5.26	A.J.S. H. & A.J. Stevens	Pushrod end
272,361	28.8.26	A.J.S. & H.C. Williams	Wireless valve holder
272,721	28.8.26	A.J.S. & H.C. Williams	Intermediate frequency transformer
273,925	28.8.26	A.J.S. & H.C. Williams	Assembly of wireless receiver (7 valve superhet)
273,326	28.8.26	A.J.S. & H.C. Williams	Variable capacitor and drive
278,800	13.7.26	A.J.S. & H. Taylor	Thermionic valve
281,367	28.8.26	A.J.S. & H.C. Williams	Inductance coil
286,478	29.3.27	A.J.S., A.J. & H.Stevens	Oil feed to big-end
288,025	29.3.27	A.J.S., A.J. & H.Stevens	O.H.C. engine
288,804	29.3.27	A.J.S., A.J. & H.Stevens	O.H.C. shaft arrangement
290,413	29.3.27	A.J.S., A.J. & H.Stevens	Crankcase oil filter
298,751	10.9.27	A.J.S. & H.C. Williams	Loudspeaker
313,738	5.6.28	A.J.S. & A.J. Stevens	Oil tray cast into timing chain case
318,566	5.6.28	A.J.S. & A.J. Stevens	Speedo drive from gearbox
320,496	29.8.28	A.J.S. & J. Stevens	Steering damper in steering head
321,582	8.12.28	A.J.S. & A.J. Stevens	Crankcase oil filter
325,198	6.11.28	A.J.S. & H. Stevens	Rear hub cush drive using rubber
328,101	6.4.29	A.J.S. & A.J. Stevens	Slipper type piston
333,413	29.8.29	A.J.S. & H. Stevens	Saddle with water deflector
335,700	29.8.29	A.J.S. & H. Stevens	Front wheel taper roller bearings
342,037	19.11.29	A.J.S. & H. Stevens	Oil tank

Stevens Bros. (Wolverhampton) Ltd.

397,913	26.1.33	Stevens Bros. & H. Stevens	3 wheeled vehicle
399,067	26.1.33	Stevens Bros. & H. Stevens	3 wheeled vehicle - steering

Appendix 3

A.J.S. Commercial Vehicle Chassis Lists

These lists are as complete as distance of time allows, detailing all known vehicles. Quite often the body builder is not known, these would be one of many, small such manufacturers existing at that time. Except from photographs, it is not possible to distinguish between normal and forward control versions of the 'Pilot'. As a rule the normal control would seat not more than twenty four, above this capacity should be forward control. If the owner's name is in brackets, the first owner is not known; that given is the first subsequent owner.

The standard body code as used by historians is used either side of the seating capacity.

Prefix letter.

B   Service Bus
C   Luxury Coach
DP Dual purpose (coach seats in a bus shell)
F   Full fronted bodywork

Suffix Letter

F   Front entrance
R   Rear entrance (behind rear axle)
D   Dual entrance

'Pilot'

Chassis Number	Registration Number	Bodybuilder and Number	Seating Details	Entered Service	First Owner
101	VR 3646		C26	10/29	(A.A.Mason, Leicester).
102	UY 5436		Goods		Accles & Pollock Ltd., Oldbury.
103	UT 5634	Willowbrook 2284	B24F	7/29	H.Bircher, Ibstock.
104	RF 5813		B26	5/29	R.W.Stevens, Stafford.
105	VO 2118		C26F	8/29	Retford Coachways, Retford.
106	TM 5935		B26	11/29	E.J.Cooper, Elstow.
107	TE 8025		C26	5/29	
108	CK 4171		C26F	7/29	J.G.Hodgson, Preston.
109	WX 348		C26R	5/29	C.A.Whiteley, Maltby.
110					
111	VH 2219		C R	/29	G.Chapman, Huddersfield.
112					
113	DE 7121	Thomas & Thomas	B26F	7/29	D.H.Roberts & Son, Newport, Pembs.
114					
115	VO 1774	Taylor	C26F	6/29	Retford Coachways, Retford.
116	DT 1534		C26	6/29	E.A.Heath, Doncaster.
117	UP 3000		20	6/29	(Mrs.S.J.Knight, Denton).
118	WX 3935		B20	3/30	J.Hardcastle, Tanshelf.
119					
120	PG 9785		C26	/30	F.E.Tapp, Coulsdon.
121	VY 1122		C26D	6/29	R.Whithead, York.
122	UW 9414	Waveney	C20D	12/29	Ruthven, S.W.1.
123	UW 9413	Waveney	C20D	12/29	Ruthven, S.W.1.
124	GS 2452	Crerar	B24	3/31	P.Crerar, Crieff.
125	RF 7045		C26	4/30	C.Collier, Bilston.
126	UW 9412	Waveney	C20D	12/29	Ruthven, S.W.1.
127					
128	BR 7572	Blagg	B26	9/29	G.W.Hetherington & Co., Coundon.

129					
130					
131	UW 9415	Waveney	C20D	11/29	Ruthven, S.W.1.
132	VJ 2039		B26F	7/29	P.B.Davies, Bodenham.
133	UP 3173	Duple 1625	C20	7/29	J.E.Smith, Bishop Auckland.
134	WX 856	Lewis & Crabtree	C26D	7/29	Wilson Haigh, Holmfirth.
135	FV 399		26	7/29	D.Roberts, Empire Hotel, Blackpool.
136	YC 7988		B26	12/29	E.L.Ford, Alcombe.
137					
138	VX 3305		B24	12/29	J.A.Mazengarb, Goodmayes.
139					
140	VX 2120	Petty	DP26F	8/29	Wickford Carriage Co., Wickford.
141	TH 619		24	4/30	Bevan Bros., Clynderwen.
142					
143	WH 2404			3/30	Thomas, Bolton.
144	UT 9407	Willowbrook 2369	C24	7/31	J.Walker, Shepshed.
145	UT 8110	Willowbrook 2368	B26	12/30	C.W.Bishop, Asfordby.
146	UT 8095	Willowbrook 2376	B24	12/30	L.Wood, Ratby.
147	VR 6479		C26	3/30	Prestwich Garage Co. Ltd., Openshaw.
148	BR 7573		B26F	9/29	G.W.Hetherington & Co., Coundon.
149	UT 6328		B26F	1/30	F.R.Wadd, Syston.
150	VO 6246	Willowbrook 2377	B24	7/31	J.Gibson, Mansfield.
151	UT 7639	Willowbrook 2378	B26	8/30	A.Underwood, South Wigston.
152	SK 1658		B20	7/30	J.J.Robertson, Wick.
153	WH 2416		C26	3/30	J.J.Battersby, Bolton.
154	EN 4419		C20	2/30	Auty Brothers, Bury.
155	TG 2990		24	3/32	W.T.Jones, Bryncethin.
156					
157	FV 1045		C26	5/30	Waddington & Son, Blackpool.
158					
159	VR 6634		C26	4/30	R.Connolly, Gorton.
160					
161	UT 7017	Abbott	B26F	4/30	J.H.B., H.B. & R.L.Watson, Waltham-on-the-Wold.
162	UK 9157		C26	7/30	A.J.S. Demonstrator.
163					
164	YD 2142		C26	6/31	E.L.Ford, Alcombe.
165	VC 4718		C26F	5/30	A.Cox, Coventry.
166					
167					
168					
169					
170	GF 5288	Reall	FC26R	4/30	Mansford, E.2.
171	EX 2590	United 1975	C26D	4/30	W.J.Haylett, Great Yarmouth.
172	EA 4370		C26	3/30	G.Hill, West Bromwich.
173	TF 1741			5/30	
174	EX 2863	United 2587	C26	6/31	W.J.Haylett, Great Yarmouth.
175	VX 4253	Metcalfe	B25D	2/30	A.E.Blane, Romford.
176	RF 7083	Willowbrook 2384	B26R	4/30	J.Lomas, Leek.
177	UT 7301	Willowbrook 2376	B20	5/30	J.Walker, Shepshed.
178	VH 3014			/30	G.Chapman, Huddersfield.
179	VX 5344		B26	4/30	T.Webster & Sons, Laindon.
180	SX 3037		24	/30	J.Beuken & Son, Whitburn.
181	JN 341		20	7/30	Rochford & District Motor Services.

182	EN 4600		C20	6/30	Auty Brothers, Bury.
183	RP 8974	Grose	B26	6/30	M.E.Jelley, Cosgrove.
184	VR 7518		26	5/30	(Neal, Newtown).
185	VX 7659	Petty	C25F	9/30	G.Barney, Grays.
186	MW 7564		C26F	6/30	N.King & R.Jones, Bromham.
187	HB 3730	Willowbrook 2440	B26	5/30	Jones Brothers, Treharris.
188	WX 3229		B26F	3/30	A.C.Staff, Upton.
189	AG 7081	Duple 2403	B26F	/31	C.B.Law, Prestwick.
190	LG 4068		26	4/30	H.Sykes, Sale.
191					
192	UR 7002	Petty	DP24F	6/30	D & E Petty Demonstrator.
193	LG 4321		C26	5/30	J.Pye, Heswall.
194	VX 7495	Petty	C25	9/30	G.Barney, Grays.
195	VO 4130		C26F	6/30	(A., A.E.& F. Blackbourn, Grimsby).
196					
197	CC 9341		26	6/30	J.Williams & Son, Llandudno.
198	TF 1598		B	4/30	
199					
200	JN 485		B26	10/30	Rochford & Disrict Motor Services.
201	UR 8528	Petty	B24F	1/31	A.B.Johnson, Watford.
202	VX 7227		B24	8/30	A.J.Springett, Rayleigh.
203	VX 7031		B24F	7/30	Mrs E.S.Furber, Colchester.
204	NV 274		26	5/31	Mrs.S.J.Knight, Denton.
205					
206					
207	VJ 3056		C26	7/30	P.B.Davies, Bodenham.
208					
209	NV 549			8/31	A.Basford, Greens Norton.
210	KX 6376		C24	2/31	F.H.Crook, Booker.
211	WD 1778	Petty	B24	1/31	J.Edwards, Bishops Itchington.
212					
213	OU 8832	Petty	B26F	5/31	W & C Stacey, Odiham.
214					
215	PL 7661	Petty	C26	/31	F.E.Tapp, Coulsdon.
216					
217	VT 6619		Goods	6/31	Beech's Garage, Hanley.
218	FV 1710	Burlingham	C20D	3/31	Leamington Touring Services, Blackpool.
219					
220	TG 3014		20	3/32	W.T.Jones, Bryncethin.
221					
222	NV 416		24	7/31	C.E.Charles, Middleton Cheney.
223	KX 7469	Petty	B20F	8/31	W.J.Cassels, Chesham.
224	DG 4390	London Lorries	C24F	5/32	H.F.Warner, Tewkesbury.
225					
226	HA 7200		C26F	4/31	Gilbert & Houghton, Smethwick.

Improved 'Pilot'

1001	VD 230	Stewart	B26F	10/30	G.Greenshields, Salsburgh.
1002	HX 3507		C26	4/31	C.J.Maillon, Staines.
1003	NV 388		26	6/31	W.Kingston, Blakesley.
1004	OU 6047	Petty	B26F	6/30	Mrs E.G.Kent, Kingsclere, Hampshire.
1005	PG 9385	Petty	B26R	/30	J.R.Fox, Woking.
1006	TF 2985		B	8/30	T.W.Pusill, Penketh.
1007	JN 692		B26	12/30	Rochford & District Motor Services.
1008	VX 7574	Petty	DP26F	9/30	A.J.Springett, Rayleigh.

1009	TF 3767		B	12/30	T.W.Pusill, Penketh.
1010	TH 1292		B26	9/30	S.t.Treharne, Ponthenry.
1011					
1012	DG 3156		C26F	8/31	H.H.Lewton, Wotton-under-Edge.
1013					
1014	EV 1785	Petty	C26F	6/31	F.H. & D.J. Rose, Chelmsford.

The following are known as 'Pilots'; chassis numbers cannot be detected. 201 is a duplication.

201	CK 4350			5/30	Woodcock? Heskin?
	CH 8750		B F	11/29	B.F.Polkerd, Derby.
	FV 399		26	7/29	D.Roberts, Blackpool.
	LG 4044			/3-	
	LG 4048			/3-	
	MT 5634			/29	
	OU 6047	Petty	B26F	5/31	Mrs E.G.Kent, Baughurst.
	RB 3372			1/31	(E.Stanton, Tipton).
	RF 8840		20	8/31	D.R.Fox, Lichfield.
	RV 851			3/31	Mrs. M.V.Fuger, Warsash.
	SC 4807		C20D	/29	W.M. Herd, Edinburgh.
	UP 3141			/29	F.G.Cowey, Coundon.
	UP 3487			/29	F.G.Cowey, Coundon.
	VB 6556	Waveney	FC24F	/30	Southern Limited Stop Motor Services, Croydon.
	VB	Waveney	FC24F	/30	Southern Limited Stop Motor Services, Croydon.
	VD - - 94		20	1/30	(W.Rendall, Broxburn).
	VR 6146			/3-	A.E.Lingley, Sale.
	VR 8871			/3-	W.A.Strowger, Manchester.

'Admiral'

3001					
3002	SC 7566	Hayward	C20D	/30	W.M.Herd, Edinburgh.
3003	FV 2541		C20	3/32	Leamington Touring Services, Blackpool.
3004	BU 6869		C26	5/31	H.Shearing, Oldham.
3005					
3006	TF 4635		20	3/31	(C.Smith, Blackpool).
3007	TF 5494		C	5/31	(Howards, Southport).
3008	VC 8426	Auto-Cellulose	C26D	5/31	B.Sephton, Coventry.

'Commodore'

5000	JV 550		C32F	/31	W.& A.E.Blackbourn, Grimsby.
5001	VX 3765		C26D	1/30	J.A.Mazengarb, Goodmayes.
5002	RP 8235		B32F	12/29	Mrs.S.J.Knight, Denton.
5003	BU 5374		C32	3/30	T.F.Shaw, Oldham.
5004	WX 2538		B32	1/30	J.J.Granter, Upton.

5005	VX 3976		C27	1/30	A.J.Evans, Ilford.
5006	UT 6792		B26	3/30	F.R.Wadd, Syston.
5007	HA 6361	Auto - Cellulose	FC32C	2/30	Gilbert & Houghton, Smethwick.
5008					
5009	VX 3977		C27	1/30	A.J.Evans, Ilford.
5010	UP 5614			5/31	G.W.Hetherington & Co., Coundon.
5011	RV 559		C32	5/31	H.W.B.Hewitt, Southsea, Hampshire.
5012	VO 5941	Willowbrook 2505	C32F	5/31	W.H.Hursthouse, Mansfield.
5013					
5014	VH 2950		B30F	/30	G.Chapman, Huddersfield.
5015	EB 8491		B32F	3/30	B.Washington, Littleport.
5016	EA 4464	Buckingham	C30D	4/30	G.Hill, West Bromwich.
5017	VR 7637			4/30	(W.Harris, Argoed).
5018	VX 3978		C27	1/30	A.J.Evans, Ilford.
5019	JV 535		Goods	7/31	G.Coggan, Grimsby.
5020	DE 7690	Thomas & Thomas	32	5/30	Edwards Brothers, Crymmych.
5021	GH 3049		C30	7/30	Pilot Coaches, S.W.1.
5022	SX 3074		B32	/30	Campbell Brothers, Whitburn.
5023	GF 7521		C32F	4/30	(S.Allison, Cleethorpes).
5024	HE 4870	Warwick Motor Bodies	C32D	4/30	Cooper & Hollinsworth, Barnsley.
5025	WM 5013		32	5/30	Bullock & France, Southport.
5026	UK 9640	Hayward	B32D	/30	A.J.S. Demonstrator.
5027	DH 7935		C32	4/30	G.H.Turner, Walsall.
5028	VX 5543		C26D	4/30	J.A.Mazengarb, Goodmayes.
5029	RF 8518		C32	5/31	Queen Street Motors, Bilston.
5030	VJ 2756		C30	4/30	P.B. Davies, Bodenham.
5031					
5032	NV 434	Petty		7/31	Mrs S.J.Knight, Denton.
5033	PG 8380		B30	/30	F.E.Tapp, Coulsdon.
5034	HB 3996		B26	8/31	Jones Brothers, Treharris.
5035	HX 4032		30	5/31	C.J.Maillon, Staines.
5036	SX 3254	Roberts	B32F	/31	W.Rendall & Company, Broxburn.
5037					
5038	DJ 502B		C30	7/31	W.S.Ellison, St.Helens.
5039	GP 3398		32	7/31	(Mrs.S.J.Knight, Northampton).
5040					
5041					
5042	EV 2459	Petty	C30F	7/31	F.H. & D.J.Rose, Chelmsford.
5043					
5044	JV 611		Goods	7/31	T.J.Holmwood.
5045	YD 2822	Bence	C32F	7/31	Binding & Payne, Clevedon.
5046					
5047					
5048	KX 7575		B32F	10/31	F.H.Crook, Booker.
5049	DM 7538	Hayward	B32F	7/31	E.Jones, Flint.
5050	WX 8418	Petty	C30F	11/31	Lancashire & Yorkshire Motors, Shafton.

5051	EA 5181	Buckingham	C30C	3/32	G.Hill, West Bromwich.
5052	DE 8693	Thomas & Thomas	B32R	3/32	D.H.Roberts & Son, Newport, Pembs.
5053	MV 1134		C30	12/31	C.J.Maillon, Staines.
5054					
5055					
5056					
5057					
5058					
5059					
5060	DE 8771	Thomas & Thomas	B32R	5/32	Edwards Brothers, Crymmych.
5061					
5062					
5063	DJ 5137		C30	8/31	W.S.Ellison, St.Helens.
5064	NV 598		32	12/31	C.E.Charles, Middleton Cheney.

Further 'Commodores' for which chassis numbers are not known.

JD 383	Wycombe	C32F	4/30	A.J.Evans, E.15.
JV 550		32	/31	A., A.E. & F. Blackbourn, Grimsby.
RV 559		32	/31	H.W.B.Hewitt, Southsea.
VD 1138		32	11/31	I.Hutchison, Overtown.

Great Witley 'Commodores'.

1	DAB 341	Moore	C32F	6/39	A.Moore & Sons, Great Witley.
2	EWP 476	Harrington	C32F	6/46	A.Moore & Sons, Great Witley.
3	GWP 20	Moore	C33F	6/48	A.Moore & Sons, Great Witley.
4	HWP 569	Moore	C33F	12/49	A.Moore & Sons, Great Witley.

The following vehicles are known to have existed, type and chassis numbers are unknown.

VX 7580	Petty	C24F	9/30	G.Barney, Grays.
JD 547		C26	5/30	Johnson & Shepherd, E.15.
KX 5901		B26	10/30	A.V.Jones, Sands.
MW 6161		B26	12/29	W.C.King & Son, Nomansland.
RF 8499		C	5/31	C.J.Tilstone, Stafford.
RF 8717		C	7/31	J.Worthington, Stafford.
UK 5054		Goods	1/30	A.J.S. Demonstrator.
UK 8221 or UK 8281		32	1/30	A.J.S.Demonstrator.
UK 8446		32	3/30	A.J.S.Demonstrator.
UP 3093		C20F	1/30	J.E.Smith, Bishop Auckland.
VR 303		24	5/29	
VR 7509			/30.	

Appendix 4

A.J.S. Motorcycle Model Specifications

YEAR	MODEL	No. Cylinders	Engine Type	Bore/Stroke (mm.)	Capacity (c.c.)	Speeds	Drive	Carburettor	Ignition	Machine Weight (lbs.)	Price	Serial N°s
1910-11	A	1	S.V.	70 x 76	292	1	Chain/Belt	Brown & Barlow	U.H. Magneto	110	37 Gns (£38.85)	UNKNOWN
	B	"	"	"	"	2	Chain	"	"	120	44 Gns (£46.20)	
1912	A	1	S.V.	70 x 82	315	1	Chain/Belt	AMAC	U.H. Magneto	132	37 Gns (£38.85)	Frame 300 — Engine 1300 — G/Box 150 —
	B	"	"	"	"	2	Chain	"	"	140	44 Gns (£46.20)	
	D	2	"	"	631	2	"	"	"	208	60 Gns (£63.00)	UNKNOWN
1913	B	1	S.V.	70 x 91	349	2 or 3	Chain	AMAC	U.H. Magneto	150	46 Gns (£48.30) 51 Gns (£53.55)	Frame 1000 — Engine 2000 — G/Box 2000 —
	D	2	"	74 x 81	696	3	"	"	"	255	69 Gns (£72.45)	Frame 917 Engine — G/Box —
1914	B Standard	1	S.V.	70 x 91	349	2 or 3	Chain	AMAC	U.H. Magneto	160	47 Gns (£49.35) 50 Gns (£52.50)	Frame 2900 — Engine 2700 — G/Box 2700 —
	B Sporting	"	"	"	"	"	"	"	"	"	47 Gns (£49.35) 50 Gns (£52.50)	
	D	2	"	74 x 87	748	3	"	"	"	276	70 Gns (£73.50)	All Matching 4318 - 4396
1915	A	2	S.V.	65 x 83	550	3	Chain	AMAC	Splitdorf Magneto	236	66 Gns (£69.30)	5701 - 6299
	B Standard	1	"	74 x 81	349	2 or 3	"	"	Thompson Bennett Magneto	160	47 Gns (£49.35) 50 Gns (£52.50)	5056 - 5685
	B Sporting	"	"	70 x 91	"	"	"	"	"	160	47 Gns (£49.35) 50 Gns (£52.50)	
	D	2	"	74 x 87	748	3	"	"	Splitdorf Magneto	280	72 Gns (£75.60)	6418 - 7200

YEAR	MODEL	No. Cylinders	Engine Type	Bore/Stroke (mm.)	Capacity (c.c.)	Speeds	Drive	Carburettor	Ignition	Machine Weight (lbs.)	Price	Serial N°s
1916	A	2	S.V.	65 x 83	550	3	Chain	AMAC	Dixie Magneto	236	£76 - 0s - 0d	5701 – 6299
	B	1	=	74 x 81	349	2 or 3	=	=	Thompson Bennett Magneto	160	£55 - 0s - 0d £58 - 0s - 0d	7201 – 7317
	D	2	=	74 x 87	748	3	=	=	Dixie Magneto	280	£84 - 0s - 0d	UNKNOWN
1917-18	D War Model	2	S.V.	74 x 87	748	3	Chain	AMAC	Dixie Magneto	280	£84 - 0s - 0d	7318 – 10624
1919-20	D Passenger Combination	2	S.V.	74 x 87	748	3	Chain	AMAC	Thompson Bennett Magneto	280	£142 - 0s - 0d to £200 - 0s - 0d	10625 – 11750 12581 – 14086
1921	B	1	S.V.	74 x 81	349	3	Chain	AMAC	Thompson Bennett Magneto	212	£95 - 0s - 0d	16001 – 16633
	D Passenger Combination	2	=	74 x 93	799	=	=	=	=	310	£159 - 10s - 0d (£159.50)	14790 – 15467
	B	1	S.V.	74 x 81	349	3	Chain	AMAC	Lucas Magneto	212	£85 - 0s - 0d	16634 – 17317
1922	B1 Standard Sporting	=	=	=	=	=	=	=	=	208	=	19001 – 20285
	B2 Stripped Sporting	=	=	=	=	=	=	=	=	197	=	21001 – 21179
	D Passenger Combination	2	=	74 x 93	799	3	=	=	Thompson Bennett Magneto	310	£175 - 0s - 0d	15468 – 16000 22001 – 22377
1923	B	1	S.V.	74 x 81	349	3	Chain	AMAC	Lucas Magneto	214	£77 - 0s - 0d	18800 –
	B1 Standard Sporting	=	=	=	=	=	=	=	=	210	=	
	T.T. Model	=	O.H.V.	=	=	=	=	=	=	204	£83 - 0s - 0d	

YEAR	MODEL	No. Cylinders	Engine Type	Bore/Stroke (mm.)	Capacity (c.c.)	Speeds	Drive	Carburettor	Ignition	Machine Weight (lbs.)	Price	Serial N°s
1923	D Passenger Combination	2	S.V.	74 x 93	799	3	Chain	AMAC	Thompson Bennett Magneto	336	£152 - 10s - 0d (£152.50)	22378 - 23500
	B	1	S.V.	74 x 81	349	3	Chain	AMAC	Lucas Magneto	214	£62 - 0s - 0d	26130 - 27129
	B1	=	=	=	=	=	=	=	=	212	=	31831 - 34559
	B3	=	O.H.V.	=	=	=	=	=	=	210	£65 - 0s - 0d	40080 - 41322
1924	B4 Racing	=	=	=	=	=	=	=	=	=	=	21853 - 23801
	B5	=	S.V.	-	=	=	=	=	=	198	£52 - 0s - 0d	36058 - 38849
	D Passenger Combination	2	=	74 x 93	799	=	=	=	Lucas Magdyno	336	£130 - 0s - 0d	23530 - 24382
	D1 Passenger Combination	=	=	=	=	=	=	=	Lucas Magneto	316	£95 - 0s - 0d	42001 - 43131
1925	E1 Passenger Combination	2	S.V.	74 x 93	799	3	Chain	Binks	Lucas Magdyno	336	£115 - 0s - 0d	24383 - 24586 24753 - 25390
	E2 Passenger Combination	=	=	=	=	=	=	=	Lucas Magneto	316	£90 - 0s - 0d	43132 - 43380 43484 - 43836 44001 - 44423
	E3	1	=	74 x 81	349	=	=	=	=	214	£57 - 0s - 0d	27269 - 27334 27634 - 28657
	E4	=	=	=	=	=	=	=	=	212	=	34560 - 35000 51001 - 52547 52601 - 53051
	E5	=	-	=	=	=	=	=	=	207	£49 - 10s - 0d (£49.50)	38850 - 39000 39438 - 44000 55001 - 57310 57401 - 58000
	E6	=	O.H.V.	=	=	=	=	=	=	218	£60 - 0s - 0d	41323 - 41524 41881 - 42000 47120 - 48895 49101 - 49226

YEAR	MODEL	No. Cylinders	Engine Type	Bore/Stroke (mm.)	Capacity (c.c.)	Speeds	Drive	Carburettor	Ignition	Machine Weight (lbs.)	Price	Serial N°s
1925	E7 Special Sports	1	O.H.V.	74 x 81	349	3	Chain	Binks	Lucas Magneto	210	Subject to Specification	46056 - 46149 46160 - 46205 46250 - 46265
	G1 Passenger Combination	2	S.V.	74 x 93	799	3	Chain	Binks	Lucas Magdyno	336	£98 - 0s - 0d	24587 - 24600 25391 - 25720 25801 - 26000 60001 - 60338
	G2 Passenger Combination	=	=	=	=	=	=	=	Lucas Magneto	316	£80 - 0s - 0d	43836 - 44000 44424 - 44745 44801 - 45200
	G3	1	=	74 x 81	349	=	=	=	=	214	£49 - 15s - 0d (£49.75)	28658 - 29495 29500 - 29601
	G4	=	=	=	=	=	=	=	=	212	=	52548 - 52600 53052 - 55000 72001 - 72979 73100 - 73108
	G5	=	=	=	=	=	=	=	=	207	£44 - 10s - 0d (£44.50)	57311 - 57400 58001 - 60000 77001 - 79706
1926	G6	=	O.H.V.	=	=	=	=	=	=	218	£53 - 0s - 0d	48896 - 49100 49227 - 50000 83001 - 83587 83601 - 84136
	G7 Special Sports	=	=	=	=	=	=	=	=	210	Subject to Specification	46206 - 46249 46266 - 46300
	GR7 Racing	=	=	=	=	=	=	=	=	203	=	46304 - 46357 46420 - 46423
	G8	=	=	84 x 90	498	=	=	=	=	274	£62 - 10s - 0d (£62.50)	85001 - 89500 90000 - 90248 90276 - 90279
	G10 Racing	=	=	=	=	=	=	=	=	250	Subject to Specification	89501 - 89558 89753 - 89841
1927	H1 Passenger Combination	2	S.V.	74 x 93	799	3	Chain	Binks	Lucas Magdyno	336	£95 - 0s - 0d	25721 - 25800 60339 - 60787 60888 - 60971
	H2 Passenger Combination	=	=	=	=	=	=	=	Lucas Magneto	316	£80 - 0s - 0d	44746 - 44800 45201 - 45657 45719 - 45752
	H3	1	=	74 x 81	349	=	=	=	=	214	£48 - 10s - 0d (£48.50)	29496 - 29500 29602 - 30000 68001 - 68126 68176 - 68267

YEAR	MODEL	No. Cylinders	Engine Type	Bore/Stroke (mm.)	Capacity (c.c.)	Speeds	Drive	Carburettor	Ignition	Machine Weight (lbs.)	Price	Serial N°s
1927	H4	1	S.V.	74 × 81	349	3	Chain	Binks	Lucas Magneto	214	£48 - 10s - 0d (£48.50)	72981 - 73099 73109 - 76115 76252 - 76546
	H5	=	=	=	=	=	=	=	=	210	£44 - 0s - 0d	79566 - 79599 79707 - 83000 110001 - 110707 110801 - 110979
	H6	=	O.H.V.	=	=	=	=	=	=	220	£53 - 0s - 0d	83588 - 83600 84137 - 85122 100001 - 100926 101011 - 101082
	H7 Racing	=	=	=	=	=	=	=	=	204	Subject to Specification	46358 - 46419 46424 - 46516 46644 - 46661
	H8	=	=	84 × 90	498	=	=	=	=	274	£62 - 10s - 0d (£62.50)	90249 - 90275 90280 - 92240 92463 - 92500
	H9	=	S.V.	=	=	=	=	=	=	=	£56 - 0s - 0d	95001 - 98067 98076 - 98190
	H10 Racing	=	O.H.V.	=	=	=	=	=	=	250	Subject to Specification	89559 - 89594 89600 - 89619 89842 - 89905 89977 - 90000
1928	K1 Passenger Combination	2	S.V.	74 × 93	799	3	Chain	Binks	Lucas Magdyno	336	£95 - 0s - 0d or £73 - 0s - 0d Solo	61000 -
	K2 Passenger Combination	=	=	=	=	=	=	=	Lucas Magneto	316	£80 - 0s - 0d or £63 - 0s - 0d Solo	
	K3	1	=	74 × 81	349	=	=	=	=	230	£47 - 0s - 0d	76500 -
	K4	=	=	=	=	=	=	=	=	=	=	
	K5	=	=	=	=	=	=	=	=	215	£43 - 10s - 0d (£43.50)	
	K6	=	O.H.V.	=	=	=	=	=	=	226	£50 - 0s - 0d	101200 - 103400
	KR6 Racing	=	=	=	=	=	=	=	=	209	Subject to Specification	

205

YEAR	MODEL	No. Cylinders	Engine Type	Bore/Stroke (mm.)	Capacity (c.c.)	Speeds	Drive	Carburettor	Ignition	Machine Weight (lbs.)	Price	Serial Nºs
1928	K7	1	O.H.C.	74 x 81	349	3	Chain	Binks	Lucas Magneto	225	£62 - 0s - 0d	UNKNOWN
	K8	=	O.H.V.	84 x 90	498	=	=	=	=	275	£59 - 10s - 0d (£59.50)	
	K9	=	S.V.	=	=	=	=	=	=	=	£55 - 0s - 0d	99200 –
	K10	=	O.H.C.	=	=	=	=	=	=	265	£73 - 0s - 0d	UNKNOWN
	K12	=	S.V.	65 x 75	248	=	=	=	=	191	£39 - 17s - 6d (£39.87½)	
1929	M1	2	S.V.	84 x 90	996	3	Chain	Amal	Lucas Magdyno	385	£76 - 10s - 0d (£76.50)	61140 –
	M2	=	=	=	=	=	=	=	Lucas Magneto	345	£66 - 0s - 0d	45988 – 46000 50126 –
	M3	1	=	74 x 81	349	=	=	=	=	264	£48 - 10s - 0d (£48.50)	68726 –
	M4	=	=	=	=	=	=	=	=	261	=	UNKNOWN
	M5	=	=	=	=	=	=	=	=	253	£45 - 0s - 0d	
	M6 Single Port	=	O.H.V.	=	=	=	=	=	=	266	£52 - 0s - 0d	103288 – 103312 103563 –
	M6 Twin Port	=	=	=	=	=	=	=	=	273	£54 - 10s - 0d (£54.50)	
	MR6 Special Sports	=	=	=	=	=	=	=	=	256	£62 - 0s - 0d	
	M7	=	O.H.C.	=	=	=	=	=	=	260	=	46775 –

YEAR	MODEL	No. Cylinders	Engine Type	Bore/Stroke (mm.)	Capacity (c.c.)	Speeds	Drive	Carburettor	Ignition	Machine Weight (lbs.)	Price	Serial N°s
1929	M8 Single Port	1	O.H.V.	84 x 90	498	3	Chain	Amal	Lucas Magneto	303	£59 - 10s - 0d (£59.50)	93406 – 93430 94681 –
	M8 Twin Port	=	=	=	=	=	=	=	=	312	£62 - 0s - 0d	
	M9	=	S.V.	=	=	=	=	=	=	300	£54 - 0s - 0d	130151 –
	M10	=	O.H.C.	=	=	=	=	=	=	297	£72 - 0s - 0d	120072 – 120100 89620 – 89752
	M12	=	S.V.	65 x 75	248	=	=	=	=	193	£39 - 17s - 6d (£39.87½)	122851 –
1930	R2	2	S.V.	84 x 90	996	3	Chain	Amal	Lucas Magneto	345	£63 - 0s - 0d	Export 50542 – Home 50236 –
	R4	1	=	74 x 81	349	=	=	=	=	262	£44 - 10s - 0d (£44.50)	114899 – 115251 –
	R5	=	=	=	=	=	=	=	=	210	£40 - 0s - 0d	
	R6	=	O.H.V.	=	=	=	=	=	=	276	£53 - 0s - 0d	106410 – 106300 –
	R7	=	O.H.C.	70 x 90	346	=	=	=	=	290	£76 - 0s - 0d	UNKNOWN
	R8	=	O.H.V.	84 x 90	498	=	=	=	=	319	£59 - 10s - 0d (£59.50)	143718 – 143851 –
	R9	=	S.V.	=	=	=	=	=	=	303	£52 - 10s - 0d (£52.50)	132125 – 132301 –
	R10	=	O.H.C.	79 x 101	495	=	=	=	=	316	£86 - 0s - 0d	UNKNOWN
	R12	=	O.H.V.	65 x 75	248	=	=	=	=	217 ¾	£40 - 0s - 0d	135498 – 135926 –

YEAR	MODEL	No. Cylinders	Engine Type	Bore/Stroke (mm.)	Capacity (c.c.)	Speeds	Drive	Carburettor	Ignition	Machine Weight (lbs.)	Price	Serial N°s	
	S2	2	S.V.	84 x 90	996	3	Chain	Amal	Lucas Magneto	356	£63 - 0s - 0d	Export 69066 –	Home 69309 –
	S3	2	=	65 x 75	498	=	Shaft/Chain	=	Lucas Coil	353	£65 - 0s - 0d	150020 –	
	S4	1	=	74 x 93	399	=	Chain	=	Lucas Magneto	278	£44 - 10s - 0d (£44.50)	Export 145668 –	Home 145940 –
	S5	=	=	74 x 81	349	=	=	=	=	214 ½	£40 - 0s - 0d	116170–	116586 –
	S6	=	O.H.V.	=	=	=	=	=	=	291	£53 - 0s - 0d	108327–	108267 –
	S7	=	O.H.C.	70 x 90	346	=	=	Binks	=	290	£80 - 0s - 0d	145114 –	145262 –
	S8	=	O.H.V.	84 x 90	498	=	=	Amal	=	323	£59 - 10s - 0d (£59.50)	62466 –	62195 –
1931	S9 Light	=	S.V.	=	=	=	=	=	=	293	£49 - 0s - 0d	133479 –	133501 –
	S9 Heavy	=	S.V.	=	=	=	=	=	=	308	£52 - 10s - 0d (£52.50)		
	S10	=	O.H.C.	79 x 101	495	=	=	Binks	=	316	£90 - 0s - 0d	140210 –	89654 –
	S12	=	O.H.V.	65 x 75	248	=	=	Amal	=	219 ½	£40 - 0s - 0d	138001 –	137675 –
	SA4	=	S.V.	74 x 81	349	=	=	=	=	278	£44 - 0s - 0d		
	SA5	=	=	=	=	=	=	=	=	221	£40 - 0s - 0d	UNKNOWN	
	SB6 'Big Port'	=	O.H.V.	=	=	=	=	Bowden	=	222	£45 - 0s - 0d		
	SB8 'Big Port'	=	O.H.V.	84 x 90	498	3	Chain	=	Lucas Magneto	291	£49 - 17s - 6d (£49.87½)		
	SA12	=	=	65 x 75	248	=	=	Amal	=	223 ¼	£40 - 0s - 0d		

208

Appendix 5.

Timing Charts for A.J.S. Motorcycle Engines

1919 - 1928 MODELS	INLET Opens before T.D.C.	INLET Closes after B.D.C.	EXHAUST Opens before B.D.C.	EXHAUST Closes after T.D.C.	Ignition Max. Adv. before T.D.C.	Tappet Clearance Ex.	Tappet Clearance In.
6 h.p. 1919-20: Front Cylinder	0°	30°	54°	0°	35½°	·008"	·006"
Rear Cylinder	0°	30°	50°	12°	35½°	·008"	·006"
3·49 h.p. Touring S.V., 1921	8½°	48°	58°	25°	37°	·008"	·006"
3·49 h.p. Sporting S.V., 1921	21½°	60°	60°	32½°	37°	·008"	·006"
3·49 h.p. Touring S.V., 1922-24	8½°	48°	58°	25°	37°	·008"	·006"
3·49 h.p. Sporting S.V., 1922-24	17½°	60°	53°	27°	42½°	·008"	·006"
7 h.p., 1921-8: Front Cylinder	0°	27°	54½°	0°	34°	·008"	·006"
Rear Cylinder	0°	27°	51°	0°	34°	·008"	·006"
3·49 h.p. O.H.V., 1923-27	15°	58°	50°	25°	47°	·008"	·006"
3·49 h.p. Sporting S.V., 1925-27	15°	58°	50°	25°	37°	·008"	·006"
3·49 h.p. Touring S.V., 1925-27	15°	58°	50°	25°	38°	·008"	·006"
4·98 h.p. O.H.V., 1926-27	10°	33°	51°	5°	37°	·008"	·006"
4·98 h.p. S.V., 1927	15°	58°	50°	25°	38°	·008"	·006"
3·49 h.p. K3 S.V., 1928	20°	48°	48°	35°	34°	·008"	·006"
3·49 h.p. K4 & K5 S.V., 1928	20°	48°	48°	35°	43°	·008"	·006"
3·49 h.p. K6 O.H.V., 1928	20°	50°	50°	35°	46°	·008"	·006"
3·49 h.p. & 4·98 h.p. K7 & K10 O.H.C., 1928	30°	55°	50°	25°	52°	·018"	·016"
4·98 h.p. K8 O.H.V. & K9 S.V., 1928	20°	51°	61°	12°	37°	·008"	·006"
2·48 h.p. K12 S.V., 1928	17°	44°	41°	27°	39°	·008"	·006"

1929 - 1930 MODELS	INLET Opens before T.D.C.	INLET Closes after B.D.C.	EXHAUST Opens before B.D.C.	EXHAUST Closes after T.D.C.	Ignition Max. Adv. before T.D.C.	Tappet Clearance Ex.	Tappet Clearance In.
9·96 h.p. M1 & M2, 1929	20°	51°	58°	13°	35°	·008"	·006"
3·49 h.p. M3 Touring S.V., 1929	20°	51°	50°	35°	37°	·008"	·006"
3·49 h.p. M4 & M5, Sporting S.V. 1929	20°	51°	50°	35°	40°	·008"	·006"
3·49 h.p. M6 O.H.V., 1929	30°	55°	50°	35°	45°	·008"	·006"
3·49 h.p. M7 O.H.C., 1929	20°	51°	50°	25°	53°	·018"	·016"
4·98 h.p. M8 O.H.V., 1929	20°	51°	50°	35°	37°	·008"	·006"
4·98 h.p. M9 Touring S.V., 1929	20°	51°	50°	35°	35°	·008"	·006"
4·98 h.p. M10 O.H.C., 1929	30°	55°	50°	25°	49°	·018"	·016"
2·48 h.p. M12 S.V., 1929	20°	51°	58°	13°	38°	·008"	·006"
9·96 h.p. R2 Touring S.V., 1930	20°	51°	58°	13°	35°	·008"	·006"
3·49 h.p. R4 & R5 Touring S.V., 1930	20°	51°	50°	35°	41°	·008"	·006"
3·49 h.p. R6 O.H.V., 1930	20°	51°	50°	35°	46°	·008"	·006"
3·46 h.p. R7 O.H.C., 1930	20°	55°	68°	25°	50°	·018"	·016"
4·98 h.p. R8 O.H.V., 1930	20°	51°	50°	35°	38°	·008"	·006"
4·98 h.p. R9 S.V. Touring, 1930	20°	51°	50°	35°	39°	·008"	·006"
4·95 h.p. R10 O.H.C., 1930	20°	55°	68°	25°	47°	·018"	·016"
2·48 h.p. R12 O.H.V., 1930	20°	51°	50°	35°	39°	·008"	·006"

1931 MODELS							
9·96 h.p. S2 Touring S.V.	20°	51°	58°	13°	35°	·008"	·006"
3·99 h.p. S4 S.V. & 3·49 h.p. S5 S.V.	20°	51°	50°	35°	41°	·008"	·006"
3·49 h.p. S6 O.H.V.	20°	51°	50°	35°	46°	·008"	·006"
3·49 h.p. S7 O.H.C.	20°	55°	68°	25°	50°	·018"	·016"
4·98 h.p. S8 O.H.V.	20°	51°	50°	35°	38°	·008"	·006"
4·98 h.p. S9 S.V.	20°	51°	50°	35°	39°	·008"	·006"
4·98 h.p. S10 O.H.C.	20°	55°	68°	25°	47°	·018"	·016"
2·48 h.p. S12 O.H.V.	30°	51°	30°	35°	39°	·008"	·006"

Appendix 6

A.J.S. Wireless Receivers

YEAR	MODEL	Nº Valves	Circuit	Cabinet Type	Finish	Dimensions (in) L x W x H	Price Complete
1923	Sloping Panel	4	HF / DET / 2LF Single Loading Coil	Exposed Sloping Panel Face	Oak, Walnut or Mahogany	17 x 9 x 13½	£30 - 17s - 6d (£30.87½)
	Table De Luxe	"	"	Enclosed Table Top Cabinet	Oak or Walnut	18½ x 16½ x 12	£36 - 5s - 0d (£36.25)
	Pedestal	"	"	Free Standing Cabinet with Enclosed Horn L/S & Battery Compartment	Oak or Mahogany	21 x 19¼ x 43½	£75 - 0s - 0d
1924	Type D	2	HF / DET Optional Coil Unit Volt Meter to Monitor Accumulator	Exposed Sloping Panel Face	Walnut or Mahogany	13½ x 8½ x 11	£17 - 10s - 0d (£17.50)
	Type E	3	HF / DET / LF Optional Coil Unit Volt Meter to Monitor Accumulator	"	"	15½ x 9 x 12½	£22 - 5s - 0d (£22.25)
	Type F	4	HF / DET / 2 LF Optional Coil Unit Volt Meter to Monitor Accumulator	"	"	17 x 9 x 13½	£27 - 5s - 0d (£27.25)
	Type F Unitop Cabinet	"	"	Enclosed Table Top Cabinet	Oak, Walnut or Mahogany	21 x 19¼ x 8	£31 - 10s - od (£31.50)
	Type F Pedestal	"	"	Free Standing Cabinet with Enclosed Horn L/S & Battery Compartment	Oak or Mahogany	21 x 19¼ x 43½	£52 - 10s - 0d (£52.50)
1925	Type Z	2	DET / LF	Lidded Table Top Panel	Mahogany	14 x 9 x 11¼	£13 - 18s - 6d (£13.92½)
	Type D6	"	HF / DET	Exposed Sloping Panel Face	Oak or Mahogany	13½ x 8½ x 11	£16 - 17s - 6d (£16.87½)
	Type E6	3	HF / DET / LF	"	"	15½ x 9 x 12½	£21 - 13s - 6d (£21.67½)
	Type F6	4	HF / DET / 2LF	"	Mahogany	17 x 9 x 13½	£26 - 15s - 0d (£26.75)
	Type T.M.I. De Luxe	"	"	Enclosed Table Top Cabinet	"	21¼ x 19½ x 13¼	£35 - 0s - 0d
	Type T.M.2. Standard	"	"	"	Oak or Mahogany	"	£30 - 10s - 0d (£30.50)
	Pedestal P1 De Luxe	"	"	Free Standing Cabinet with Enclosed Horn L/S & Battery Compartment	Mahogany	21 x 19¼ x 43½	£65 - 0s - 0d
	Pedestal P2 Standard	"	"	"	Oak or Mahogany	"	£52 - 0s - 0d
	Console S1	"	"	Free Standing Cabinet with Enclosed Horn L/S & Cupboards	Mahogany and Rosewood	39 x 21 x 39	£75 - 0s - 0d
	Unit Pedestal	"	"	Free Standing 3-Piece Unit Construction Cabinet with Enclosed Horn L/S & Battery Cupboard	Oak or Mahogany	21 x 19¼ x 43½	£51 - 18s - 0d (£51.90)
1926-28	Symphony Two	2	T.R.F.	Lidded with Exposed Controls	Mahogany	22 x 14 x 11	£17 - 10s - 0d (£17.50)
	Symphony Three	3	"	"	"	"	£25 - 0s - 0d
	Symphony Five Table Model	5	Superheterodyne using short indoor or outdoor aerial	"	"	"	£45 - 0s - 0d
	Symphony Five Bureau Model	5	"	Free Standing Lidded Cabinet with Exposed Controls	"	23¼ x 15½ x 39½	£52 - 10s - 0d (£52.50)
	Symphony Seven Table Model	7	Superheterodyne with two interchangeable frame aerials	Lidded with Exposed Controls	"	23¼ x 15½ x 21½	£60 - 0s - 0d
	Symphony Seven Bureau Model	7	"	Free Standing Lidded Cabinet with Exposed Controls	"	23¼ x 15½ x 39½	£67 - 10s - 0d (£67.50)
	Symphony Five Portable Model	5	T.R.F.	Portable with Carrying Handle	Oak	16 x 8½ x 13½	£22 - 10s - 0d (£22.50)

Key to Abbreviations: HF - High Frequency Stage. **DET** - Detector Stage. **LF** - Low Frequency Stage. **TRF** - Tuned Radio Frequency ('Straight') Receiver.

Appendix 8

A.J.S. Light Car

MODEL	FOUR DOOR FABRIC SALOON	FOUR DOOR COACHBUILT SALOON	COACHBUILT OPEN TWO SEATER	FOUR DOOR RICHMOND FABRIC SALOON
PRODUCTION SPAN	August 1930 to October 1931	October 1930 to October 1931	October 1930 to October 1931	February 1931 to October 1931
ENGINE	COVENTRY CLIMAX & A.J.S.			
TYPE	S.V.			
Nº CYLINDERS	4			
BORE & STROKE (mm)	60 x 90			
CAPACITY (c.c.)	1018			
R.A.C. RATING	8.92 h.p.			
POWER OUTPUT	24 b.h.p. @ 3000 r.p.m.			
IGNITION	LUCAS 12v COIL			
CARBURETTOR	SOLEX			
GEARBOX	THREE SPEED + REVERSE			
WHEELBASE & TRACK	7' 7" x 3'9"			
WEIGHT	16 cwt (1792 lbs)	15 cwt (1680 lbs)	14 cwt (1568 lbs)	16 cwt (1792 lbs)
PRICE	£230 - 0s - 0d	£240 - 0s - 0d	£210 - 0s - 0d	£197 - 0s - 0d

Appendix 7

A.J.S. Commercial Vehicles

MODEL	PILOT	COMMODORE	ADMIRAL
CHASSIS Nºs	101 – 226 / 1001 – 1014	5000 – 5064	3001 – 3008
PRODUCTION SPAN	February 1929 to October 1931	October 1929 to October 1931	February 1931 to October 1931
ENGINE	Meadows 6 ERC	Coventry Climax L6	Coventry Climax L6
TYPE	O.H.V.	S.V.	S.V.
Nº CYLINDERS	6	6	6
BORE & STROKE (mm)	82.5 x 120.7	98.4 x 127	98.4 x 127
CAPACITY (c.c.)	3800	5748	5748
R.A.C. RATING	25 h.p.	36 h.p.	36 h.p.
POWER OUTPUT	54 b.h.p. @ 2000 r.p.m.	75 b.h.p. @ 2000 r.p.m.	75 b.h.p. @ 2000 r.p.m.
IGNITION	Magneto	Magneto	Magneto or Coil
CARBURETTOR	Solex	Solex	Solex
GEARBOX	Three Speed + Reverse	Three Speed + Reverse	Three Speed + Reverse
WHEELBASE & TRACK	15' 6" x 5' 10¾"	16' 6" x 5' 10¾"	16' 2" x 5' 10¾"
CHASSIS WEIGHT	2 Tons - 6cwt (5152 lbs)	3 Tons - 2 cwt (6944 lbs)	2 Tons - 17 cwt (6384 lbs)
MAX SEATING CAPACITY — Normal Control	24	–	28
MAX SEATING CAPACITY — Forward Control	26	32	–
PRICE — Normal Control	£685 - 0s - 0d	–	£795 - 0s - 0d
PRICE — Forward Control	£705 - 0s - 0d	£850 - 0s - 0d	–

211

Appendix 9

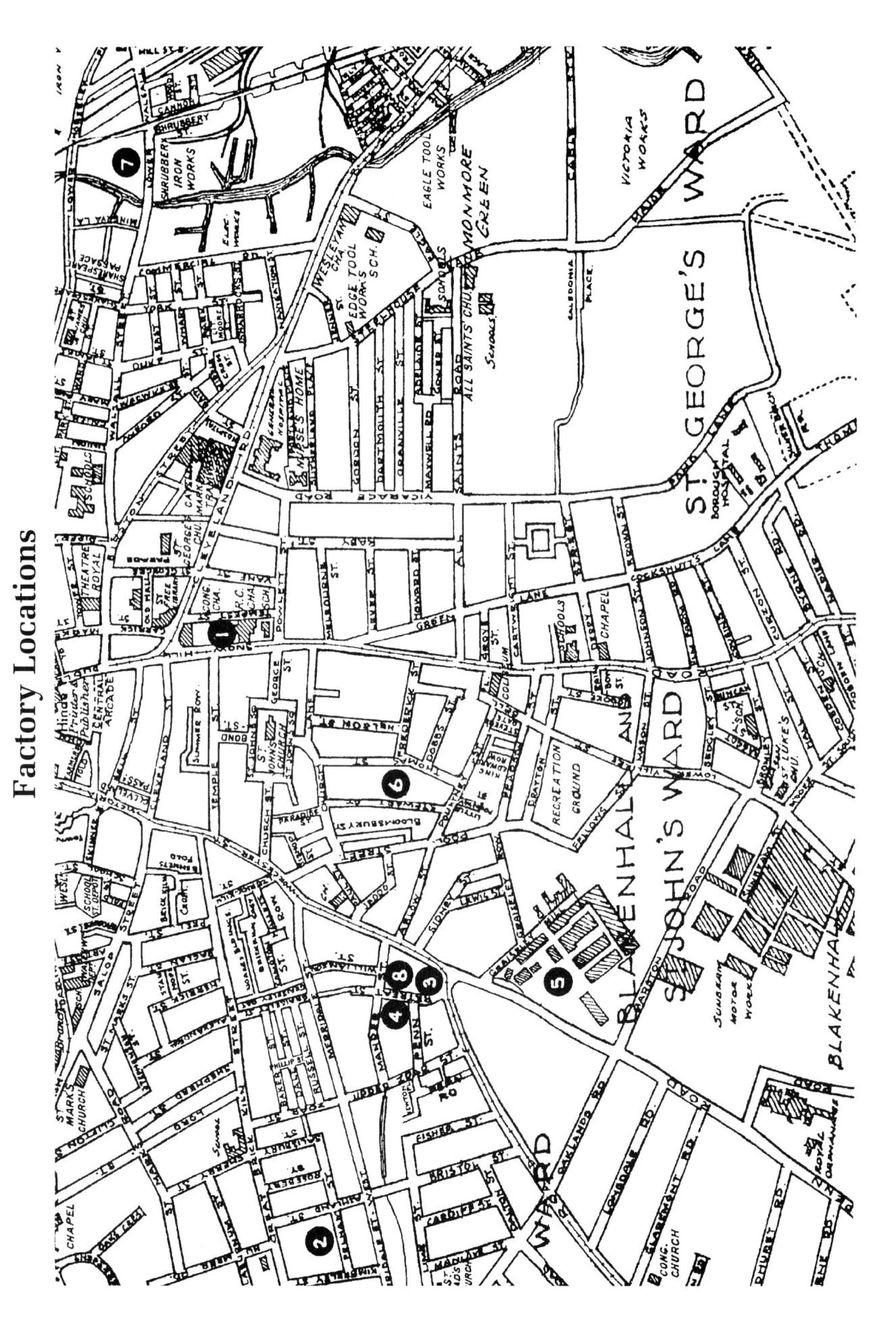

Factory Locations

Map reproduced from 'Alfred Hindes' map of Wolverhampton, originally printed in the Wolverhampton Red Book and Directory 1928.

Map copied by kind permission of Wolverhampton Central Library.

	Address.	Period of Occupation.	Company Title.
1.	Tempest Street	1894 - 1898	J. Stevens & Co.
		1899 - 1904	The Stevens Motor Manufacturing Company.
2.	Pelham Street	1904 - 1910	The Stevens Motor Manufacturing Co. Ltd.
		1906 - 1908	The Stevens Screw Co. Ltd.
		1909 - 1910	A.J. Stevens & Co. Ltd.
3.	Retreat Street	1908 - 1972	The Stevens Screw Co. Ltd.
4.	Retreat Street	1909 - 1914	A.J. Stevens & Co. Ltd.
		1914 - 1915	A.J. Stevens & Co. (1914) Ltd
		1915 - 1931	The Stevens Screw Co. Ltd.
		1932 - 1992	Stevens Brothers (Wolverhampton) Ltd.
		1972 - 1992	The Stevens Screw Co. Ltd.
5.	Graiseley Hill	1915 - 1931	A.J. Stevens & Co. (1914) Ltd.
6.	Stewart Street	1920 - 1922	C.W. Hayward.
		1925 - 1928	A.J.S. (Wireless & Scientific Instruments).
7.	Lower Walsall Street	1922 - 1930	C.W. Hayward.
		1923 - 1927	A.J.S. (Wireless & Scientific Instruments).
		1927 - 1931	A.J.S. (Commercial Vehicles).
8.	Retreat Street	1933 - 1956	Stevens Brothers (Wolverhampton) Ltd.

Appendix 10

Club Information

THE VINTAGE MOTOR CYCLE CLUB LTD.

FOUNDED BY C.E. ALLEN, B.E.M., IN 1946.

Allen House, Wetmore Road, Burton upon Trent, Staffordshire. DE14 1SN. Tel: 0283 540557 Fax: 0283 510547.

A.J.S. & Matchless Owners Club

Affilated to the British Motorcycle Federation.

AJS & MOC Administration Officer.
25, Victoria Street,
Irthlingborough,
Northants.
NN9 5RG.

British Vintage Wireless Society

Enquiries to the Editor:
63 Manor Road, Tottenham,

Robert Hawes. Tel: 081 808 2838
London. N17 0JH.

The AJS nine Car Club.

Membership Secretary:
Peter Hubbard.
The Chestnuts
Chequers Road,
Tharston,
Long Stratton,
Norwich.
NR15 2YA.
Tel: 0508 30072

THE PSV CIRCLE

Contact:
Andrew G. Johnson.
30 Bonnersfield Lane, Harrow,
Middlesex. HA1 2LE.

214

Index

A
Accles & Pollock Ltd. 119, 183.
A.E.C. 166.
Agar, Bates, Neal & Co. 106.
A.J.Stevens & Co. Ltd. 20, 43, 109.
A.J.Stevens & Co. (1914) Ltd. 43, 104, 111, 120.
A.J.S. 'Admiral'. 100, 168, 169.
 – 'Commodore'. 92, 100, 164-171.
 – 'Nine'. 96, 99, 100, 106, 120, 174-180.
 – 'Pilot'. 91, 92, 99, 159-166, 168, 174.
 – 'Richmond'. 178, 179.
A.J.S. Social & Sports Club Ltd. 75.
A.J.S. Wireless & Scientific Instruments. 66, 136.
A.J.W. 184.
Albion. 166.
A.M.A.C. 25, 35, 46, 54, 56, 123, 126, 154.
Amal. 94, 100, 104, 132, 149, 186.
Ariel. 66, 119.
Arthur, Frank. 91.
Austin. 89, 159, 172.
Austin. Seven. 115, 172.
Auto Cycle Union. 23, 26, 27, 30, 35, 37, 39, 65.
Auto Machinists Ltd. 183.
Autovac. 176.
Avon. 176.

B
Baldwin, Captain Oliver M. 92, 94, 153-155, 157.
Barker, E. 39.
Barnes, George A. 19.
Barnett, Arthur. 71.
Barnett, W. 19.
Barrett, Gladys. 190.
Barrow, C.S. 96.
Bedford. 165.
Bennett, Alec. 62, 66, 86.
Berrington, Richard, Evans, Willoughby. 43.
Best & Lloyd. 46.
Binks. 68, 75, 126, 128, 147.
Blackburne. 66.
B.M.W. 92, 154.
Booth, Arthur G. 91, 172, 174.
Bowden. 103, 133, 147, 149, 181, 183, 186.
Brampton. 103.
Brewster, D. 103.
Bristol. 166.
British Broadcasting Company. 66, 135, 136, 138.
British Motor Cycle Racing Club. 73.
British Thompson-Houston. 135.
Briton Motor Co.Ltd. 66, 106, 114, 170.
Brooklands. 31, 43, 58, 61, 63, 73, 83, 92, 125, 150, 151, 154.
Brooks. 58, 59, 70, 128.
Broom, Mick. 104.
Brough. 119, 157, 190.
Brough, George. 119, 189, 190.
Brown & Barlow. 22.
Brown, Cecil. 91.
B.S.A. 13, 20, 62, 106, 145.
Bullus, Tommy. 103.
Burman. 181, 186, 187.

C
Carter, G.S. 73.
Castrol. 154.
Chambers, Herbie. 66.
Chillington Fields. 66.
Clark, R.O. 57.
Clarke, Albert. 16.
Clarke, Jack. 113.
Clarke, William. 14, 20.

Clayton-Dewandre. 161, 165.
Clyno. 20, 22, 84, 85, 89, 91, 117, 120, 159, 172-174, 178.
Cohen, L.R. 86.
Commer. 166.
Commercial Autocar Co. 22.
Cooper, Frank. 189.
Corke, J.D. 23.
Cotton. 67.
Coventry Climax. 92, 96, 100, 165, 169, 174, 175, 180.
Cox-Atmos. 172.
Craig, Joe. 72.
Crossley. 166.
Crystal Palace. 14, 16.
Curran, Arthur. 56, 71.

D
Daimler. 166.
Dance, George. 62.
Davenport, Leo. 71, 88, 92, 96, 127, 149, 152.
Davies, Howard R. 55-58, 61-63, 65, 66, 71, 106, 122.
Deadman, Tommy. 189.
De Dion-Bouton. 109.
de la Hay, Tommy. 62.
Denly, Bert. 92, 93, 96, 150-152, 154.
Dennis. 165, 166.
Diamond Motors. 106, 120, 121.
Dixie. 49.
Dixon, Freddie. 62, 70.
Docker, Bernard (Sir). 106.
Docker, Dudley. 106.
Dodson, Charlie. 88, 148.
Douglas. 30, 38, 66, 70-72, 91.
Douglas, Billy. 36.
Downie, A.F. 73.
Downie, A.L. 73.
Driscoll, L.P. 151.
Druid. 59, 65, 75, 110, 123, 130, 132, 147, 184.
Dunlop. 128, 154, 185.
Dutch T.T. 88, 149, 152.

E
Earls Court Exhibition. 190.
Ebblewhite, A.V. 147.
Edmond, Freddie. 62.
Enfield. 30, 38.
Ever Ready Co. 105, 106.
Excelsior. 119.

F
Fernihough, Eric. 157.
Firth Cleveland Group. 159.
Fourreau, Charles. 72.

G
General Electric Co. 135.
German T.T. 149.
Giles, Adelaide. 73, 117.
Giles, Frank. 63, 68, 73, 83, 117.
Gilford. 162, 166.
Gnesa, Enesto. 67.
G.P.O. 136.
Graiseley Hill Works. 49, 51, 52, 54, 59, 64, 66, 68, 75, 80-83, 87, 88, 96, 105, 106, 114, 117, 119, 120, 159, 174, 180, 181.
Graiseley House. 43, 49, 51, 52, 54.
Grand Prix, Austrian. 83, 88, 92, 96, 148, 149, 152.
 – Belgian. 67, 72, 77, 83, 96, 148.
 – Brooklands. 83.
 – Czecoslovakian. 88.

Grand Prix d'Europe. 83, 92, 148, 150.
 – French. 67, 72, 73, 96, 152.
 – German. 79, 96, 149, 152.
 – Hungarian. 96.
 – Italian. 67.
 – of the Nations. 103.
 – Swiss. 83, 148.
 – Ulster. 83, 88, 92, 96, 149, 152.
Greenshields, G. 163.
Greenwood, Cyril. 71.
Gregory, A.W. 73.
Grinton, George. 66, 71.
Guthrie, Jimmy. 96, 103, 104, 152, 155.
Guy. 166, 168.

H
Hackett, Walter. 183.
Haddock, Bert. 30, 34-36, 38, 39.
Haden, W.H. 19.
Handley, Wal. 88, 92, 149, 151.
Hardy Spicer. 101, 176.
Harris, H.F. 56, 57, 61, 62, 66, 67.
Hartford. 174.
Hatch, Ike. 152.
Hatch, Tommy. 88.
Hayward, Charles. 26, 64, 79, 89, 110, 114, 115, 119, 137, 159.
Hayward, C.W. & Co. 26, 45, 66, 84, 85, 110, 114, 117, 120, 121, 136, 172.
Hayward, Daisy. 117.
Hayward, F.R.W. 19.
Heath, Phil. 104.
Heaton, Billy. 26, 27, 30, 31, 35, 36, 38, 40.
Henne, Ernst. 92, 154, 155.
Herd, W.M. 164, 169.
Hicks, Ernie. 181.
Hicks, Freddie. 96, 102-104, 125, 149, 151, 152.
Hill, Frank. 79.
Hill, G. 167.
Hill, Rowland (Sir). 43.
Himing, George. 103.
Holder, Alec. 121.
Hollowell, Billy. 67, 72, 73.
Hough, Charlie. 70, 71, 73, 88, 89, 147, 148.
Humphries, E.C. 184.
Hunt, Tim. 103, 104.

I
Indian. 62.

J
Jackson, S. 77.
James. 73.
J.A.P. 66, 91, 154.
Jenner, Edward. 159.
Johnson, Paddy. 96.
Jones, Billy. 33, 34, 37-39, 43.
Jones, Daisy. 190.
Jones, Sidney. 121.
Jowett, E.T.H. & W.H. 157.

K
Kelly, George. 61, 62, 66.
Kershaw, B. 73.

L
Lamb, Edgar E. 79, 140.
Lamont, Billy. 91.
Letts, William (Sir). 106.
le Vack, Bert. 66.
Levis. 57, 66.
Lewis, John Todd. 106.

Leyland.	165, 166, 171.
Lind, J.G.	152.
Lloyd, S & Sons.	183.
Lodge, Oliver (Sir).	140.
Longman, Frank.	66, 67, 70-73, 77.
Longuemare, Georges.	72.
Low, A.M. (Professor).	140.
Lowe, T.E.	19, 20.
Lower Walsall Street Works.	66, 68, 74, 84, 85, 89, 91, 96, 105, 106, 115-120, 135, 136, 138, 139, 144, 159, 172-174.
Lucas.	49, 54, 61, 70, 90, 102, 123, 133, 147, 174, 182, 185, 186.
Lycett.	154.

M

Marconi.	135, 136.
Marston, John.	22, 110.
Mason, Hugh.	37.
Matchless.	106, 155.
Maudslay.	165, 166.
McDiarmid, Dan.	104.
Meadows, Henry & Co.	92, 100, 160, 162, 169.
Merryweather.	117.
Metropolitan Vickers Electric Co.	136.
Midland Bank.	104.
Mills & Fulford.	106.
Ministry of Aircraft Production.	190.
Ministry of Munitions.	50, 52, 114.
Mitchell.	13, 14.
M.L.	152, 157.
Modern Machine Tool Co.	181.
Moore, Arthur & Sons.	170, 171.
Morcom, Edgar L.	79.
Morris.	89, 159, 165, 172.
Morris Minor.	159, 172.
Morrison, D.J.	163.
Mortimer, Charles (Snr).	155, 157.
Motosacoche.	149.

N

National Association of Radio Manufacturers and Traders.	140.
National Motorcycle Museum.	190.
National Radio Exhibition.	79.
New Hudson.	73.
New Imperial.	66.
Nock, Harold.	121.
Norton.	66, 71, 72, 103, 104, 119, 130, 148, 151.
N.S.U.	103.

O

O.E.C.	154.
OK-Supreme.	96, 184.
Olsson, V.	61, 62.
Olympia Exhibition.	22, 23, 25, 52, 65-67, 109, 122, 176.

P

Parkinson, Ronnie.	86.
Pelham Street Works.	19, 22.
Petty, D & E.	165.
Peugeot.	50.
Pilgrim.	75, 80, 86, 97, 101, 102, 126-128, 130, 132, 147.
Powerplus.	155, 157.
Prescott, H.V.	57.
Pullin, Cyril.	66.

R

Radio Communication Co.	135.
Raleigh.	181.
Rendall, W & Co.	168.
Renold.	61.
REO.	165.
Retreat Street Works.	22, 25, 30, 43, 45, 46, 49, 52, 110, 181, 191.
Roberts, D.H. & Son.	163.
Rose Brothers.	169.
Rowley, George.	70, 71, 73, 77, 86, 88, 89, 92, 96, 103, 126, 149.
Rudge.	88, 91.
Ruthardt.	20.

S

Sackville Co.	98, 133.
Scott.	62, 88, 119.
Scott, I.H.R.	70.
Scottish Motor Traction Co.Ltd.	164, 168.
Senspray.	35.
Shakespeare, Bob.	36, 37, 41, 56, 71, 152.
Sheard, Tom.	57, 62, 66.
Shell.	154.
Silvers, Tommy.	183.
Simcock, Arthur.	96, 149.
Simpson, Jimmy.	67, 70, 71-73, 77, 83, 86, 88, 103, 147, 148.
Simpson, William.	190.
Smith, Ailwyn.	20, 22.
Smith, Frank.	20, 22.
Smiths.	102, 132, 174.
Sociable.	112, 113.
Solex.	176.
Spann, Tommy.	86, 88, 96, 97, 103, 148.
Specialist Coach Co.Ltd.	121.
Splitdorf.	46, 49.
Spring, R.M.N.	92, 93, 96, 150-152.
St. John, Geoffrey.	157, 158.
Staffordshire Engineering & Boiler Covering Co.Ltd.	66.
Stanley Show.	20.
Star Aluminium Co.Ltd.	106.
Star Cycle Co.	114.
Star Engineering Co.	159.
Star 'Flyer'.	162.
Stevens, Albert John (Jack).	13, 18, 20, 21, 23, 34, 35, 37-40, 45, 47, 49, 50, 59, 64, 79, 92, 128, 152, 154, 155, 183, 191.
– Alec.	191.
– Annie.	113, 114.
– Daisy.	13, 16, 20, 45, 190.
– Ethel.	13, 16, 45.
– George.	13, 19, 21, 22, 37, 40, 41, 45, 48, 50, 64, 65, 79, 86, 90, 96, 181, 184, 189.
– Hanford.	72.
– Harry.	13, 16, 19, 21, 22, 31, 40, 45, 50, 55, 56, 61, 62, 64, 67, 79, 80, 109, 113, 114, 122, 135, 136, 181, 184.
– Jim.	191.
– Joe (Jnr).	13, 20, 21, 37, 39, 40, 45, 50, 64, 66, 71, 79, 89, 106, 119, 122, 130, 159, 183, 191.
– Joe (Snr).	13, 17, 19, 20, 45, 52, 112, 114, 191.
– Lily.	13, 16, 17, 20, 45, 190.
– Lucy.	13, 45.
– Millie.	72, 73, 75, 76, 96, 97, 99.
– William. (Billie).	13, 45, 46, 54, 184, 190, 191.
Stevens, Brothers (Wolverhampton) Ltd.	181, 186.
Stevens, J & Co.	13, 19.
Stevens Light Commercial Vehicle.	181-185, 189.
Stevens Motor Manufacturing Co.	13, 19.
Stevens Motor Manufacturing Co.Ltd.	19, 109.
Stevens Protected Carburettor.	16, 17.
Stevens Screw Co,Ltd.	19, 20, 46, 52, 54, 181, 186, 190, 191.
Stewart Street Works.	64, 66, 75, 84, 89, 114, 115, 138, 139, 141, 142, 143-145, 159.
Stratford, A.G.	73.
Sturmey -Archer.	103, 132, 133, 152.
Sunbeam.	22, 26, 62, 66, 86, 88, 110, 119, 130, 159, 168.
Swallow Coachbuilding Co.	119.
Symphony Gramophone & Radio Co.Ltd.	145.

T

Taylor, Bert.	71.
Taylor, H & Co.	23, 27, 49.
Tempest Street Works.	13, 15.
Terry.	75, 85, 128.
Thompson Bennett.	46, 54, 56, 61.
Thompson, John, Motor Pressings Ltd.	160, 174.
Thornycroft.	162, 166.
Toghill, Edward.	159.
Trials A.C.E. M.C. Midland Daily Telegraph.	77.
– A.C.U. Six Days 1000 mile Stock Machine.	70, 73, 83, 88.
– Alan Trophy.	96.
– Colmore Cup.	77, 83, 88.
– Cork 'Twenty' Reliability.	89.
– International Six Days.	73, 77, 89, 92.
– Kickham Memorial.	83, 89.
– Leicester-Cardiff.	89.
– London-Edinburgh.	83, 89.
– London-Exeter.	88.
– London-Lands End.	77, 83, 89.
– Manville Trophy.	77.
– Matchless Cup.	63.
– Scottish Six Days.	68, 70, 73, 77, 83, 88, 92, 96.
– Travers Trophy.	77, 83.
– Victory Cup.	77, 83, 88, 119.
– Western Centre Open.	77.
Triumph.	62, 130.
Turley, Frank.	96.

U

U.H.	46.

V

Velocette.	86, 149.
V.M.C.C.	104.

W

Wade, J.E.	86.
Wade, Ossie.	57, 61, 66.
Walker, F.J.	38, 39.
Walker, Graham.	88, 96, 97.
Walker, Murray.	96, 97.
Wearwell Cycle Co.Ltd.	14, 15, 113.
Wearwell Motette.	17, 19.
Wearwell Motor Carriage Co.Ltd.	14, 16, 20, 109.
Wearwell-Stevens.	15, 17, 18.
Webb.	102, 132.
Weight, Charles Aaron.	66, 106, 170.
Weller Chain Tensioner.	83, 101, 146.
Weston Electric Co.	136.
Weston, Harry.	81.
Weymann.	117.
Whalley, Jim.	62, 72.
Whatmough.	174.
Williams, Cyril.	26, 27, 30-40, 42, 43, 56, 57.
Williams, Eric.	22, 30, 34, 35, 38, 39, 41, 43, 46, 56, 57, 61, 62.
Williams, S.M.	70, 71, 73.
Willis, Harold.	86.
Willys-Overland Crossley.	106, 180.
Wise, Clarrie.	71, 89, 92, 96.
Wood, Jabez.	45, 79.
Woods, Stanley.	67, 104.
Wolf.	19, 20, 23.
Wolverhampton Corporation.	166, 168.
Wolverhampton Die Castings Co.	106.
Wolverhampton Motor Cycling Club.	43.
Wright, Joe.	154-157.

Z

Zenith.	39.